Inconsistent Treatment p. 17	Unemphatic Writing p. 21	Weak Conclusion p. 25	Inappropriate Title p. 26		
¶10 Faulty Connection p. 55	**¶11** Inconsistent in Person, Number, Tense pp. 56-57	**¶12** Lack of Effectiveness p. 57	**¶13** Indentation p. 61	**¶14** Quotation Improperly Paragraphed pp. 61-63	
S9 *SEQUENCE* Position of Modifiers pp. 99-103	**S9** Clauses Not Related p. 111	**S9** Improper Subordination p. 111	**S9** *CONSISTENCY* Position of Antecedent p. 96	**S9** Faulty Parallelism p. 105	**S9** Ineffective Order pp. 112-113
D6 Vagueness p. 144	**D6** Repetition p. 145	**D6** Mixed Figure p. 148	**D6** Triteness p. 149	**D6** Jargon and Slang pp. 151-154	**D6** Colloquialisms p. 154
G10 Case of Personal, Interrogative, or Relative Pronoun p. 223, 226	**G10** Genitive Case of Noun p. 227	**G12** Tense Sequence pp. 230, 233	**G13** Indicative for Subjunctive p. 234	**G14** Illogical Comparison p. 236	**G15** Split Infinitive p. 236

Glossary of Usage p. 333

Glossary of Grammatical Terms p. 254

DASH
3 Incomplete sentence, p. 273
6 Parenthetical material, p. 291
10 Break in thought, p. 300

HYPHEN
15 Compound words, p. 314
15 Syllabic division, p. 314

PERIOD
3 p. 271

COLON
5 p. 286

QUESTION MARK
P3 p. 271

EXCLAMATION POINT
P3 p. 272

BRACKETS
P6 p. 291

PARENTHESES
P6 p. 292

CAPITAL LETTERS
P14 First word of sentence, p. 311
P14 First word of line of poetry, p. 311
P14 First word of quoted sentence, p. 311
P14 Proper names, etc., p. 312

ITALICS
P13 For emphasis, p. 310
P13 Titles, p. 311
P13 Names of ships, etc., p. 311
P13 Foreign words, p. 311
P13 Words and letters as such, p. 311

Sp8 Dropping Final e p. 323	**Sp8** Words Ending in y p. 324	**Sp8** Plurals p. 324	**Sp9** Spelling Accepted But Not Preferred p. 324	**Sp10** Spelling Inappropriate For Formal Use p. 325	Word Division p. 181

SCRIBNER
HANDBOOK
OF
ENGLISH

Scribner Handbook of English

BY

ALBERT H. MARCKWARDT

Professor of English
University of Michigan

SECOND EDITION

IN COLLABORATION WITH
FREDERIC G. CASSIDY

Associate Professor of English
University of Wisconsin

CHARLES SCRIBNER'S SONS
New York   Chicago   Atlanta   San Francisco

New edition, completely reset

PREFACE TO THE SECOND EDITION

*T*HE FIRST EDITION of the *Scribner Handbook of English* was an experiment. It is reassuring to find that an honest approach to the problems of the freshman English course—an approach based upon an objective examination and scientific presentation of the facts of the English language—has found favor with instructors the country over. The Second Edition of the *Scribner Handbook* is based upon an inventory of the experiences which many of these instructors have shared with the authors.

But first of all a word of reassurance: there has been no change whatever in the objective approach to present-day English usage, which was the point of departure of the first edition. Judgments of the acceptability of disputed expressions are still based upon the most authoritative collections of the facts of the English language. We continue to believe in the merit of intensive corrective drill on a relatively small number of language habits. We continue to believe that cultivated informal English should not be disparaged. We still believe that students can comprehend and appreciate simple explanations of the fundamental linguistic processes.

We have altered much of the illustrative material and many of the exercises throughout the book in the interests of variety and timeliness. Some of the grammatical explanations have been re-stated for greater simplicity. The correction chart has been revised with the same end in view. The most important change is the re-ordering of the various chapters of the book. This reorganization accentuates the basic distinction between achievement of mere mechanical acceptability in writing and stimulation of self-expression, independence of thought, and originality.

Therefore, those chapters designed to help the student to express his own thoughts clearly are placed at the beginning of the text under *Effective Writing*. Within this division the order of chapters has been left unchanged; the chapters proceed from the larger unit of expression to the smaller, an order which we believe to be psychologically and pedagogically sound.

Part Two, *Standards of Modern Writing,* has as its primary aim the achievement of correctness. It seeks also to aid the student in making intelligent decisions for himself on matters of unsettled usages. Chapters are devoted to *The Dictionary, Grammar, Punctuation and Mechanics, Spelling,* and *Usage.* This section may be taught chapter by chapter or may be employed as a reference work.

The authors recognize that the focus of many beginning composition courses is the long paper based upon individual investigation. Part Three gives full directions and models for this type of writing, with emphasis upon such mechanical details as footnotes and bibliography. It also aids the student in gathering, classifying, and synthesizing the information upon which his paper is based.

In its present form, the *Scribner Handbook* is designed to satisfy the basic objectives on which freshman English courses throughout the country are in general agreement: the improvement of the student's ability to read with comprehension and the establishment and fortification of correctness in his writing. Above all, the *Scribner Handbook* is concerned with developing the ability to express ideas clearly and forcefully and with stimulating creative powers through experience in the discipline of writing.

We wish to thank the periodicals, publishers, and authors that have given us their kind permission to reprint. Special acknowledgment of our indebtedness is given in the footnotes accompanying the selections.

PREFACE TO THE SECOND EDITION

It is appropriate here for us to express our great indebtedness to Thomas J. B. Walsh of Charles Scribner's Sons for his kind encouragement, his wise counsel and able assistance in preparing this work for the press.

ALBERT H. MARCKWARDT
FREDERIC G. CASSIDY

CONTENTS

CONTENTS

x

CONTENTS

CONTENTS

CONTENTS

APPENDIX

PART I

Effective Writing

*A*LL OF US use language constantly. We have been using it ever since we were small children. We employ it to satisfy the simplest necessities of our lives, to secure food, clothing, and shelter. At the other extreme language serves us as the vehicle for the expression of ideas as abstract and complex as the theory of relativity, and as beautiful as those contained in a lyric by Rossetti or a sonnet by Edna St. Vincent Millay.

Most of us, however, are neither physicists nor poets. We spend at least part of our daily lives in business, following various trades, or in the professions. We use language for making explanations, analyzing situations, or discussing the relative merits of one procedure or another. To be successful, these language activities demand precision and forcefulness. Consequently we must all learn to express ourselves clearly and effectively.

In college too you will find that clear and effective expression is a daily necessity. Often it constitutes the difference between a brilliant and an average recitation. It is an equally important factor in reading and laboratory reports, term papers, and examinations.

The kind of writing that we most often need to do is called *exposition* or *expository* writing. To "expose" something is to set it forth or to explain it. Directions for mixing and applying the newest type of lacquer are exposition. So too is an account of the various interacting parts of the United Nations organization. You may explain why corn is detasseled in growing the hybrid seed, or how the meter of a sonnet suits the expression of its ideas. You may set forth the merits of one or another type of labor union or sales campaign. All these are examples of exposition.

Chapter I contains some practical suggestions for expository writing.

CHAPTER I

THE WHOLE THEME

1. CHOOSING A SUBJECT

A. Choose a subject within your range of experience.

You would scarcely attempt to describe an ocean voyage if you had never taken one. Even with the help of reference material it is almost as futile for a student who has never seen the inside of a factory to write on industrial problems, or for one who has never been west of the Hudson River to attempt to discuss the problems of the Middle-Western farmer.

This does not rule out imagination in the choice of a topic. It is wholly permissible to picture the world a thousand years from now, to describe the United States at the present time if the South had won the Civil War, to portray the married life of Romeo and Juliet assuming that their tragedy had not occurred. But you will do well to handle even such imaginative topics in the light of things you know or have experienced.

B. Be constantly on the lookout for suggestions for theme topics.

Most of us, teachers as well as students, encounter every day—every hour, almost—enough material to suggest dozens of themes. Unfortunately we do not observe closely enough, nor do we give our imaginations sufficient play over what we do observe. The apparently uneventful happenings of a single day may, as in James Joyce's *Ulysses*, be developed into a long novel. Percy Marks in a discussion of this same point once listed sixteen possible theme topics arising from a student's walk down town. His list included such diversified subjects as *College Slang, A Popcorn Machine,* and *Is Lying Ever Justified?* A glance at the "Talk of the Town" section of the *New Yorker* magazine will illustrate the exceptional ingenuity of its authors in selecting random subjects for comment and discussion. In a single issue, for example, there is:

1. A description of the electronic carillon atop the Empire State Building, and some comparisons with old-style bells.

2. An account of the legal tangles involved in shooting movie sequences on the sidewalks of New York.

3. The misunderstanding that arises from an overheated conversation until the hearer sees who the speakers are.

4. A rapid-fire write-up on Pakistan.

5. A humorous incident arising from the housing shortage.

6. The account of a window display on the atomic bomb, and the stages by which the display grew.

7. A story of an Australian who thought he could speak better American since he had broken his nose.

Readers look forward eagerly every week to this department, largely because its authors recognize that many of the trivial and commonplace incidents of everyday life have story material in them. Conversations, group discussions, any situation where there may be a conflict of opinion or desires is likely to prove a fruitful source of subject matter. Above all, write on something that interests you.

C. Limit your topic so that you may treat it adequately in the space at your disposal.

4

GATHERING IDEAS

Radio Broadcasting, The Coal Industry in America, The Foreign Policy of Soviet Russia are examples of topics too broad for satisfactory treatment in a theme. But a single aspect of any of these would be entirely appropriate. Instead of writing on *Radio Broadcasting* in general, the student might better select such a subject as *An Evening at the Short Wave Dial, My Favorite Sports Announcer, A Broadcasting Station I Have Seen, An Instance of Radio Censorship, Homemade Directional Antennas, How F-M Works.*

EXERCISE 1. Limit the following topics sufficiently for treatment in less than one thousand words:

Sports	Fraternities
Magazine Advertising	Chief Justice Vinson
The Steel Industry	Swimming
Japan	Debating
Labor Relations	The Constitution

2. GATHERING YOUR IDEAS

Much of the work of a successful composition has been done before the first word of the theme proper is ever written. After the topic has been properly limited, think about your subject from as many points of view as possible, and put down every idea, fact, or observation that comes to you. Suppose you were planning a theme on showing your pedigreed dog and taking a prize with him. Your preliminary list of rough ideas might look like this:

1. Pedigree of my dog.
2. Making out the entry blank.
3. Training for the show.
4. Avoiding distemper at the show.
5. Food at the show.
6. Proper diet to secure a glossy coat.
7. Reducing diet.

8. Care of coat at the show.
9. Whether or not to hire a handler.
10. Judging in the ring.
11. Points upon which ratings are made.
12. Past champions.
13. Dog show politics.
14. Thrill of the decision.

One of the best ways of gathering your ideas is to think in terms of your reader. The reader wants to be informed; you have the information. What questions would he ask that you can answer? He may never have seen a dog show, and may have heard only vaguely about pedigrees and handlers. You need to anticipate his questions, then, and answer them for him.

3. ARRANGING YOUR IDEAS

The foregoing topics have been set down in the haphazard order in which they might occur to you when you are preparing to write. Your first task is to see how many major divisions or classes of facts or ideas are represented in the list. An examination shows that (1) certain items deal with what the exhibitor must know before he enters the show, (2) certain others deal with preparing the dog for the show, (3) a third group contains directions for caring for the dog at the show, (4) the fourth group relates experiences of the actual judging. With this basic grouping in mind, you must now sort out the fourteen rough ideas. A rearrangement of them—still tentative—might look something like this:

I. First steps, or What I had to know beforehand.
   1. Pedigree of my dog.
   2. Making out the entry blank.
  11. Points upon which ratings are made.
  12. Past champions.

II. Preparing the dog for the show.
    3. Training for the show.
    6. Proper diet to secure a glossy coat.
    7. Reducing diet.
    9. Whether or not to hire a handler.

III. Caring for the dog at the show.
    4. Avoiding distemper.
    5. Food.
    8. Care of coat.

IV. The judging.
    10. Judging in the ring.
    11. Points upon which ratings are made.
    13. Dog show politics.
    14. Thrill of the decision.

Notice that this is not yet a workable outline:

1. None of the items under the main headings are yet in an order which would make for effective presentation.

2. Some important items may have been left out. Glancing at division III, a reader may well inquire, "What did you do with the dog at night?"

3. Some items may be unnecessary or inharmonious with the general tone of the composition. After you get a clearer notion of what your theme is to be, you may decide to omit all discussion of dog show politics, feeling perhaps that this is not in keeping with the general atmosphere of the theme. Notice also that item 10 under IV is little more than a re-statement of the main heading.

The next step is to consider each of the main divisions carefully, placing the sub-topics in the most effective order possible, and allowing the topics that are already there to suggest others which may be necessary to round out the discussion. The topics already under division I might be rearranged and expanded to make a more complete outline which would read:

I. Entering the show.
    A. Acquisition of a pedigreed Irish setter.
    B. Details of the pedigree.
        1. Champions in the father's line.
        2. Champions in the mother's line.
    C. Qualifications of a champion.
        1. Matters of measurement.
            a. Length.
            b. Height.
            c. Weight.
        2. Matters of build.
            a. Shape of head.
            b. Placing of ears.
            c. Stance.
    D. Decision to enter the show.
        1. Entry in the proper class.
        2. Registration fee.

Each of the main divisions should be re-worked and expanded in exactly this fashion.

4. AN OUTLINE IS NECESSARY

You will notice that when we finished organizing the ideas for the theme on exhibiting a dog, an outline for the theme was the product. The chief argument for outlining is that better balanced and more carefully conceived compositions are the result.

The only satisfactory alternative to writing from an outline is to write the first draft immediately after your choice of a subject. Then you are still in the white heat of your early enthusiasm for it. After the first draft is written, subject your theme to a number of thorough and careful revisions.

Upon analysis this second process is not so very different from working from an outline. The first draft, supposedly written at a fever pitch of creative energy, is little more than the Gathering of Ideas, but written in connected sentences rather than in note form. Careful revision will then entail the same sort of activity as was illustrated on pp. 6, 7, *Arrangement of Ideas*. The student should attempt both methods, to see which is best suited to him.

For the form of the outline, see Chapter XII. If your theme topic sets forth an opinion or point of view, you will find it helpful to precede your outline with a single sentence, stating as precisely as you can the gist of what you intend to say in your theme. This is usually referred to as the *theme sentence*.

The following might serve as a *theme sentence* for "On Exhibiting My Dog":

> The grin of triumph with which I received the prize for my dog in last year's show was well earned, for I had worked hard and gone to a lot of trouble to enter him, prepare him, and care for him at the show grounds.

Notice that the theme sentence need not be the opening one; but it is always wise, somewhere near the beginning of the essay, to indicate its scope and purpose with such a sentence.

EXERCISE 2. Choose any one of the topics listed and set down whatever ideas it suggests. Organize and revise these into a theme outline. The suggested topics may be limited or modified to conform to your own experience.

1. Freshman registration.
2. My boarding house.

3. What makes a good movie.
4. The prospects of our football team for the coming season.
5. My last summer's job.
6. First impressions of my professors.
7. An unusual picnic.
8. My own experience with the labor question.
9. Traveling in a strange country.
10. My most eccentric acquaintance.

5. BEGINNING THE COMPOSITION

The student knows that no matter how inauspiciously any theme of his may begin, the instructor is duty bound to wade through it to the end. This is not true of other writing, that which is done outside of the college classroom. The opening of any piece of writing, be it a novel, an essay, an advertisement, or even a letter of application for a position, must be arresting. If it starts in a dull or uninteresting fashion, it is not likely to catch the attention of the reader, and may remain unread.

Observe the following methods of securing your reader's attention:

A. State briefly and simply the central purpose of what you are planning to write about.

"The method of scientific investigation is but the expression of the necessary mode of working of the human mind."

B. Concrete details easily grasped by the reader may be introduced.

1. Begin with some vivid description.

"Nothing much remains to me of my birthplace but a sense of warm winds mixing the tang of salt with the sweetness of jasmine, and the warm negro laughter coming from the back-yard buildings."

2. Begin with an incident.

"This afternoon I watched a squirrel on our front lawn collecting acorns and burying them. For a time he carried them one by one to some cache; but now he was burying each where he found it, without bothering to mark the spot."

3. Introduce one or more characters.

"Imagine if you can the New York of 1948. A young man just out of college is laying siege to the city desks of the metropolitan papers. He has good legs, but his past record includes nothing more substantial than having been fired out of college and having worked during vacations on a small city paper upstate, also on a Hearst-owned Chicago paper."

C. Some form of writing which gives the impression of conversation is often helpful.

1. Begin with a fragment of dialogue.
2. Begin with a quotation, either direct or indirect, of what someone else has said.

" 'Romance is dead, the cave man said—.' And there we go quoting Kipling, which dates *us,* all right."

"It has been said many times, and always with an air of authority, that there is no tragedy in the modern drama."

3. Ask a question or a series of questions.

"Is there such a thing as modern biography? Can one name a year in which suddenly the old biography ceased to exist and modern biography came into being? And if so, what is the difference between old and modern biography?"

D. The element of surprise may be employed.

1. Make a startling statement.

"If an inquiring microbe should ask me to explain what I know about the sun, he would understand part of my description."

2. Put the reader in suspense.

"When I met Captain Alvin at the airport, I took the opportunity to question him about the 'flying saucers' which he claimed to have seen."

3. Parody a familiar quotation.

"It is not my intention here to praise Hollywood or to bury it."

4. Make a paradoxical statement.

"If you stop to think about it, you probably know very few people who have ever seen the sun."

6. DEFINITION OF TERMS

If you are writing an argumentative essay in which the soundness of the conclusion depends upon the interpretation of some of the terms you use, you must be certain to define all such terms at the beginning of your discussion. If you were seeking to prove that isolationism was a greater menace to America than Communism, you could not begin your argument until you had made perfectly clear what was meant by the terms *isolationism* and *Communism*.

It is necessary to define terms in a non-argumentative paper on a subject that your readers cannot be expected to know much about. In a theme dealing with present-day educational trends in American universities you would have to explain what you meant by the *humanities* and an *integrated curriculum;* if you were writing about governmental policies, you might have to define or describe such terms as the *SEC,* the *REA, parity.*

EXERCISE 3. 1. Examine the beginnings of ten articles, two from each of the following magazines: *Harper's, Current History, New Yorker, Fortune, Time.* What devices are used to gain the reader's attention? Classify them on the basis of the information you have been given. Do you find any devices that were not mentioned in the foregoing treatment?

2. Examine the beginning of any one book by each of the following: Walter Scott, William Makepeace Thackeray, Thomas Hardy, Mark Twain, Sinclair Lewis, John Galsworthy, John Steinbeck, Clarence Day, John Hersey. Answer the same questions which were asked in respect to the magazine articles in the preceding question.

3. Examine in any single issue of a newspaper such as the New York Sunday *Times* both the news stories and the articles in the magazine section. How do these stories begin?

4. Write beginning sentences employing several of the devices mentioned for each of the theme topics listed on pages 9 and 10.

7. SEQUENCE IN THOUGHT

Assuming your paper is off to an effective start, it must move in a straight line to its conclusion. It must have continuity. It should include nothing that is inconsequential (notice that *sequence* is the root of this word).

Here are several ways of attaining an orderly sequence:

A. Ideas or events may be arranged in chronological order:

"During the Pliocene period, which lasted at least six million years and terminated with the onset of the glacial

13

epoch, perhaps a million years B.C. . . . Before the end of the glacial period, perhaps 25,000 years ago . . . After the final glacial retreat, perhaps not more than eight to ten thousand years ago . . ."

B. The composition may be organized according to the relative position of whatever objects or ideas are treated:

"Since the brass goods industry in Connecticut's Naugatuck valley demands a high percentage of skills, the logical place for our examination to begin is Thomaston. . . . This accords very neatly with the situation in Baltimore. . . . In Greenville, South Carolina, it is the same story over again. . . ."

C. Begin with a general statement and proceed with its application to specific details:

"Rivalries have often existed between groups or certain social, economic, or racial orders within the same region. . . . When the Anglo-American civilization struck the Spanish culture in the Southwest . . . The English colonists came into contact with a French civilization in Canada. . . . New England Puritans met and mingled with the German settlers of the Old Northwest. . . ."

These examples illustrate only a few of the possible plans of organization. There are many others. You might proceed from the *abstract* or *general* to the *concrete* or *specific,* from what is *familiar* to the reader to that which is *unfamiliar,* from the *more* to the *less important.*

The method of organization you employ will necessarily be determined by the nature of the material you are writing about. The important thing is to have a plan and to follow it scrupulously.

EXERCISE 4. 1. Write a list of topics for one of the theme subjects listed below, using the chronological order.

2. Write a similar list using the familiar-to-the-unfamiliar order.

3. Do the same using the general-to-the-specific order.

4. Make preliminary plans for themes on any two of the topics which you have not used in answering the foregoing questions.

> Baseball, then and now.
> Our campus.
> My most eventful year.
> Planning a meal.
> Should I join a fraternity?
> Extra-curricular activities.
> Did my high school educate me?
> What I expect from college.
> Music I like.
> My latest hobby.

8. CONNECTING THE VARIOUS PARTS

There would be little point in drawing a map of some territory if you were the only one who could interpret it. So it is with the organization of your composition. Make this so clear that your reader will be able to follow your plan in a single reading.

The following devices may be employed to couple one division of a theme to another:

A. Word and phrase connectives may be used:

"Many serious-minded persons are urging us to prohibit strikes and lockouts. . . ."

"*While* the justifications for this proposal are persuasive, it has limitations. . . ."

15

"Moreover, the very nature of the process of compulsory arbitration . . ."

"In conclusion, it is extremely probable . . ."

Connecting words and phrases may be sorted according to the functions they perform. Some useful ones follow:

1. Those which show that a similar, supplementary point is being made: *Furthermore, in addition, moreover, besides, in like manner, and so again, next, again.*

2. Those which show that a contrasting point is being made: *Yet, still, on the contrary, on the other hand, however, in spite of this, but, nevertheless, despite this, nonetheless.*

3. Those which show relationships of space, time, or importance: *Beyond, above, around, formerly, hitherto, in particular, foremost.*

4. Those which show the stages in your argument or in your marshaling of evidence: *To begin with, from the start, at the outset, initially, so far, up to now, lastly, finally, in conclusion, after all, to sum up.*

B. A portion of the preceding division may be repeated:

"Clearly, if there is any substitute for war, it must lie in the *pacific settlement of controversies* out of which wars grow. . . ."

"As against these policies based upon power, the intermittent suggestion of securing *pacific settlement* by using among nations the agencies worked out in the domestic policy of civilized states . . ."

"From its beginning the United States has had an attitude favoring the *pacific settlement of international controversies.* . . ."

C. Certain key words and phrases may be used to show the proposed development of your argu-

ment. These can then be repeated at the beginning of each division:

"We shall discuss the *present status* of the securities market, the *causes* for the prevailing conditions, and whatever *remedies* seem to suggest themselves. . . ."

"At *present* the *status* of . . ."

"Turning now to the *causes* . . ."

"What are the *remedies* which may improve . . ."

D. Divisions may be numbered:

"Of the details of that lesson, we can name and illustrate *three* of some technical importance. . . ."

"The *first* is oneness of tone or pitch. . . ."

"Let me approach a *second* and more specific agent of unity. . . ."

"*Thirdly,* the modern craftsman has learned . . ."

The writer must be careful to avoid tiresome and repetitious division numbers or key words. Connectives should do their work unobtrusively, showing the reader the pattern or order of the essay without calling attention to themselves.

EXERCISE 5. 1. Examine the magazine articles read in Exercise 3, p. 13. Make a list of the connectives which you find in each.

2. Supply appropriate connecting sentences for the lists of topics you worked out in Exercise 4, p. 15.

9. CONSISTENCY

Consistency may be characterized as that quality which gives the reader a sense of a harmoniously planned composition, all the parts of which form an organic unity. In practice this means that, when writing, you must keep always in mind a sense of the total essay. (Here is the great value of an outline, which insures that the subject has been thought through.) Do not begin to write until you know pretty clearly what you intend to say—not, of course, every detail, but the general pattern and the main parts. This sense of the whole will help you to avoid straying.

A. Maintain the same physical point of view throughout.

If you were attempting to give your reader some notion of the buildings and business establishments which were clustered about the public square in your home town, you would scarcely jump from one side of the square to the other six or seven times in your account.

FAULTY: The house which Doctor King has just built is a model of compactness and economy of space. It consists of a dining room, living room, and kitchen on the first floor, three bedrooms and a bath on the second. The stair is enclosed as it used to be in original colonial houses, and there is no waste passage around it. The kitchen region of the house dexterously includes an inside entry and a breakfast alcove. The bedrooms all have plenty of closet space and there is cross-ventilation in each of them as well as useful wall space for furniture. The living room is sixteen by twenty-eight feet and is reached through a small entryway which has a lavatory adjoining.

REVISED: The house which Doctor King has just built is a model of compactness and economy of space. It consists of a dining room, living room, and kitchen on the first floor, three bedrooms and a bath on the second. The living room is sixteen by twenty-eight feet and is reached through a small entryway which has a lavatory adjoining. The kitchen region of the house ingeniously includes an inside entry and a breakfast alcove. The stair is enclosed as it used to be in original colonial houses, and there is no waste passage around it. The bedrooms all have plenty of closet space and there is cross-ventilation in each of them as well as useful wall space for furniture.

B. Maintain the same chronological point of view throughout.

In describing a process or telling a story it is important to relate the stages or events in the order in which they occurred. A skillful writer may at times choose to relate a comparatively recent event before he tells some things which happened earlier, but for the beginner it is preferable to adhere to a straight chronological order.

FAULTY: Three months ago I began the study of Latin and at present I am beginning to read small selections from Cæsar. The declensions and verb forms seemed hard at first, but now my chief difficulty is the word order. This is not my first experience with a foreign language, since I studied French for two years when I was in high school. I am gradually becoming accustomed to the vocabulary, but expect to have difficulty as I come upon more new words.

REVISED: My first experience with a foreign language was in high school, where I studied French for two years. Three months ago I began the study of Latin. At first the declensions and verb forms seemed difficult, but now, as I am beginning to read small selections from Cæsar, my chief difficulty is with word order. I am gradually becoming accustomed to the vocabulary, but I expect to have difficulty as I come upon more new words.

C. Maintain the same logical point of view throughout.

Inexperienced writers and speakers frequently shift the logical situation, thereby confusing the reader or hearer. They may change without cause from singular to plural, from active to passive, or in many other ways. The whole point of grammatical agreement is to avoid such inconsistency. For a full treatment see Chapter VI, Grammar.

One glaring type of fault, the confusion of pronouns, will suffice for illustration here. Notice the shift from personal *you* to impersonal *one*, and from singular *he, himself* to plural *those, their*.

FAULTY: *You* may be liberal in essentially four ways, namely with respect to social, economic, political, and religious matters. If *one* is liberal in each of these four fields, *he* may call *himself* a liberal in the true sense of the word. . . . In short, liberals are *those people* who are willing to give *their* serious thought to those proposals which may further human progress.

REVISED: *One* may be liberal essentially in four ways, namely with respect to social, economic, political, and religious matters. If *one* is liberal in each of these four fields, *he* may call *himself* a liberal in the true sense of the word. . . . In short, a liberal is *one* who is willing to give *his* serious thought to those proposals which may further human progress.

D. Maintain the same tone throughout.

If you were listening to a humorous story, you would consider it jarring if the teller inserted in the middle of it a serious reflection on the virtues of thrift, and then went back to finish his story. Avoid such breaks in your own writing.

If you are writing a formal composition, don't become cheaply witty or colloquial. If you are writing in an emotional mood, don't suddenly become satirical. One or two ill-chosen words are enough to mar consistency of tone.

FAULTY: In addition to the advantages to the student which I have mentioned, there are those which are enjoyed by the corporation. The principal one is undoubtedly the infusion of new blood into the corporation machinery, since it is necessary for every corporation to keep abreast of progress if it is to survive. Of course, every corporation needs some *old-timers* who *know the ropes,* but that is not enough to keep a company going.

Notice that this is not a condemnation of the expressions *old-timer* and *know the ropes.* In another setting (informal) they might be wholly apropos, but here they are out of keeping.

Conversely one or two words that are too dignified or literary may spoil the flavor of a vigorous but simply written passage:

FAULTY: The hardest problem that a foreign student has to face at the beginning of the school year is that of finding a room. He may have to look for a long time before he will find a landlady who will take him in. There are several reasons for this. The lady of the house may be afraid that she will be unable to rent the rest of her rooms if it becomes known that a foreigner is *residing at her domicile.*

10. EFFECTIVENESS

You have noticed, perhaps a little enviously, that some of your acquaintances can tell a story or express an opinion so effectively that everyone listens to them. There are also effective writers, writers who arrest and hold the interest of their readers.

How does one become an effective writer? The answer lies partly in the personality of the writer, but there are a few useful principles which may be consciously studied.

A. Use concrete illustrations whenever possible.

You have only to leaf through the advertisements of any magazine to see what is meant by the use of definite illustration. Compare the two examples which follow and note the difference in the effect achieved by the appeal to the senses and the imagination.

INEFFECTIVE: John was unsuccessful as a student partly because of his inability to concentrate on his work and partly because he could always be persuaded to neglect his studies in favor of some trifling amusement.

EFFECTIVE: John is a hopeless student. Picture him at his books after dinner on a winter's evening. He reads for ten minutes. Then he looks about him. He drums on the table. He gets up and walks about the room. After an unrewarding glance out of the window, he returns to his volume, but not for long. A good program on the radio, he has suddenly recalled, is to begin in ten minutes. Better turn it on now while he thinks of it. Adjusting the dial to the proper station, he turns to go back to his desk, but a new popular song on the present program attracts him. The next one is not new but is a favorite and worth listening to anyway. By this time books and assignments are out of mind except for one fleeting resolution to get at them tomorrow.

The use of illustrative incidents to make a point or idea clear is always an effective device. Lincoln was given to these simple and homely methods of driving home a point. His well-known comment about the danger of swapping horses midstream is effective because it puts an idea in terms of an incident, even though the incident itself is not told.

B. Vary your style to avoid monotony.

1. Do not use sentences which are too much alike in length or construction:

WEAK: I offer as an example my own father. My father's parents had little money. They provided a grade school education for their children. Then the children were forced to shift for themselves. My father had two brothers. Today he has achieved success in his field and is considered equal to those around him. His brothers are still where they were when they finished school. They all had the same opportunities, the same intelligence. Perhaps they had even more intelligence. However, he had initiative and a desire for success. They had none.

BETTER: I offer the experience of my father and his two brothers as an illustration of this point. Their parents had little money and were able to give the children only a grade school education. After they finished the eighth grade, the children were forced to shift for themselves. My father has achieved success in his field and is considered equal to those around him. The brothers are still where they were when they finished school. All three had the same opportunities, the same intelligence; possibly the unsuccessful brothers were even more intelligent than my father. However, he had initiative and a desire for success where they had none.

2. Dialogue and direct quotation are sometimes helpful:

WEAK: Long before I had the notion of attending a university for the purpose of educational advancement, I had the curiosity to ask some of the older men with whom I worked what a college education meant to them. I was frequently told that college training was not an absolute essential in acquiring intellectual and cultural training. Most of my co-workers, however, seemed to value most highly the social contacts and friendships which they had made in college.

BETTER: Long before I had the notion of attending a university for the purpose of educational advancement, I had the curiosity to ask some of the older men with whom I worked what a college education meant to them. The typical answer was that of a man who is recognized as a successful person intellectually, financially, and socially:

"If you have sufficient energy and real interest in the cultural and intellectual aspects of life, you can get just as much help, and can progress just as well right here at the Public Library as you would at college. After fifteen years the thing that means most to me from having gone to college is the social contact and friendships built up while I was there."

3. Use questions and explanations where necessary:

WEAK: The same holds true for professors and students. Of course, it is impossible to expect an equality between professors and students because the former are more learned and are here to teach the less learned, but the student body should be given equal rights among themselves, and these rights should be respected by the professors. When I say equality among the students I do not mean absolute equality because I believe that their rights should be equally respected and justice equally dispensed. There can be no justice when superficialities are allowed to enter into the weighing of the worth of an individual.

BETTER: Should not all students be treated equally by their professors? Should any distinctions be made among the student body? I believe we will agree that equal rights are due to all and these rights ought to be respected by the faculty. Yet some professors show a degree of favoritism to certain students. What are the reasons? Sometimes the student's personality especially appeals; there may be a similarity of ideas that attracts the professor's attention. Or perhaps the student has an eagerness not shown by the rest of the class; he immediately grasps the point which the professor is trying to make, while others merely sit through the hour. It is not surprising that the professor

24

should appreciate such a student, but even so, should we excuse discrimination in his favor? Other professors tread lightly on the toes of the child from an influential or wealthy family, or the child of an old friend. This, too, while certainly understandable, is even less pardonable.

C. Use the active voice whenever possible.

Notice the difference in effectiveness here:

(passive)   The ball was advanced six yards by Quarterback Jones.

(active)   Quarterback Jones advanced the ball six yards.

D. Strive for proportion in your composition.

1. Omit everything that does not contribute definitely to the purpose of your theme.

2. Give each idea the space it deserves, no more. The introduction and conclusion should be shorter than the body of the theme. Give less space to subordinate ideas, and the most space to the most important phases of your theme.

See pages 51–53 for illustrations of this principle applied to the individual paragraph.

11. ENDING THE THEME

Many a good theme is spoiled by a clumsy ending. The writer may be too obvious, he may run off the track, he may trail away to nothing. Student themes in particular sometimes seem to end merely because the assigned number of words have been written, or because the writer collapsed from fatigue. Yet it is a psychological fact that the reader is most strongly impressed with the last thing he has read. Thus an effective conclusion is quite as important as a striking beginning.

There is no one right way to end a theme; the choice must depend on the writer's purpose. Nonetheless, there should usually be some attempt, direct or implicit, to summarize the content or the argument, or to leave the main point sticking in the reader's mind. Some of the most useful ways of concluding are the following:

a. After a formal argument, you may restate what you have proved.

b. You should end an emotional or persuasive piece of writing strongly or intensely.

c. You may end with a rhetorical question.

d. You may end with a question or remark which opens for the reader the further implications of the subject.

e. Occasionally you may find an abrupt break effective.

f. You may find irony or paradox effective sometimes.

See pages 57–59 for illustrations of effective and ineffective conclusions of individual paragraphs.

EXERCISE 6. 1. Study the conclusions of the same ten magazine articles which you read in connection with Exercise 3 of this chapter. Classify these conclusions as to type.

2. Study the conclusions of the same newspaper articles which you examined in Exercise 3. Do they differ in type from the magazine articles?

12. WRITING THE TITLE

A. A good title should suggest the limits of your subject.

The title is a sort of promise to the reader. If it promises more than the theme gives, the reader will feel cheated; if less, he still has a right to feel misled. When you finish writing a theme, look back to your title and make certain that it does not promise too much or too little. Some writers write the title last.

B. A good title is always applicable.

Usually, in expository and argumentative writing, the title tells exactly what the selection is about or what it sets out to do. For imaginative types of writing a title that hints is frequently more striking than one which merely labels. *Ariel,* the title of a biography of the poet Shelley, is effective not because it announces that that particular book is a life of Shelley, but rather because it indicates in a single, superbly chosen word just what conception the author had of his subject.

C. A good title should be short.

A count of the number of words in the titles of sixty essays contained in a modern collection gives an average of five words per title. Of the sixty essays, there were two with titles containing eight words; none was longer than this. A short title impresses by its conciseness and can be remembered with ease. A lively phrase is usually to be preferred to a clause.

D. Keep the title of the theme separate from the opening sentence. The meaning of the first sentence should not depend on a reference to the title.

FAULTY: *Patriotism and Militarism.* In many men these two -isms have a similar origin.

BETTER: *Patriotism and Militarism.* In many men militarism and patriotism have a similar origin.

OR: *Two Related -Isms*. Patriotism and militarism have, in many men, a similar origin.

EXERCISE 7. 1. From the book review section of the New York *Times* or a similar newspaper, choose ten books which have just appeared. Read the reviews and form an idea of the contents of the book. In each case decide whether the title is appropriate and appealing, and point out the factors which do or do not make it so.

THE PARAGRAPH

*I*NTELLIGENTLY and skillfully employed, the paragraph can be an aid in setting forth the organization of your ideas and the development of your thought. It is necessary, therefore, to find out what the paragraph is and how it is put together.

1. HISTORY OF THE WORD

The word came originally from the Greek, formed from the prefix *para*, "by the side" and *graphos*, "written." It referred to a symbol or character, now usually written ¶, which indicated the end of one section or part of a narrative or discourse, and the beginning of a new one. It was generally placed in the margin or at the beginning of the line as a *guide to the eye*.

Later the term *paragraph* came to be applied to written matter which was introduced by the mark ¶. Then indentation became established as the accepted mode of marking a section of written matter. Finally the symbol ¶ ceased altogether to be used for this purpose.

The fact that the paragraph was originally a mark or sign suggests that it belongs primarily to the written language. We talk in sentences much as we write in sentences, the period, as a point of punctuation in writing, corresponding to the short silence or pause at the end of a spoken sentence. But there is nothing equally definite in speech corresponding to the break in the line which concludes one paragraph, or the indentation which begins the next. Thus the paragraph is much more a matter of the eye and hand than of the ear and tongue.

2. SPECIMEN PARAGRAPHS

Study the following modern paragraphs carefully in the light of the questions concerning them on page 33.

[A] At various times polls have been made of consumer needs, desires and eccentricities. And the answers show why there is plenty of room for all kinds of stores, from independents to chains, and from gigantic department stores to little specialty shops.

One segment of the consuming public is primarily interested in price. It compares the prices of competing retailers and always goes where the most is offered for the money.

Another segment is interested in certain trade-marked brands, and buys only in stores which carry those it favors.

Still another segment places service high on the list of its requirements. It wants delivery of goods to the home, the charge account privilege, a very liberal policy in exchanges, and it is willing to pay the added costs that these and other services entail.

Under the free competitive system—which is the American system—there is a store to meet every demand. Every kind and character of consumer commodity is stocked, and a long list of brands is offered. If one store can't meet some buyer's standards, another store down the street will. And every merchant who keeps up with the times will get his share of the business. American retailing is geared to serve the varying wishes of the 140,000,000 Americans who patronize it.

—From the Bessemer (Mich.) *Herald,* August 28, 1947.

[B] The patron we want, then, is one who will help us to preserve our flowers from decay. But, as his qualities change from age to age, and it needs considerable integrity and conviction not to be dazzled by the pretensions or bamboozled by the persuasions of the competing crowd, this business of patron-finding is one of the tests and trials of authorship. To know whom to write for is to know how to write. Some of the modern patron's qualities are, however, fairly plain. The writer will require at this moment, it is obvious, a patron with the book-reading habit rather than the play-going habit. Nowadays, too, he must be instructed in the literature of other times and races. But there are other qualities which our special weaknesses and tendencies demand in him. There is the question of indecency, for instance, which plagues us and puzzles us much more than it did the Elizabethans. The twentieth-century patron must be immune from shock. He must distinguish infallibly between the little clod of manure which sticks to the crocus of necessity, and that which is plastered to it out of bravado. He must be a judge, too, of those social influences which inevitably play so large a part in modern literature, and able to say which matures and fortifies, which inhibits and makes sterile. Further, there is emotion for him to pronounce on, and in no department can he do more useful work than in bracing a writer against sentimentality on the one hand and a craven fear of expressing his feeling on the other. It is worse, he will say, and perhaps more common, to be afraid of feeling than to feel too much. He will add, perhaps, something about language, and point out how many words Shakespeare used and how much grammar Shakespeare violated, while we, though we keep our fingers so demurely to the black notes on the piano, have not appreciably improved upon *Antony and Cleopatra*. And if you can forget your sex altogether, he will say, so much the better; a writer has none. But all this is by the way—elementary and disputable. The patron's prime quality is something different, only to be expressed, perhaps, by the use of that convenient word which cloaks so much—atmosphere. It is necessary that the patron should shed and envelop the crocus in an atmosphere which makes it appear a plant of the very highest importance, so that to misrepresent it is the one outrage not to be forgiven this side of the grave. He must make us feel that a single crocus, if it be a real crocus, is enough for him; that he does not want to be lectured, elevated, instructed, or improved; that he is sorry that he bullied Carlyle into vociferation, Tennyson into idyllics, and Ruskin into insanity; that he is now ready to efface himself or assert himself as his writers require; that he is bound to them by a more-than-maternal tie; that they are twins indeed, one dying if the other dies, one flourishing if the other flourishes; that the fate of literature depends upon their happy alliance—all of which proves, as we began by saying, that the choice of a patron is of the highest importance. But how to choose rightly? How to write well? Those are the questions.

—Virginia Woolf, *The Common Reader*.[1]

[C] The bank has its offices in Washington, and its able president, John J. McCloy, is an American. But the fine staff makes it truly international in management. Key posts in the bank are filled by experts from England, Canada, France, Holland, Belgium, and many other countries. A Board of Governors, one member from each nation, controls the bank. The first meeting of the board was held in Washington in September 1946; the second in London in September 1947. Both France and China asked for the 1948 meeting.

The bank will not call upon the member nations to put up more cash to be lent. The money the bank lends will come from the sale of its securities to private investors here and, later, in other countries. The quarter billion dollars' worth of bonds sold the other day represented only the first of many such sales to the investing public. Incidentally, the

[1] Reprinted by courtesy of Harcourt, Brace and Company.

$250,000,000 was the exact amount of the first loan the bank made, a loan to France.

The bank is a genuine effort to help the world recover from war, but it is also a piece of enlightened self-interest from the American point of view. Since the United States is almost the only source from which the devastated nations can get the materials and equipment with which to rebuild their productive capacity, the bank is a tremendous instrument for building up the sale of our products and thus maintaining employment here at home. At the same time, it is a powerful force for building up the capacity of other nations to produce the wealth which they can exchange for our products.

—Eugene Meyer, "The World Bank Gets Down to Business," *The Readers Digest,* October, 1947.[2]

At this point we are examining paragraphs for the purpose of learning how they are organized and how much they contain. These specimens, drawn from the three great classes of printed matter, the newspaper, the book, and the magazine, differ markedly. Consider them in the light of the following questions:

1. How do these specimens compare in length?
2. How do they compare in the number of sentences they contain?
3. Do all the paragraphs deal with but a single or central idea—are they unified in content?
4. In any of the specimen selections, do two or more successive paragraphs treat the same idea?

3. LENGTH

The longest paragraph of the three selections, by Virginia Woolf, is from a printed book. The twenty-two sen-

[2] Reprinted by courtesy of *The Readers Digest*.

tences contain 560 words. The passages taken from the magazine and the newspaper have much shorter paragraphs: the magazine paragraphs here illustrated average about four sentences; the newspaper paragraphs are generally only two sentences in length.

Many modern books are written with short paragraphs, and with little searching, one could turn up examples of newspaper and magazine paragraphing quite out of keeping with these illustrations. Nevertheless it is generally true that newspaper paragraphs are shorter than those in magazines or books, and that paragraphs in magazines are often shorter than those in books. In our college composition classes the general limits of the paragraph are often defined as ranging between one hundred and three hundred words; newspaper style books generally place the maximum limit of the paragraph at one hundred words and the average at sixty or thereabouts.

Our conclusion, then, is that paragraph length is extremely variable, depending upon the kind of material that is written and the medium in which it appears. Evidently the hasty and highly factual character of newspaper writing will result in shorter paragraphs, since topics are seldom completely developed.

If we remember that the paragraph is essentially a guide to the eye, another reason for the variations in paragraph length suggests itself. The newspaper is printed in small type, set in narrow columns averaging about six words to the line and nine lines, or a little more than fifty words, to the column inch. A paragraph of two hundred and fifty words would then require about five column inches. Without question, readers would find material so printed fatiguing to the eye. Magazines, on the other hand, while they often employ the narrow columns, invariably use larger type and can admit longer paragraphs. Books, using large type and a page-wide line, can afford to be least concerned about length.

In student papers, or in the informal writing of the average person, factors such as the size of the paper, the size of the handwriting, whether the manuscript is hand written or typewritten, all play a part in determining paragraph length.

4. CONTENT

To what extent are the specimen paragraphs unified? Do they treat of one topic or more than one? Is the topic under discussion fully developed in the one paragraph?

Mrs. Woolf's paragraph seems to be capable of division into three parts. True enough, the whole long paragraph is devoted to the discussion of a single topic: the qualities desirable in a patron of literature. However, the first six sentences are devoted to the education and interests he should possess; the next eight sentences concern his moral and social attitudes; the remaining eight deal with what the author calls atmosphere. Though in a large sense the paragraph is unified, its contents are certainly capable of division into smaller units.

Conversely, are the extremely short newspaper paragraphs in Selection A entities or full divisions in themselves? If any two or more of them were combined, would the resulting paragraph still treat a single topic? A rereading will show that the second, third and fourth paragraphs could be combined, since they briefly describe the types of consumer demand alluded to in the first paragraph, but do not get into the implications regarding our whole economy. It would be possible to combine these three, thus reducing the number of paragraphs from five to three.

Of the three examples, selection C, by Mr. Meyer, best maintains the topical unity of the paragraph. The first paragraph tells of the international composition of the World Bank's management; the second tells how it works

financially; the third describes its goal in relation to United
States economy.

5. STANDARDS OF PARAGRAPHING

In summary, we may conclude:

1. Paragraphs were originally intended to give visual assistance to the reader.

2. The length of the paragraph varies according to the subject treated and to the mechanics of writing or publication.

3. Paragraphs may include more than one topic; or more than one paragraph may be devoted to a single topic.

How are you going to paragraph *your* writing? Are you to adopt the newspaper style of short, choppy paragraphs or the opposite style of long, diffuse paragraphs? We have seen that the length and organization of the paragraph was dependent upon the nature of the material treated and upon the kind of reader for whom it was intended. Your paragraphs should be governed by the same two factors.

Usually you are writing directly to a very specific audience, your instructor. Whether the class be in the social sciences or in English, the one thing your instructors will be especially interested in is your capacity to think. Are you able to organize your ideas? Are you capable of logical analysis?

Paragraphing here is a helpful device. It is a visual aid, but effectively employed it can be more than a mere eye-rest! The indented break in the monotonous regularity of the printed page should correspond in each instance to the introduction of a new unit in thought or the insertion of a new idea.

Write from an outline. You will have less trouble with paragraphing than if you depend upon the inspiration of the moment.

6. UNITY WITHIN THE PARAGRAPH

A. Do not treat more than a single topic or an aspect of a topic within a paragraph.

Your paragraph should show singleness of purpose.

NOT UNIFIED: The plot, showing how people do not always want to be realistic but like to have some fantasy in their lives, is very ingenious. An old man is harmlessly obsessed with the idea that he is Santa Claus. He turns up at just the right moment to save a Christmas parade from failure by taking the position of Santa Claus in the sleigh, and acts the part with such sincerity that he is asked to continue in it for a large department store. He becomes the friend of a little girl whose mother (also employed in the store) does not want her to be deceived by anything imaginary or imaginative. But again the old man's sincerity works against the mother's educational theory, and the little girl wants very much to believe him genuine. Finally, by a clever piece of work in court, a young lawyer wins a decision that there is a Santa Claus, and that this old man is he. The plot shows how the mother finally realizes that her child needs to use her imagination as well as to be true to facts. In the movie, however, she seems to be making a little cynic out of her daughter before the Santa Claus episode makes her see the other side. The young lawyer also helps to change her mind, since he is in love with her, but disagrees with the way she is raising the little girl.[3]

This paragraph lacks unity because it mixes together the outline of the plot and the writer's commentary upon it.

[3] In all fairness to the authors quoted to illustrate this aspect of the paragraph, it must be said that it is quite unfair to judge any paragraph apart from its context. What may seem not unified when examined by itself may be quite justifiably unified when seen along with the paragraphs adjacent to it.

UNIFIED: The plot, showing how people need fantasy in their lives as well as realism, is quite ingenious. An old man, harmlessly obsessed with the belief that he is Santa Claus, turns up at just the right moment to save a department store Christmas parade from failure by taking the place of Santa Claus in the sleigh. He acts the part with such sincerity that he is asked to continue it for the store. He also becomes the friend of a little girl whose mother (employed at the store) does not want the child to be deceived by anything imaginary or imaginative. But the old man's sincerity again has its effect: the child wants to believe in him. Finally, by a clever piece of work in court, a young lawyer (in love with the child's mother) "proves" not only that there is a Santa Claus, but that this old man is he. Everything ends happily with the mother admitting the child's need of make-believe.

The story is obviously arranged to bring out this underlying idea. The mother's theory that fantasy is a kind of trickery has already begun to make the child a cold-eyed little cynic. The old man revives for the child the world of "let's pretend." His sincerity, coupled with that of the young lawyer, wins the mother over when she sees her daughter thriving on the affection of the two men. She admits at last that the world cannot be all stark realism; and she has come to see that fantasy has its place, especially for children.

B. Do not paragraph too frequently.

While overlong paragraphs make the most interesting material seem dull and long-winded, paragraphs that are too short give an impression of incoherence. They suggest that the writer has not sufficient mental stamina to develop a thought completely.

Short paragraphs may be used tellingly in a narrative when an effect of haste, excitement, indignation, or any

strong emotion is desired. Do not use them in a delibera-
tive or reflective composition.

NOT UNIFIED: Petrillo and the recording industry! These
great opponents are foremost in the minds of people who
depend on music for a living.

Petrillo represents an organization in this country aimed
at protecting part of America's thousands of musicians.

The big recording companies, and their chief customer,
the radio business, have always sought to reduce their de-
pendence on the musicians, and so have come into conflict
with their union and its leader.

Notice that all four sentences might be more profitably
combined into a single paragraph.

NOT UNIFIED: The old-fashioned idea that college is an unnecessary luxury is now fading in the minds of most people.
The demand for high-school and college diplomas has increased greatly, for an education is needed even in many
of the simpler fields.

The persons who considered college unimportant in the
past, with the growth of their families have come to see
the importance of a college education and all that it offers.

NOT UNIFIED: Government, as it exists today, plays a large
role in the life of the private individual. It is certainly an
indispensable institution. There are two reasons for this.
First it gives protection. Our police departments, fire departments, health services, and many other government
institutions are absolutely necessary for the maintenance of
a successful community, and not only a successful community but a livable one. The same is true of the external
protection governments maintain in the form of an army,
navy, and merchant marine.

Secondly, government offers, or rather controls, institutions for the betterment of society as a whole, such as

schools, aid for the poor, and protection for various groups such as farmers.

The writer of the last two paragraphs has reached a broad conclusion based on two sets of facts. Two courses are open to him: he may paragraph his conclusion separately and then give a paragraph to each of the sets of facts upon which it is based; or he may place all the material, conclusion and reasons, in a single paragraph. Either of these is preferable to placing the conclusion and the first set of facts in one paragraph and paragraphing the second set of facts separately.

EXERCISE 1. Break up these passages into shorter, unified paragraphs:

[A] The most difficult fear to overcome, so far, has been fear of the sea. Our first attempt to take the boy into the sea was at the age of two and a half. At first, it was quite impossible. He disliked the cold of the water, he was frightened by the noise of the waves, and they seemed to him to be always coming, never going. If the waves were big, he would not even go near to the sea. This was a period of general timidity; animals, odd noises, and various other things caused alarm. We dealt with fear of the sea piecemeal. We put the boy into shallow pools away from the sea, until the mere cold had ceased to be a shock; at the end of the four warm months, he enjoyed paddling in shallow water at a distance from waves, but still cried if we put him into deep pools where the water came up to his waist. We accustomed him to the noise of the waves by letting him play for an hour at a time just out of sight of them; then we took him to where he could see them, and made him notice that after coming in they go out again. All this, combined with the example of his parents and other children, only brought him to the point where he could be *near* the waves without fear. I am convinced that the fear was instinctive; I am fairly certain there had been no suggestion to cause it. The following summer, at the age of three and a half, we took the matter up again. There was still a terror of going actually into the waves. After some unsuccessful coaxing, combined with the spectacle of everybody else bathing, we adopted old-fashioned methods. When he showed cowardice, we made him feel that we were ashamed of him; when he showed courage, we praised him warmly. Every day for about a fortnight, we plunged him up to the neck in the sea, in spite of his struggles and cries. Every day they grew less; before they ceased, he began to ask to be put in. At the end of a fortnight, the desired result had been achieved: he no longer feared the sea. From that moment, we left him completely free, and he bathed of his own accord whenever the weather was suitable—obviously with the greatest enjoyment. Fear had not ceased altogether, but had been partly repressed by pride. Familiarity, however, made the fear grow rapidly less, and it has now ceased altogether. His sister, now twenty months old, has never shown any fear of the sea, and runs straight in without the slightest hesitation.

—Bertrand Russell, *Education and the Good Life.*[4]

[B] That evening we were busily occupied completing catalogues and other written work. The camp was very still and Ben and Bassi had long since departed into the blackness of the night with the shotguns and the torch. A shot rang out some distance away and was followed almost immediately by a quick left and right. After a short pause there came further firing. Suddenly I developed a keen desire to see the spoils and decided to slip out of camp and join the hunt. Taking the spare torch, I crept away unobserved and was soon weaving my way among the trees and creepers in the direction from which the occasional shots still rang out. When I was some distance from the

[4] Reprinted by courtesy of the Liveright Publishing Corporation.

position of the last shot fired, I entered an area where a considerable number of animals were noisily moving through the trees above me, apparently shifting from the centre of danger. I shone the beams of the torch upwards in the hope of catching a glimpse of them. When I did so my whole inside gave a clutch with excitement and delight as I gazed upward, for suspended from a branch almost directly above me was an animal of the most curious though unaccountably lovable appearance. This statement may sound mad, but to those whose childhood was spent among Teddy bears it may perhaps be intelligible. It was upside down, with an eager little round face peering down over its back at me. So low down was it, indeed, that I could only watch fascinated while it licked its pink nose with a tiny pink tongue to match. The rest of the body was compact, brown and woolly. It blinked at me in the glaring light and then began laboriously clambering forward in the direction of the tree trunk, still suspended upside down like a sloth. A presumably natural urge prompted me to attempt a climb so that I could come to closer quarters with this adorable little toy of the forest and perhaps even capture it. The climb was not an easy one, though it was a miracle that there were any branches at all to allow of an ascent. This was difficult, as I had to keep the torch beam on the animal all the time so that it would not disappear among the tangled foliage, and the whole procedure evolved into a race between myself and the potto (for that was what it was) to reach the angle between the branch and the trunk. Most unfortunately I got there first.

—Ivan Sanderson, *Animal Treasure*.[5]

2. Combine these paragraphs into longer and more unified paragraphs:

[A] The traffic problem in the United States has become one of the greatest problems of the day. The national gov-

[5] Reprinted by courtesy of the Viking Press.

ernment, the state, and the city are all working as one to solve this all important problem.

Each year the national government sets aside sums of money to be used for traffic-benefiting devices.

The state also plays a large part in helping to regulate traffic. Large sums of money have been given to make hard-surfaced roads. Roads have been widened and stop-and-go lights have been placed in small towns that could not afford them.

The state also provides officers who see that the drivers of cars obey the traffic regulations, and these officers are a very great help in eliminating traffic congestion on holidays and Sundays.

The city, I think, plays the greatest part in regulating the traffic. It provides many ways of helping the motorist and at the same time safeguarding the pedestrian.

The city provides parking places for motorists. There are stop-and-go lights to eliminate officers and reduce municipal expense. Traffic laws also provide that fire plugs be marked so that in case of fire there will be no difficulty in getting to the most convenient plug.

Traffic by water is much older than that by auto. Therefore its traffic problems have been largely solved. Yet the United States government has spent millions of dollars in making harbors, dredging rivers, and digging canals.

Undoubtedly the Panama Canal is one of the greatest engineering feats ever accomplished. .Why did the United States build it? Because the traffic was getting so heavy that it was necessary. Like other traffic devices, it was made to save time.

[B] In Sweden, information is assembled from private business so that a tolerably clear picture is available at the beginning of each year as to the probable volume of private investment in the next twelve months.

This enables the government to plan public works, public improvement projects and housing, so as to bring the total volume of capital outlays, public and private, up to the required level.

This is responsible public finance.

If we in the United States are to avoid mass unemployment and give our magnificently productive economy a chance to operate at full employment, we must: (a) raise to much higher levels the volume of mass consumption; (b) encourage a high level of private investment, and (c) plan ahead an adequate volume of useful and productive public investment which can be timed to offset fluctuations in the private sector.

To raise the level of mass consumption, we must raise wages as rapidly as increases in man-hour productivity permit.

Also, we must raise the level of public school education in the backward parts of our country. It is intolerable that millions of American citizens should continue to be "functional illiterates."

This is a national problem. The poorer states and localities are already taxing their people, in proportion to income, more heavily than the rich states. Yet the level of education is intolerably low. There is no solution except federal aid for public education.

We need greatly expanded public health facilities to stamp out disease.

We must extend our social security program to provide adequately for old age, unemployment, and loss of work through sickness.

We need better housing. In every town and city, we should plan, over the next two decades, an attack upon slum and blighted areas. We need to rebuild these areas on a planned basis, providing ample open spaces to prevent overcrowding.

This redevelopment, except for needed public building and some low-cost housing would be undertaken by private development companies. Urban redevelopment along these lines will protect the financial values of new structures. It will stop the continued spread of slum and blight which progressively is driving our cities into an intolerable financial position.

All these measures act as a great irrigating system distributing mass purchasing power throughout the country.

Without mass purchasing power, we cannot find markets for our mass production industries.

—Alvin Hansen, "Financing the United States," Chicago *Sun*, April 25, 1944.

7. TOPIC STATEMENT

In writing that is primarily argumentative or expository, each paragraph often contains a sentence or statement which gives the gist of that particular division of the whole composition. A topic statement may *announce* the topic to be treated, or it may *summarize* the contents of the paragraph. Though it usually comes at or near the beginning, it may come anywhere in the paragraph. Following are paragraphs whose topic statements have been put in italics:

A more popular and lasting basis of a humorous story is the theme of mistaken identity. Mr. Jones is mistaken for Mr. Brown, whereupon all things may happen. This is especially the case if the two people confused are really of utterly different categories—if an Egyptologist is mistaken for a plumber or a bishop gets mixed up with a janitor, or a lunatic at large is mistaken for all sorts of people.

—Stephen Leacock, *How to Write.*[6]

Hardened—I beg your pardon—softened first-nighters to whom I have put this riddle have never been able to give me very satisfactory answers. *Your true first-nighter, I can only presume, is born with a passion for the theatre;* he loves it always, for its own sake, blindly (for love is

[6] Copyright 1943, by Dodd, Mead & Company, Inc.

blind), uncritically. He pays his money at the box office, he leaves his judgment in the cloak-room along with his great-coat, hat and walking stick, and takes his seat, certain that he will enjoy himself, whatever may happen on the stage. The stuffiness and the crowd, the dark, expectant hush and then the apocalyptic rising of the curtain, the glitter and the shining, painted unreality—these are enough in themselves to make him happy. He does not ask for more. I envy him his easily contented mind.

—Aldous Huxley, *Along the Road.*[7]

The private life of Lincoln continued, and for many years increasingly, to be equally marked by indiscriminate sociability and brooding loneliness. Comfort and the various influences which may be associated with the old-fashioned American word "elegance" seem never to enter into it. What is more, little can be discerned of positive happiness in the background of his life, as the freakish elasticity of his youth disappeared and, after a certain measure of marked success, the further objects of his ambition though not dropped became unlikely of attainment and seemed, we may guess, of doubtful value. *All along he was being moulded for endurance rather than for enjoyment.*

—Lord Charnwood, *Abraham Lincoln.*[8]

When you come to write you will find that the parts of your outline suggest the topic statements. Do not slavishly repeat the phrases of the outline; you do not want the skeleton to show through the flesh. Try to introduce each point in an interesting way, and vary the position of the topic statements. A whole series of paragraphs, each commencing with a topic statement, becomes tiresome and gives the impression of amateurishness.

[7] Reprinted by courtesy of Harper & Brothers.
[8] Copyright, 1917, by Henry Holt and Co., Inc. Published by Henry Holt and Co., Inc.

EXERCISE 2. 1. Select the topic statement in each of the following paragraphs:

[A] If, as I have said, the things already listed were all we had to contribute, America would have made no distinctive and unique gift to mankind. But there has been also the *American dream,* that dream of a land in which life should be better and fuller and richer for every man, with opportunity for each according to his ability or achievement. It is a difficult dream for the European upper classes to interpret adequately, and too many of us ourselves have grown weary and mistrustful of it. It is not a dream of motor cars and high wages merely, but a dream of a social order in which each man and each woman shall be able to attain to the fullest stature of which they are innately capable, and be recognized by others for what they are, regardless of the fortuitous circumstances of birth or position. I once had an intelligent young Frenchman as guest in New York, and after a few days I asked him what struck him most among his new impressions. Without hesitation he replied, "The way that every one of every sort looks you right in the eye, without a thought of inequality." Some time ago a foreigner who used to do some work for me, and who had picked up a very fair education, used occasionally to sit and chat with me in my study after he had finished his work. One day he said that such a relationship was the great difference between America and his homeland. There, he said, "I would do my work and might get a pleasant word, but I could never sit and talk like this. There is a difference there between social grades which cannot be got over. I would not talk to you there as man to man, but as my employer."

—James Truslow Adams, "The American Dream." [9]

[9] Reprinted by permission of Atlantic Monthly Press (Little, Brown & Co.).

[B] Their popularity was a result of the changing social and economic scene. A century earlier it would not have been possible. The increased leisure and generally higher standard of living of the laboring masses in the first instance made possible the rôle of these diversions in modern life, but equally important was the new attitude toward amusement which was itself born of this economic progress. By the opening of the twentieth century, recreation had become fully accepted in this country as a natural right of people of whatever social status. The concept of democracy coalesced with the profitable economy of mass production to flood the land with moving pictures, automobiles, and radios. It was not by accident that in no other country of the world did any comparable diffusion of these new means of amusement take place among the masses of the people.

—Foster R. Dulles, *America Learns to Play*.[10]

[C] It would, however, be a great mistake to suppose that all our "popular" terms are of native origin, and that all foreign derivatives are "learned." The younger and less cultivated members of a community are naturally inclined to imitate the speech of the older and more cultivated. Hence, as time has passed, a great number of French and Latin words, and even some that are derived from the Greek, have made themselves quite at home in ordinary conversation. Such words, whatever their origin, are as truly popular as if they had been a part of our language from the earliest period.

—J. B. Greenough and G. L. Kittredge,
"Learned Words and Popular Words." [11]

[D] Again the plainest diet seems the fittest to be preceded by the grace. That which is least stimulative to ap-

[10] Reprinted by permission of D. Appleton-Century Co.
[11] Reprinted by permission of the Macmillan Company, publishers.

petite leaves the mind most free for foreign considerations. A man may feel thankful, heartily thankful, over a dish of plain mutton with turnips, and have leisure to reflect upon the ordinance and institution of eating; when he shall confess a perturbation of mind, inconsistent with the purposes of the grace, at the presence of venison or turtle. When I have sate at rich men's tables, with the savoury soup and messes steaming up the nostrils, and moistening the lips of the guests with desire and a distracted choice, I have felt the introduction of that ceremony to be unseasonable. With the ravenous orgasm upon you, it seems impertinent to interpose a religious sentiment. It is a confusion of purpose to mutter out praises from a mouth that waters. The heats of epicurism put out the gentle flame of devotion. The incense which rises round is pagan, and the belly-god intercepts it for his own. The very excess of the provision beyond the needs, takes away all sense of proportion between the end and means. The giver is veiled by his gifts. You are startled at the injustice of returning thanks—for what?—for having too much, while so many starve. It is to praise the Gods amiss.

—Charles Lamb, "Grace Before Meat."

2. Supply topic statements for each of the following:

[A] It is true, of course, that a genius may, on certain lines, do more than a brave and manly fellow who is not a genius; and so, in sports, vast physical strength may overcome weakness, even though the puny body may have in it the heart of a lion. But, in the long run, in the great battle of life, no brilliancy of intellect, no perfection of bodily development, will count when weighed in the balance against that assemblage of virtues, active and passive, or moral qualities, which we group together under the name of character; and if between any two contestants, even in college sport or in college work, the difference in character on the right side is as great as the difference of intellect or strength the other way, it is the character side that will win.

—Theodore Roosevelt, *The Strenuous Life*.[12]

[B] Thus it was left to the white man to recover this lost Indian history. Yet this was only one of many puzzles the New World offered as a challenge to European intelligence. On a more material level it offered opportunity, wealth and adventure. All the old families of white America, whose traditions made our culture what it is, are the descendants of explorers and adventurers whose legends are so deeply rooted in our scheme of life that the first thing one of us thinks of doing when he attains a little leisure is to go off on an expedition. Great popular award and acclaim go to the explorer who finds something new. To discover dinosaur eggs is more popular than to lead an army to victory. And how the mystery of the Indian stirs one! The first white scholars in Europe and America assumed that the Indian came from the Old World. After Russian explorers in the north Pacific Ocean made it clear that Alaska almost touched the mainland of Asia, wise men said the Indian came from that continent. You will find such statements in the oldest books upon the subject. In 1739 a great portrait painter named Smibert came to Boston to paint the colonial governors. He had painted at the Russian Court and so was familiar with the Siberians who appeared there from time to time. When Smibert saw Indians he pronounced them Mongolians. From that day to this, notwithstanding the intensive research of specialists, everything points to a Mongoloid ancestry for the Indian. Even the oldest human bones found in America have been pronounced Mongoloid. So one question is answered: the first man to discover America came from Siberia. This may not be the final answer, but since nothing to contradict it has

[12] Reprinted by permission of the D. Appleton-Century Company.

been discovered since 1492 we must accept it as the best answer.

—Clark Wissler, *Indians of the United States.*[13]

3. Write a paragraph developing one of the following topic statements:

    a. Writing makes an exact man.
    b. A game is never lost until the final whistle blows.
    c. The newspaper is the poor man's university.
    d. Architecture is frozen music.
    e. The evil that men do lives after them.
    f. A jammed landing gear does not leave one much choice.
    g. The noise of the machines was terrific, but not without variety.

8. SELECTION OF MATERIAL

A. Avoid any omission of material that is relevant, especially facts or assumptions which form important links in your general argument.

FAULTY: In not going to college I missed the opportunity of association and friendship with men of wide culture and high ideals in an atmosphere of quiet and detachment. It was many years before I ever had the opportunity of close and friendly contact with men whose intellect and culture were superior to my own. I know that it would have broadened and enriched my life if I had been exposed at an impressionable age to the example of men who had read, studied, and traveled.

REVISED: In not going to college I missed the opportunity of association and friendship with men of wide culture and high ideals in an atmosphere of quiet and detachment.

[13] Copyright, 1940, by Doubleday & Company, Inc.

I went to work when I was sixteen years old because at that age it seems important to eat ravenously and regularly— seems more important than it really is. My associations thenceforth were with folk who were neither scholars nor gentlemen. It was many years before I ever had the opportunity of close and friendly contact with men whose intellect and whose culture were superior to my own. I know that it would have broadened and enriched my life if I had been exposed at an impressionable age to the example of men who had read, studied, and traveled.

Note that the second paragraph is more effective because it fills in the gap between the first and second sentences of the faulty version. The sentences inserted tell us why the author didn't go to college, and its consequences.

B. Exclude all facts or statements which do not contribute directly (1) to the purpose for which you have designed the paragraph or (2) to the conclusion you are attempting to reach.

FAULTY: The modern automobile has proved its value to the American people both for usefulness and pleasure. Think of the amount of business and the number of businesses which depend on motor transportation. Think of the distances we have to cover in so large a country and how inaccessible much of our population would be if it were not for cars. Of course there are other means of transportation, and we all have our preferences. Some prefer trains, and some would rather fly. The Sunday drive, too, is a great American institution, taking us to see our friends and getting city people out into the country for a healthful change.

REVISED: The automobile has proved its value to the American people for both usefulness and pleasure. Think of the amount of business and the number of businesses which depend on motor transportation. Think of the distances we have to cover in so large a country and how inaccessible much of our population would be if it were not for cars. Thanks to them, too, the Sunday drive has become a great American institution, taking us to see our friends and getting city people out into the country for a healthful change.

EXERCISE 3. 1. Exclude from the following paragraph whatever material you consider superfluous:

More than ever before youth should be the object of our solicitude. All over the world the enthusiasm of youth, the restlessness of the parent reflected in the young, the flaming desire of boys and girls to spring to the relief of their distressed families, all have brought about a new problem which we must solve. Our youth eagerly, anxiously are seeking new opportunity. Despite temporary limitations, they will find their goal if we but preserve to them the thing rightfully theirs—the opportunity and the means for a sound education. Would that we fathers and mothers gathered here today had been afforded the same opportunity as the present-day youth. At this point I feel it incumbent upon me to address a word to both boys and girls and their parents in relation to the vital and ever-growing need for vocational education. Each year there has been graduated in the past and will continue to be graduated in the future a very large number of students from your high school here in Stonington. Many of these young boys and girls are fortunate enough to have both the means and the inclination to matriculate further and obtain college degrees, and many also have neither the means nor the inclination to pursue a college education. It is to the latter group that I speak today, because I have experienced an increasing concern for the future welfare of these boys and girls. I cannot urge too strongly, therefore, these boys and girls and their parents to take advantage of every opportunity for vocational training that will be afforded in this fine new institution, the new Stonington High School. It is quite true that we have in this great country of ours today an increasing number of unemployed, but the basic reason for this unemployment is the lack of training on the part of our youth. And so I say to those of you who do not plan to attend universities and seek professions, equip yourselves for your future, at any cost. You have before you some of the most revolutionary industries of the age still in their infancy: air conditioning, the radio, and television, industries almost unheard of when most of our boys and girls were babies. And to the parents I say have your children take advantage of the splendid opportunities afforded in these industries to make their future secure and the future of the fine families they will contribute to their communities.

9. SEQUENCE OF THOUGHT

Present your ideas in the most logical order.

FAULTY: In any country or age architecture is limited by the building materials which are available. In turn these various materials give rise to different types of construction. Wood must be held together through beams jointed into framing; stone must be assembled in blocks; clay is held by continuous aggregation. In forest country wood will, of course, be the chief material. If the country is rocky, stone buildings will be developed. In open country without trees or stone, the builders often resort to clay for material.

REVISED: In any country or age the nature of the architecture is determined by the building materials which are available. In a forest country wood will, of course, be the chief material. If the country is rocky, stone buildings will be developed. In a country that is without trees or stone, the builders often resort to clay for material. In turn these various materials give rise to different types of construction. Wood must be held together through beams jointed into framing; stone must be assembled in blocks; clay is held together by continuous aggregation.

EXERCISE 4. These sentences have been intentionally disarranged. Put the sentences in their proper order in a paragraph.

(1) Of course there is nothing new about this. (2) Farmers in this country too, in the days before rural electrification became a reality, used wind motors for pumping water. (3) Such projects present difficult engineering problems. (4) We refer to the use of wind for power production. (5) But only in the past decade have schemes for commercial power production by wind engaged the planners of public utilities. (6) In the windswept areas of Holland windmills have for centuries added their picturesque silhouettes to the landscape. (7) The exploitation of climatic "income" has also spread in another direction. (8) To adjust the variable wind to the variable load is so complicated that many engineers have rejected the scheme as impractical. (9) Economical power production, however, is based on maintaining proper levels for the fluctuating load requirements. (10) The wind in most localities is quite variable in direction and intensity.

10. CONNECTION

Connect your material in such a way that the relation of the various elements of the paragraph to one another will be clear.

Use the devices which were suggested on pages 15–17 on the whole theme. Observe these connectives:

While I do not believe in *these* restrictive measures and paying for not raising crops, I decided it was no worse than the rest of the bill and I would let it go by without too much objection. *However,* when I began to inquire about the bill and put the question to its author as between early rose and late rose potatoes, I found it did not apply. I found it was not the early or late variety that counted, but where the potatoes were raised. *For example,* potatoes raised in Pennsylvania would receive the 4-cent rate, but over the state line in Maryland the bonus would be 6 cents. *This* extra pay of 2 cents a bushel would be forthcoming to all who danced to the fiddler, and all of the way south from the Pennsylvania and Maryland state line as far as our domain extends, *this* 6-cent rate would prevail.

11. CONSISTENCY

Re-read the paragraphs illustrating consistency on pages 17–21. Notice the following paragraphs:

UNNECESSARY SHIFT IN PERSON: When men feel patriotic toward their country, they feel that the only way for that country to exist and to become great is through having an army. Although such is not so widely the case in the United States, one sees it throughout Europe where conditions are different. Here, we feel that we are quite safe from war, and that we can become great economically. In Europe, however, many large competing countries are close together, countries which have no love for each other. To be patriotic means to love your country, to love your country means to want to protect it, and certainly plenty of protection is needed by European countries.

UNNECESSARY SHIFT IN NUMBER: In adjusting myself to fraternity life, I have been faced with a number of problems. The chief of these is maintaining an open mind. One of the first things to consider is the fellows that we are associated with and their ideas. In many cases they may have very little initiative of their own and just let the other fellow do their thinking for them. This soon becomes a habit and is passed on to the new member.

UNNECESSARY SHIFT IN TENSE: The best movie produced in the last three months, in my opinion, is *The Miracle on Thirty-Fourth Street,* in which Edmund Gwenn starred. Mr. Gwenn played the part of Santa Claus with something close to perfection. The part is made rather difficult by the fact that he really thinks he is Santa Claus even when not in costume.

12. EFFECTIVENESS

A. An effective paragraph has a clear and concisely worded topic statement.

See pages 45, 46.

B. Pay particular attention to the beginning and ending of your paragraphs to avoid unemphatic or inconclusive writing.

INEFFECTIVE BEGINNING: I shall attempt to discuss the free recreational facilities provided by the city. A city as large and populous as New York needs a multiplicity of parks, playgrounds, swimming pools, and the like.

INEFFECTIVE CONCLUSION: Both young and old alike sometimes wanted more exciting recreation, turning to petty thievery, which in later years could turn them into criminals. As a result of these poorer children trying to find excitement, juvenile delinquency became a great problem. Children were sent to reform schools, where some of them turned into hardened criminals. Perhaps it seems far-fetched to some that all the above-mentioned things result from a lack of recreational facilities, but it has happened. Of course there have been other factors involved.

INEFFECTIVE BEGINNING AND CONCLUSION: Perhaps I could refer to a very good example by going back to the days when Napoleon was running rough-shod over Europe. Since the then-divided German states were too near to his own country, it was only natural that the great French general should war with them. At the time, the citizens of the various German states were getting along none too well among themselves. There was no sense of unity; they did not think of themselves as a single nation. However, the threat of Napoleon threw them together for mutual protection, and they no longer thought of themselves as separate states. They became patriotic Germans. Furthermore, was it not also natural for them to become militaristic under such circumstances?

EFFECTIVE BEGINNING AND CONCLUSION: Perhaps the men of genius are the only true men. In all the history of the race there have been only a few thousand real men. And the rest of us—what are we? Teachable animals. Without the help of the real men, we should have found out almost nothing at all. Almost all the ideas with which we are familiar could never have occurred to minds like ours. Plant the seeds there and they will grow; but our minds could never spontaneously have generated them.

—Aldous Huxley, *Along the Road,*
Young Archimedes.[14]

The whole swing of American style, for a quarter century past, has been toward greater and greater freedom in the use of essentially national idioms. The tart admonitions of English purists—as, for example, in the *Literary Supplement* of the London *Times*—are no longer directed solely or even mainly to writers who need apology at home: the offenders now include many of the best we have yet produced. And they begin to get the understanding and

[14] Reprinted by courtesy of Harper & Brothers.

approval of a larger and larger fraction of intelligent English-men.

> —H. L. Mencken, *Supplement One,*
> *The American Language.*[15]

All the English teachers in the country are trying to get their pupils to discover the varied relationships of ideas, and to range their ideas in the proper order of subordination. Hemingway is just as strenuously working to reduce all ideas to a single order of relationship, the conjunctive coördinate relationship, in which no one item is subordinated to any other. It is the great leveling democracy of the *and*. Both Hemingway and the English teachers have their reasons. The teachers are concerned with the logical structure of thought and with hoping to raise their pupils a few degrees in their level of understanding. The writer of fiction is concerned with the aesthetic projection of images. The understanding spirals back upon itself and ties itself in subtle knots that will hold the thought firm. But the writer of fiction is telling a story, and he wants it to flow and not be lost in eddies of logic.

> —Joseph Warren Beach,
> *American Fiction, 1920–1940.*[16]

C. Vary sentence structure to avoid monotony.

FAULTY: These men know that they will receive their government checks. These checks represent buying power for the purchase of goods, although the men can buy little with the checks. Therefore the workers have little or no incentive to work, so they accomplish little towards real efficiency. On the other hand the worker in a society of equals will have no security as to a pay check. His security will depend upon the quality of his work and co-operation with other men.

[15] Reprinted by permission of Alfred A. Knopf Co.
[16] Reprinted by permission of Macmillan Co., publishers.

IMPROVED: These men know that they will receive their government checks, representing purchasing power, although not much can be bought with them. Therefore, having little or no incentive to work, such laborers scarcely attain what may be called real efficiency. In a society of equals, on the other hand, there is no such security as a pay check for a worker. Instead, the quality of his work and the extent of his co-operation with others determine his security.

D. Repetition of sentence structure may sometimes make a paragraph more emphatic.

This standpoint establishes for us a certain scale of values. In every aspect of knowledge and of living, the test of life holds. It accounts for our pleasures and our antipathies. The test of life was with us a racial thought, wordless and needing no definition or giving of reasons. It was that test of life which, instinctively I think, guided us to distrust civic civilization and uphold the rural ideal in art, life and letters, to dislike religion in our rational moments, to play with Buddhism but never quite accept its logical conclusions, and to hate mechanical ingenuity. It was that instinctive trust in life that gave us a robust common sense in looking at life's kaleidoscopic changes and the myriad vexatious problems of the intellect which we rudely ignored. It enabled us to see life steadily and see life whole, with no great distortions of values. It taught us some simple wisdom, like respect for old age and the joys of domestic life, acceptance of life, of sex and of sorrow. It made us lay emphasis on certain common virtues, like endurance, industry, thrift, moderation and pacificism. It prevented the development of freakish extreme theories and the enslaving of man by the products of his own intelligence. It gave us a sense of values, and taught us to accept the material as well as the spiritual goods of life. It taught us that, after all is said and done, human happiness is the end of all knowledge. And we arrange ourselves to make our lives happy on this planet, under whatever vicissitudes of fortune.

—Lin Yutang, *My Country and My People.*[17]

EXERCISE 5. 1. Analyze the paragraphing in the leading editorial in your newspaper for any selected day. Notice the length and unity of the paragraphs, the sequence of ideas, the way in which they are connected, and the devices used to make them forceful.

2. Do the same for advertisements in various types of magazines: fashion magazines, garden magazines, science magazines, etc.

3. Apply a similar analysis to essays in such magazines as *Harper's,* the *Atlantic Monthly, Fortune,* etc.

4. Apply this analysis to a novel you have recently read.

13. MECHANICAL REQUIREMENTS

In handwritten manuscripts the first word of each paragraph should be indented one-half inch or more, depending upon the size of the handwriting. At all times the indentation must be uniform and clearly visible. Indent five spaces when typing double-spaced manuscript. Every paragraph begins on a new line. When the last sentence of the paragraph ends before the right-hand margin of the page is reached, the remainder of the line is left blank.

14. PARAGRAPHING DIALOGUE

A. In dialogue or conversation each quotation from a new speaker is usually paragraphed, along with that portion of the sentence which introduces the speech or announces the speaker.

[17] Reprinted by permission of the John Day Co.

Once I asked him the name of the ship on which he was captain.

"It was in 1943," he said vaguely. "War time."

"What was the name of the ship?"

"Number Four."

"What kind of a ship was Number Four?"

"It was a barge, a munitions barge. It was towed between Wilmington and the Navy Yard, and I was captain."

A few modern writers vary from this standard practice, but the student will do well to master it just because it is standard. Unless innovation has positive value, avoid it.

B. In quotations within connected narrative, if the quotation demands emphasis it is paragraphed separately; if the unity between the quotation and the context is more important, the quotation is not made a separate paragraph.

Uttering cries of consternation, Ray's parents rushed after him. They found their son, still enfolded in the big boa and sagging under its weight, quietly laughing as he stroked and soothed it. A few moments more, and he had induced it to cast off and crawl peaceably into its cage.

"Oh, Ray, what a frightful sight!" his mother exclaimed weakly, as she sank into a chair.

Ray grinned. "That's a very gentle, good-tempered snake, Mama," he explained. "If ever a snake had an excuse to lose its temper and strike, that one did, the way Pop was punishing its tail."

"I never did care for snakes," John Ditmars growled, wiping beads of perspiration off his pale forehead.

—L. N. Wood, *Raymond L. Ditmars.*[18]

[18] Reprinted by permission of Julian Messner, Inc.

I got out of bed quietly so as not to wake Molly, dressed and went down the back way over to the Thomas house. There was no one stirring but I knew which room Joe's was. The window was open and I could hear him snoring. I went up and stuck my head in.

"Hey," I said, "killing frost!"

He opened his eyes and looked at me and then his eyes went shut. I reached my arm through the window and shook him. "Get up," I said. "We got to start right away."

—Caroline Gordon, "The Last Day in the Field." [19]

The cruellest thing he heard this man say was to a boy who was rather thick and fat but conscientious. "You can't draw," he said roughly. "Take my advice and go home. You'll make more money driving a wagon."

—Dreiser, *The Genius*.

C. When a quotation is introduced by a portion of a preceding sentence, paragraphing the quotation separately gives it emphasis.

Gideon rose, blinked his eyes, and followed the secretary to the office. Grant was sitting behind his desk, hunched, tired, red-eyed, a man defeated and lost and regarding the long, empty years before him without hope and without pleasure. He nodded and said:

"Sit down, Gideon," and then told his secretary, "I don't want to be interrupted."

—Howard Fast, *Freedom Road*.[20]

Holly turned her head, pointed with her little brown fist to the piano—for to point with a finger was not "well-brrred"—and said slyly:

[19] Reprinted by permission of Charles Scribner's Sons.
[20] Reprinted by permission of Duell, Sloan and Pearce, Inc.

"Look at the 'lady in grey,' Gran; isn't she pretty today?"

Old Jolyon's heart gave a flutter, and for a second the room was clouded; then it cleared, and he said with a twinkle:

"Who's been dressing her up?"

—Galsworthy, *The Forsyte Saga*.[21]

15. TYPES OF PARAGRAPH DEVELOPMENT

A good, well-rounded paragraph requires careful planning and development. The following paragraphs illustrate how good writers use various means of paragraph development:

A. Definition.

We have, then, in attempting to make more precise *our definition of socialism,* to avoid relating it in our minds to any utopian picture of the future. We can say that socialists seek the common ownership and collective control of the means of production and exchange; but we cannot say that this involves either the "nationalization" of all industries or some particular way of managing them. There are many possible forms of common ownership—nationally by the state, locally by municipalities or similar bodies, and locally or nationally by quasi-public trusts, guilds or corporations acting on behalf of the public. There are also many possible forms of administration—directly by state or municipal departments, by specially constituted boards or commissions of experts, or by representative bodies of producers or consumers or of both. All these forms of ownership and administration have had advocates among socialists, and many socialist plans embody features from several of them, or allow for diversity of experiment in different

[21] Reprinted by permission of Charles Scribner's Sons.

cases. Nor can it even be assumed that socialists wish all the means of production to be publicly owned. If the vital and basic industries and services were under public control, many socialists would be ready to leave smaller enterprises largely in private hands.

—G. D. H. Cole, in
Encyclopædia Britannica (14th ed.).[22]

B. Particularization and Exemplification.

The statement of a general truth or principle is followed by a number of specific facts which support it.

In any tree, however live and growing, the substance composing trunk and branch is inert and lifeless matter. The heartwood of a tree, the heaviest and solidest part, extending a considerable distance from the centre, is dead in every sense of the word. Its tubes no longer convey the sap upward, because their walls have become thickened and filled with lignin. In them there is not even the semblance of vital activity. From the heartwood outward to a point very near the surface we find the water-conveying structure consisting of long tubes; and these tubes are mere conduits, inert and lifeless. They serve a useful purpose in conveying the water upward, but they are not themselves alive. At first, when they were being built, there were live cells working inside of them, little bags of protoplasm; but, once they were completed, the live tenants disappeared. Interspersed among these tubes is tissue which still contains protoplasm, but it is not alive in the sense that it can grow or reproduce itself.

—Charles D. Stewart, "The Tree as an Invention." [23]

C. Generalization.

A number of specific facts are presented, and a general conclusion is drawn from them.

[22] Reprinted by courtesy of *Encyclopædia Britannica*.
[23] Reprinted by courtesy of the author.

It is a matter of course that a familiar piece of music, whether a tune you heard in your childhood or a symphony you have studied, cannot come to you otherwise than charged with associations. Herein lies a meaning of music, a meaning which technical language cannot define, yet which it would be stupid to deny. Even in music which we hear for the first time the suggestion of familiar things plays upon us continually, and with meaning. They may be things not personally but only racially familiar. The timbre of voices, the sound of instruments surely act upon us in this way. For whom could the music of bagpipes be only a sequence of sounds, their fine melodic variations only patterns in tonal design. The difference between the oboe and the flute is far more than the difference in the order of their partial tones. Each instrument is inseparable from associations that run back perhaps thousands of years. So it is with the trumpet, the drum, the guitar, and in fact, with most instruments. I cannot hold that those have less enjoyed music, have even perhaps less understood it, whose memory has drifted from their listening, whose imagination has conjured visions athwart the sound.

—Leland Hall, "The Power of Music,"
Harper's Magazine, May, 1933.[24]

D. Cause to Effect.

The most fateful mistake Venezuela made when she appeared on the political stage was beyond doubt the adoption of a regime of tolerance. The law codes by which our magistrates were guided were not designed to teach them the practical science of government. They were the compilation of certain amiable visionaries who, with an imaginary republic in mind, aimed for political perfection, and assumed the perfectibility of mankind. As a result, we had

[24] Reprinted by courtesy of *Harper's Magazine.*

philosophers for leaders, philanthropy for legislation, dialectics for policy, and sophists for soldiers.

Jules Mancini, "Bolivar's First Campaign," in
The Green Continent, ed. by German Arciniegas.[25]

E. Effect to Cause.

Unhappily, too, Thompson's verse is certainly fatiguing to read, and one of the reasons why it is so fatiguing is that the thought that is in it does not progress; it remains stationary. About the fragile life which cries somewhere in its center he builds up walls of many colored bricks, immuring his idea, hiding it, stifling it. How are we to read an ode of many pages in which there is no development, not even movement? Stanza is heaped upon stanza, page is piled upon page, and we end where we began. The writer has said endless things about something but never the thing itself. Poetry consists in saying the thing itself.

—Arthur Symons, *Dramatis Personæ.*[26]

F. Comparison and Contrast.

A European, when he first arrives, seems limited in his intentions, as well as in his views; but he very suddenly alters his scale; two hundred miles formerly appeared a very great distance; it is now but a trifle; he no sooner breathes our air than he forms schemes, and embarks in designs he never would have thought of in his own country. There the plenitude of society confines many useful ideas, and often extinguishes the most laudable schemes, which here ripen into maturity. Thus Europeans become Americans.

—Hector St. John de Crèvecoeur,
Letters from an American Farmer, III.

[25] Reprinted by permission of Alfred A. Knopf, Inc.
[26] Copyright 1923. Used by special permission of the publishers, the Bobbs-Merrill Company.

G. Elimination.

Develops what the subject is not and finally what it is.

This brings us to another kind of thought which can fairly easily be distinguished from the three kinds described above. It has not the usual qualities of the reverie, for it does not hover about our personal complacencies and humiliations. It is not made up of the homely decisions forced upon us by everyday needs, when we review our little stock of existing information, consult our conventional preferences and obligations, and make a choice of action. It is not the defense of our own cherished beliefs and prejudices just because they are our own—mere plausible excuses for remaining of the same mind. On the contrary, it is that peculiar species of thought which leads us to *change* our mind.

—James Harvey Robinson,
The Mind in the Making.[27]

[27] Reprinted by courstey of Harper & Brothers.

THE SENTENCE

*T*HE SENTENCE is the basic unit of language, a relatively complete utterance. It may be only one word long, or may run on for a hundred or more words if the thing to be expressed is complex; but whatever its length, it gives the hearer or reader a sense of relative completeness as it stands. When we speak or write our native language, we put words unconsciously into sentence patterns, which exist, just like the words, as characteristics of the language. These sentence patterns differ from language to language, but each particular language has its own stock on which its users may draw. We, for instance, without thinking consciously about it, know that if we say *I have* it means one thing, while *Have I* means another. Or in the words of the old joke, a headline saying *Dog Bites Man* is nothing, but one saying *Man Bites Dog* is *news*.

On the number of sentence patterns which a speaker or writer has at his command obviously depends the variety of ways in which he is able to express himself, the responsiveness and adaptability of his thoughts. Every native user of English knows the basic patterns already, but all of us can increase our range—and must, if we are to write better.

1. SPEECH AND WRITING

Before beginning the examination of sentences, however, we must note one big distinction in language: the difference between speech and writing. Consider the following piece of conversation, which might take place on any campus:

Morning, Mary.
Hello, Bill! Well, how'd you do on the exam?
Not too badly—made my B.

You *didn't!* Were you relieved?

Was I relieved! Means my scholarship'll be re-
newed, that's all. Now I can quit worrying
about a loan or a summer job.

Say, that's fine. So now you can celebrate.

I'm planning to. In fact, Mary—

Yes?

Well, the Frosh Fling is next Tuesday night, and I
thought maybe—

Well?

How about it? Eight o'clock, informal.

Well, I wasn't planning anything else—

It's a date then. O.K.?

O.K.

Swell! See you Tuesday. So long!

This piece of conversation, though perhaps not an example of elegance, will be recognized as typical. Actually, it
was spoken, and was directed to the ear; here it has been
written down and is directed to the eye. As a result, certain
features of sound have been translated into terms of sight.
Most obvious is the use of "punctuation" to show pauses
(commas), hesitation (dashes), emphasis (italics, exclamation points).

Less obvious, though always present and essential to
meaning, are features of the voice. Emphasis comes chiefly
from *volume:* Mary speaks more loudly when she says
"didn't" (which is emphatic also to indicate irony); Bill
reduces the volume, speaks a little softly when he begins to
make his invitation, and says "Mary—". The difference
between a question and an exclamation lies chiefly in *pitch:*
the pitch drops at the end of every exclamation, and usually
rises at the end of each question. The phrase "Were you
relieved?" clearly demands an answer, since the voice rises
in pitch at the end; but "Was I relieved!" though grammatically in the form of a question, is clearly not one, since

the pitch of the voice falls definitely at the end. So with "O.K. which is first a question, then an answer, with rising and then falling pitch. These features of voice, though essential to meaning, are inadequately indicated in writing.

There are still other features of the voice which punctuation fails altogether to show. A playwright is often forced to give directions in the script, such as, "in a whisper," "softly," "fiercely"; a narrative writer quoting dialogue frequently adds, "he growled," "she sighed," "said he with a shrug." For in speech we face each other, we react visibly, we make gestures, our voices go up and down, fast and slowly, loudly and softly. The words alone do not have to carry the burden.

In writing, apart from the help which punctuation can give, the words and sentence patterns must do all the work. The shades of facial expression, gesture and intonation are lacking; a substitute must be supplied. This is done through more careful choice of words, greater variety in the sentence patterns, and other such means.

If we look again at the conversation of Mary and Bill, we see that it is very limited in the range of patterns. There are greetings and exclamations (Morning; Swell; So long), abbreviations (made my B; See you Tuesday), fragments (In fact, Mary—; I thought maybe—), answers that are incomplete without their questions (Not too badly—; I'm planning to). These would seldom appear in writing, except as imitations of speech. There are also, however, many of the "relatively complete utterances" which are the staple of both spoken and written language (How'd you do on the exam?; the Frosh Fling is next Tuesday night; It's a date then). Speech has a considerable proportion of the fragments and abbreviations; writing depends almost wholly on the "relatively complete utterances," in a great many variations.

It should be noticed further that the informality of this conversation lies not only in its words, but in its structure.

The thing is obviously made up as it goes along; there is no deliberate phrasing. Something is said, then (often by afterthought) it is supplemented with something more (Say, that's fine. So now you can celebrate. How about it? Eight o'clock. Informal.).

The main difference between the sentences of speech and writing should now be evident.[1] Certainly, not all informal speech is as elementary as the sample (though by far the greatest part of our use of language is of this kind, as we shop and eat and chat with our friends, exchanging opinions and giving information about our doings and plans). But even when ideas are being discussed, or some serious point argued, the same basic situation prevails. Gestures, volume, pitch, tone of voice are still present to aid the words; the speakers still stop and start as the expression comes more or less fluently; they still speak in fragments as they interrupt one another, repeat things for emphasis and continuity, rephrase them as they find a better way.

Much the same process may go on inside us before we write, but it need not show in the finished product. Those trials which prove to be errors may be left aside, and we may present to our reader only the best statement of our thought of which we are capable. It will differ considerably from the uneven, irregular, somewhat haphazard thing that is conversation. For we will have had the time to choose those words and sentence patterns which will make up for the absent shadings of voice and gesture, will avoid unnecessary repetitions, give a tighter, deliberate structure to the expression, and make it far more effective.

2. STRUCTURE OF THE SENTENCE

The vast majority of sentences turn out, when we examine them, to have a single basic structure which we may

[1] Not only the sentences but the words used in conversation may differ from those of good writing. See Chapter IV.

call the conventional one. They are made up of two related parts called a *subject* and a *predicate*.[2] What with
variations and combinations of this basic structure, the
English language has developed a wide range of sentence
patterns to suit the different requirements of expression.
(It is obvious that vigorous, rapid expression will call for
one kind of sentence structure, thoughtful and deliberate
expression another, and so on. The writer must choose
whatever suits his purpose best.) There are also a few
sentence patterns not of this basic structure, which yet,
having been used frequently by able writers, are established
as acceptable. We shall first consider the conventional
sentences, and later the unconventional.

3. SIMPLE SENTENCES

A *simple* sentence is so called because it has only one
subject-predicate combination. For example:

Dogs   bark.
Subject   *Predicate*

Notice how the subject and predicate are related through
their meaning. The subject identifies *who* or *what* the
predicate is telling about, and the predicate gives a *specific
piece of information* about the subject. Without changing
this basic pattern of relationship between subject and predicate we may amplify each in various ways. First the subject:

Dogs   bark.
Simple Subject   *Predicate*

Dogs and foxes   bark.
Compound Subject

[2] When the verb of the predicate is in the imperative mood, the
subject is unexpressed. See Chapter VI.

The dogs on the farm *Simple Subject*	bark.
Angry dogs and foxes *Compound Subject*	bark.

Then the predicate:

Dogs *Subject*	bark. *Simple Predicate*
Dogs	run and bark. *Compound Predicate*
Dogs	run all over the farm. *Simple Predicate*
Dogs	run around and bark angrily. *Compound Predicate*

Or both:

Dogs and foxes *Compound Subject*	run around and bark. *Compound Predicate*

All of the above sentences are *simple* because, though the subject or predicate may have one or more parts, there is only one subject-predicate relationship in each sentence. A subject-predicate group is also called a *clause,* thus one may say that a *simple sentence* has one clause. Other kinds of sentences (*compound, complex,* and combinations of these) are made by uniting two or more clauses in various ways. But before coming to these, we must examine further the nature of the predicate.

A. The English language requires a "finite" verb as the core or basis of the predicate.

Without a finite verb the utterance would not be "relatively complete" in effect. A finite verb is a verb in one of the six tenses: present, past, future, present perfect, past perfect, or future perfect.

Dogs bark.	Present tense
Dogs barked.	Past tense
Dogs will bark.	Future tense
Dogs have barked.	Present perfect tense
Dogs had barked.	Past perfect tense
Dogs will have barked.	Future perfect tense

All these tenses are satisfactory finite forms of the verb. *Dogs are barking, Dogs did bark, or The barking was heard* still satisfy this requirement, for although the parts of the verb *bark* which are used are not finite, each has with it a finite form of an auxiliary verb (*be* or *do,* here).

Note that those non-finite forms of the verb which by themselves do not make satisfactory predicate elements may and often do take on the functions of some other part of speech. Participles and the infinitive, which function often as adjectives and noun respectively, are the chief of these. Compare the following:

Not complete sentences	*Complete sentences*
Dogs barking *Present Participle*	Dogs are barking. *Finite Verb* *Present Participle*
A dog stolen *Past Participle*	A dog was stolen. *Finite Verb* *Past Participle*
To call a dog *Infinitive*	He ought to call a dog. *Finite Verb* *Infinitive*

Although the basic element or core of the subject is usually a noun or pronoun (*Dogs* bark, *Who* cares) and that of the predicate is a verb (Dogs *bark,* Who *cares*), certain verbs require a third element to complete the thought and give meaning to the verb:

Jane was	Incomplete
Ruth bought	Incomplete
He considered this.....	Not necessarily complete

When such verbs are completed by another element, the third element is called a *complement*. Note that the first part of the words *comple*ment and *comple*te are the same.

Jane was *a good student*.	Subjective complement
Ruth bought *a new dress*.	Direct object
He considered this *a wise move*.	Objective complement

Note that the subjective complement refers to the subject, and that the objective complement refers to and completes the meaning of the direct object.

B. The participles and infinitive, when not combined with an auxiliary verb, and therefore functioning as adjectives or noun respectively, are often used to introduce additional details into the senence.

Thus: *Dogs do not bite* is a complete, simple sentence; but we may want to give further detail, so we say:

> Barking   dogs do not bite.
> *Participial Adj.*

And similarly:

> A dog,   stolen from the farm, was found   in the city.
> *Participial Adj. Adverbial Phrase*   *Adverbial Phrase*

> To call   with all the force   at one's command
> *Infinitive Noun*   *Adverbial Phrase*   *Adverbial Phrase*

> is unnecessary.

One may pile up these modifying phrases almost indefinitely (though, of course, this is easily overdone). For example, the following is still a **simple sentence.** Try to separate the subject, the predicate, and the modifying phrases, and decide what each phrase modifies.

Dogs, barking lustily on the farms in the dead of night at the approach of strangers with unfamiliar scents, and growling in their kennels for the protection of their masters asleep in their homes, do not bite at the calves of the intruders but snap at their ankles.

EXERCISE I. Select the subject, verb, and complement (if there is one) in each of the following sentences.

Examples: *The horse galloped.* Subject, *the horse;* verb, *galloped.*
The foundation appeared unstable. Subject, *the foundation;* verb, *appeared;* subjective complement, *unstable.*

1. We were certain of good results.
2. The box contained several letters.
3. A gold watch was found on the floor.
4. They elected Jones secretary.
5. Only the brave deserve the fair.
6. The directory will surely be printed.
7. Hundreds and thousands crowded the streets of the old city.
8. Even the prosperous citizens wore old suits and battered hats.
9. The waves tossed and churned.
10. Not a creature was stirring, not even a mouse.

4. COMPOUND SENTENCES

A compound sentence is so called because it is compounded or made up of what, if separate, would be simple sentences. We may want to keep separate the two simple sentences *Dogs run* and *Rabbits hop;* or we may want to indicate some closer relationship between them, and may therefore convert them into a compound sentence, joining them in some way. There are two chief ways of doing this: by using a co-ordinating conjunction (see page 215) or by placing them side by side with a semicolon between. Occasionally some other mark than a semicolon may be used; see below in this chapter, pages 89, 90. For example:

a. Dogs run   **and**   rabbits hop.
                      Conjunction

b. Dogs run   **but**   rabbits hop.
                      Conjunction

c. Dogs run   **;**   rabbits hop.
                      Semicolon

d. Dogs run   **;**   rabbits hop **;** snakes slide.
                      Semicolon   *Semicolon*

e. Dogs run   **and**   horses trot **;** rabbits hop.
                      Conjunction   *Semicolon*

Notice the variations in these compound sentences: *a, b,* and *c* have two clauses each; *d* and *e* have three clauses each. There is no theoretical limit to the number of clauses which may be in a compound sentence. (Practically, we seldom have use for more than three, since with more the sentence becomes unwieldy or monotonous.) Sentences *a* and *b* use conjunctions alone; *c* and *d* use semicolons alone; *e* combines both.

What differences, of use to a writer, are produced by these various combinations? Apart from the difference in meaning introduced by *and, but,* or the other conjunctions, the chief thing gained is the holding together of the parts so that the reader becomes aware of the relation between them. In *b, c,* and *d,* this is a relation of contrast. In *a* there is simply addition. In *e* the similar ideas of the first two clauses are combined, then this group is contrasted with the third clause.

EXERCISE 2. 1. Which of the following are simple sentences, and which are compound? Which have compound subjects or predicates?

1. Butter and eggs with toast and jam make a fine breakfast.
2. The choice of swimming or drowning lay before him.
3. Jack paddled; Mary sang and played the mandolin.
4. The grass is growing, but meantime the horse is starving.
5. Take it or leave it.
6. On the contrary, and despite his efforts, the court ruled unfavorably for his client.

2. Examine the following passages (from a story and an editorial) and decide where simple and compound sentences have been well used, or where one type would do better than the other. (Note, in the second, the use of the colon.)

And so the long afternoon wore on. But there was no change. The boat continued to rise upon the swells. The sea, blue and relentlessly glittering in the sun, rose and fell. The boat rose and fell with it. The men knew the desperation of monotony and then lapsed into dullness. The sea rose and fell. Bjorn still lay back against his thwart; his head bobbed loosely. His eyes stared. But still instinctively, or by the course of custom, his right hand grasped the tiller.

Democracy is not the same thing as equalitarianism. Equalitarianism is impossible. No two men are literally born equal. Nor can they be made equal. There is no physical equality. Some are strong. Some are weak. There is no economic equality: some have all they need; others have not enough. It will never be possible to have equality in these things. Nor would it be desirable, but there are some things in which equality is both possible and desirable. And these democracy seeks to achieve.

5. COMPLEX SENTENCES

In a compound sentence, as we have just seen, the clauses are of approximately equal importance, and can, if the sentence is broken up, stand separately. But in combining clauses we often need to show that one is more important than the other, and here we use the *complex sentence*. For example:

The dogs bark loudly.   The dogs live on the hill.

Here we have two simple sentences. As they stand, they are given about the same importance. So they would be too if they came in the opposite order, or if they were made into a compound sentence.

But if we want to suggest that the dogs' barking is more important (for our present meaning) than the place where they live, we may write a complex sentence:

The dogs *that live on the hill* bark loudly.

Here the first sentence has become the *main* or *independent clause* (since it could still stand alone), and the second, with the change of a word, has become the *dependent* or *subordinate clause* (and cannot, in this form, stand alone).

Or, on the other hand, if we want to give more importance to the place where the dogs live than to their barking, we may write:

The dogs *that bark loudly* live on the hill.

The word *that,* in each case, has taken the place of *dogs* in the subordinate clause; it depends for its meaning on its *antecedent* in the main clause (here, *dogs*), and thus connects the two clauses, putting them in the desired relation of unequal value.

There are three kinds of words used in English for subordination: 1. The *relative pronoun;* 2. Certain *adverbs;* 3. *Subordinating conjunctions.*

1. The *relative pronoun.* The *that* just used above is an example; others are *who, whose, whom, which, what,* etc. For example (the subordinate clauses italicized) :

a. I do not know *who was there.*
b. It does not matter *whose hat you took.*
c. Choose the partner *whom you prefer.*
d. *Which he chose* is immaterial.
e. He did not say *what he wanted.*

Note that in *d* and *e* the "independent" clause is not complete without the dependent, which in *d* is the subject of *is,* and in *e* is the object of *say.*

Note also that very frequently in speech, and often in writing, there occurs the so-called "omitted relative construction." For example, sentence *c* above could omit the relative *whom* and still be perfectly acceptable (though less formal) English. In such a construction, obviously, meaning is possible because the two clauses are side by side. If anything except the relative came between, it would break the connection. This construction is often useful when a writer is seeking fluency rather than strict formality; its danger is that it may lead to ambiguity.

2. Certain *adverbs: when, where, how, why, whenever,* etc. These connect the clauses by introducing the subordinate clause and modifying a word in the main clause. For example:

a. Dogs bark *when(ever) they smell a fox.*
b. *Wher(ever) they found water,* they made their camp.
c. *How you did it* does not matter.
d. He did not say *why he had come.*

Note again that in *c* and *d* the subordinate clause is necessary to complete the main clause.

3. The *subordinating conjunctions: since, because, unless,* etc. (See further, page 215.) For example:

a. *Since the clock was late,* I missed my train.
b. He likes a bungalow *because there are no stairs.*
c. *Unless this catch is released,* the trigger will not move.

Complex sentences are valuable because they allow the writer to show easily the relative importance of the various parts of his thought.

EXERCISE 3.   1. Make complex sentences from the following pairs of simple sentences, first subordinating *a* of each to *b,* then *b* to *a.* (You will have to supply conjunctions and to change the italicized pronouns and adverbs.)

a. I will not come.	b. He is angry.
a. Lincoln was great.	b. Lincoln understood kindliness.
a. He felt like a fool.	b. He apologized.
a. Nothing seems to matter.	b. You are tired.
a. She needs encouragement.	b. Her voice is good.
a. He works *there.*	b. He eats *there.*
a. You must accept *that.*	b. You deserve *that.*

2. Convert the following comparatively weak sentences into complex ones which put the parts into an effective relationship. (You may add necessary subordinating words.)

1. He will come in June and we will begin to build.
2. Eskimos live in ice houses but they keep as warm as anybody.
3. The vote must be heavy or we will not win.

4. The new director came to dinner today; I met him last week.
5. The rain began coming through the top and we patched it.

6. COMBINATIONS OF COMPOUND AND COMPLEX

Compound and complex sentence structures may be combined in a number of different ways. Examples of the main types follow:

a. The dog barks, and the cat purrs *when her fur is rubbed.*

b. The dog barks *when a stranger comes,* but the cat, *who is timid,* runs into a corner.

c. The dog, *who has guarded the house ever since we left it,* always barks *when a stranger comes.*

In *a,* a simple clause is co-ordinated by *and* with a complex element; in *b,* two complex elements of equal rank are co-ordinated with *but;* in *c,* there is only one independent clause, to which two other clauses are subordinated, the first of which itself has a dependent clause.

Entire books have been written in simple sentences—as they have, too, in words of one syllable. But this is a special feat of simplification, by no means necessary or desirable in general. Such writing is more simple even than everyday conversation; it becomes colorless and repetitious, and annoys the intelligent reader with its kindergarten style. The writer who does not "write down" in this way will find the compound and complex sentences and their combinations of great value. And, what is more, if the simple sentence is not overused it will be the more effective when it *is* used: by contrast with the more involved sentences it will gain sharpness, decisiveness, force.

EXERCISE 4.   Examine the following passage from a story by Henry James for his use of sentences. *a.* Which kinds has he used? *b.* Try to put the passage into simple sentences only. What is the effect?

I must confess that I had spent much of the interval in wondering what the disagreeable thing was that my charming friend's disagreeable cousin had been telling her. The "Belle Cuisinière" was a modest inn in a shady by-street, where it gave me satisfaction to think Miss Spencer must have encountered local color in abundance. There was a crooked little court where much of the hospitality of the house was carried on; there was a staircase climbing to bedrooms on the outer side of the wall; there was a small, trickling fountain with a stucco statuette in the midst of it; there was a little boy in a white cap and apron cleaning copper vessels at a conspicuous kitchen door; there was a chattering land-lady, neatly laced, arranging apricots and grapes into an artistic pyramid upon a pink plate. I looked about, and on a green bench outside of an open door labeled *Salle à Manger,* I perceived Caroline Spencer. No sooner had I looked at her than I saw that something had happened since the morning. She was leaning back on her bench, her hands were clasped in her lap, and her eyes were fixed upon the landlady, at the other side of the court, manipulating her apricots.

But I saw she was not thinking of apricots.

7. SUMMARY

The conventional requirements of the written sentence may be stated as follows:

A. A sentence must contain at least one subject-predicate sequence, or clause.

See pages 72–73, also. Further:

1. **The predicate must contain a finite verb.** (*Dogs bark,* not *Dogs barking.*) See pages 74–76, also.
2. **Dependent clauses must not be treated as sentences; they cannot stand alone.** (*They came in when it rained,* not *They came in. When it rained*). See page 75, also.

B. If two or more subject-predicate sequences are put into a sentence, they may be connected in various ways. If of about equal importance, they should be co-ordinated (compound sentence); if of unequal rank, the less important should be subordinated (complex sentence); or co-ordination and subordination may be combined.

See pages 110, 111, also.

EXERCISE 5.   Classify the following sentences as simple, compound, or complex, and in each of the complex sentences select the independent subject-predicate sequence (or *clause*) and those which are dependent. (Do not confuse modifying phrases with clauses.)

1. The shoes and stockings were of the same color.
2. This color, which was an unusual shade, was guaranteed not to fade.
3. The stockings were of finest silk, and the shoes had soles of heavy leather.
4. The booklet will tell you how to take delightful pictures in your home.
5. She excels in short-story writing and has just finished a novel.
6. The plan for the house grew and grew.
7. Anyone who can understand the natures of those three men can understand mine.

8. I leave it, nevertheless, in its former condition, and I do not now write unadvisedly, and think it wrong to cancel my previous statement; but it must not so remain without a few added words.

9. Lastly, let us return to the lines respecting the power of the keys, because now we can understand them.

10. Neither does a great nation send its poor little boys to jail for stealing six walnuts; and allow its bankrupts to steal their hundreds of thousands with a bow, and its bankers, rich with poor men's savings, to close their doors; and large landed estates to be bought by men making their money by going with armed steamers up and down the China seas, selling opium at the cannon's mouth.

11. When men are rightly occupied, their amusement grows out of their work, as the color petals out of a fruitful flower; when they are faithfully helpful and compassionate, all their emotions become steady, deep, perpetual, and vivifying to the soul as the natural pulse to the body.

12. I speak, therefore, of good novels only, and our modern literature is particularly rich in types of such.

13. Well read, indeed, these books have serious use, being nothing less than treatises on moral anatomy and chemistry; studies of human nature in the elements of it.

14. I suppose few people reach the middle or later period of their age without having, at some moment of change or disappointment, felt the truth of those bitter words, and been startled by the fading of the sunshine from the cloud of their life, into the sudden agony of the knowledge that the fabric of it was as fragile as a dream, and the endurance of it as transient as the dew.

15. And this is right; but it is a pity that the accuracy insisted on is not greater and required to a serious purpose.

16. He was obviously a great artist.

17. I believe that they will come when the play is over.

18. Our friends left early, but we were sorry to see them go.

19. The destination of the ship was the west coast of Africa, then a favorite cruising and training ground for the navy.

20. When our instincts warn us to be cautious, they are often overriden by our enthusiasms, and disaster results.

8. UNCONVENTIONAL SENTENCES

There are ways of expression widely used by good authors which do not conform to the requirements just summarized, but which are still acceptable in standard prose writing. It is now time to consider these. We are not referring here to "experimental" or highly individualistic writing such as some authors produce today; however interesting, that is outside the scope of this book. Yet it might be pointed out that Gertrude Stein, James Joyce, and others have not written in their less conventional manners because they *could not* write standard prose, but because they felt that their literary purpose demanded a special medium.

In college composition courses the purpose is usually different; the primary aim of the writer is to demonstrate his command of the formal, standard language—a medium which, by the way, will generally be found quite adequate to his ideas, as it has been to many minds before his. This does not mean that he should merely imitate the giants of the past any more than that he should imitate the experimenters of today. Pope's dictum is an excellent one for the beginner:

> Be not the first by whom the new is tried,
> Nor yet the last to lay the old aside.

When the student has mastered standard prose and still finds it inadequate to his purposes, he is ready for exploration outside its boundaries.

The word *unconventional*, then, refers here to the grammar of the sentences considered, not to their acceptability as standard English. They lack some things required by the conventional sentence, or they contain more than it may. Many of them are characteristic of speech, and appear in writing only when it imitates or tries to reproduce speech:

1. *Exclamations and commands:* Get it. Quick! Ouch! One round trip to Chicago. Ham on rye.
2. *Questions:* Why not? Who? What of it?

Others appear in formal writing for purposes of emphasis or economy:

3. *Transitional phrases at the beginning of a new section of a composition:* To proceed to the next issue. So much for the cause. Now for the cure.

(Nothing would be gained by saying *Let us* proceed . . . or Now *we are ready* for the cure, etc.)

4. *Words or phrases set off within a connected argument, exposition, or narrative:*

   a. No one had thought about the engines much, once the fires were out: but now they began to think of them. *Steam.* The leak was stopped now: if they had steam again to work the pumps they could snap their fingers at spray going down the hatches.   —Richard Hughes, *In Hazard.*

   b. Up North we raise our glasses and wish each other "Health! Success!" *But time to enjoy them?* How many American business men ever think of it? Some day, yes, they will retire and enjoy life. But now they must work hard. They must hurry, hurry, hurry. They must be successful. And then you read the morning paper! This dynamic young executive has dropped dead at 40, that high-pow-

ered tycoon at 45 has gone to Mayo's to have his stomach re-treaded. Havana doctors tell me that nervous breakdown from overwork is so seldom encountered they have no pat phrase for it in Spanish.
—J. P. McEvoy, ". . . And Time to Enjoy It."
The Pan-American, July-September, 1945.[2]

c. Even in such an essentially empty book as "Theatre," the pieces fall into place with a satisfying click, the expected surprises come off. The incision is so neat that one ceases to wonder, looking on, whether the operation was really necessary. *A great craftsman—a great operator—and something more.*
—Stephen Vincent Benét, "A Self-Taught Trade," *The Saturday Review of Literature,*
April 16, 1938.

d. Sannie was almost certain she could do it. *Almost but not quite.*
—Stuart Cloete, *Turning Wheels.*

These examples contain less than the conventional minimum requirements of the sentence. There are others that contain more than the conventional maximum:

5. *Short co-ordinate clauses closely connected in thought and separated only by commas.*

These are usually used when the writer wishes to show contrast, to move rapidly between associated thoughts, or to make less of a separation than would be made by a colon or semicolon. When this is done inappropriately, or done through carelessness, and therefore makes a bad connection, a **"comma splice"** is produced—that is, the clauses seem merely spliced together with commas, rather than well connected.

[2] Reprinted by permission of *The Pan-American.*

Examples of the "comma splice":

He told me about it, however I did not believe him.

He did not seek to prove that the accident was an "act of God," of that he was convinced, but he wanted to collect the insurance.

Most of the work is now done, the rest I will finish next year.

Note by contrast the following successful uses of this kind of structure:

a. Elizabeth was flushed and beautiful from the heat of the oven, and the sight of her overwhelmed me, she was so much lovelier than all my yearning dreams of her in absence had been.
—Kenneth Roberts, *Northwest Passage.*

b. Man fixed the association of colors with grief and gladness, he made ornaments the insignia of office, he ordained that fabric should grace the majesty of power.
—Agnes Repplier, *Americans and Others.*

c. Form becomes vanity, art is held a bauble, style an indulgence; strenuousness is all: and that way disaster lies.   —William Watson, *Pencraft.*

d. I do not belong to any of these organizations. I get some of their literature. Much of it is good, I read it, and am impressed by it.
—Senator Royal S. Copeland,
Congressional Record.

e. The beautiful big valve lit up, the motor whirred.
—Richard Hughes, *In Hazard.*

Note that just because they are unconventional, sentences of these five types are conspicuous, and should therefore be used sparingly. Though some conservative writers avoid them, they are established in standard usage. Handled skillfully, they should not be objectionable, and are added resources to the writer.

EXERCISE 6. Prove that you have mastered the requirements of the conventional sentence by revising these sentences from student themes. Put them into conventional sentence form. After considering each carefully, do you think any might be justified in its present form? Explain.

1. Supposing that a child has ideas for building a toy.

2. This sort of person is injuring himself to the extent that he is becoming decidedly narrow-minded, he is not able to find things out for himself.

3. One can easily see this by looking at the different types of government there are in the world. The United States with her democracy, Russia with her communism, Spain with her fascism, and England with her socialism.

4. From Robinson's essay, "On Various Kinds of Thinking," I find that I am very normal in my thinking in respect to reveries, practical decisions, and rationalizing, these are insignificant however, to creative thought, a type of progressive thinking.

5. After many hardships as a result of which the brother, guides, and woman were killed.

6. The top office said, "Cut out half your organization by June 30." We did just that in a period of a month. Twenty branch companies wiped out like trees in a forest fire.

7. The wealthy have control of all the necessities, industries, and political powers of the community and compel the poor to do their bidding. Yet how could or how can we remedy this, the author of a "A Plea for Equality" says this inequality leads in the end to revolution.

8. Under the present conditions of environment and education in the slums, the poor have an excuse for not im-

proving their conditions, they do not receive a fair opportunity.

9. I think that it has been a long time since men have been moved by these ideals. Except, perhaps, the ideal of the family which has lasted longer than the others.

10. Some of the men who were leaders in the strike movement are sorry now that they were mixed up in it. They find they are getting more work to do. That the boss is getting tougher.

11. When a person does things because his grandfather and his grandfather before him did them. Or in other words his life is ruled by custom.

12. There are many different types of people in this world. Some that are easy to get along with and others that are not so easy to get along with.

13. I would not say that rational thinking is altogether harmful, however, it remains to be seen that creative thought is much more advantageous.

14. It is by this sort of demonstration that new members are gained. A practice which is definitely undemocratic.

15. It isn't because my environment, parents, or contact with other people prevent it in fact, they encourage it. It isn't because of time I have had a sufficient quantity of it.

9. WRITING GOOD SENTENCES

As has been suggested, the types of sentences you use should depend on the kind of writing you are doing. A literary purpose will call for a wider variety of sentences, more closely adapted to the nuances of idea and emotion, than everyday expository prose will demand. But no matter where, a short, sharp sentence will differ in effect from a long, deliberate one; a compact one from a loose one; a slow or heavy one from a smooth, rapid one.

The independent clause, always the basic unit of expression, may be used by the skillful writer as a skeleton to be fleshed out in a variety of ways, as he needs to add details to the bare statement, keeping them organically related to it. Let us follow the process through which a writer might go in choosing, from many possibilities, the kind of sentence he can best use. Perhaps he begins with two simple sentences whose relationship is not apparent:

> *Man is the most perverse of creatures. Man is the most intelligent of creatures.*

He first tries to show the relationship by means of the word *but,* and makes a compound sentence:

> *Man is the most intelligent of creatures, but he is the most perverse.*

This balances well, yet it strikes him that *he* and *is* are unnecessary. He therefore reduces this to a simple sentence with a compound complement. The result now seems to him a little too obvious; he does not want to moralize so much as to show the paradox. If he merely puts the two facts side by side, he will make his point. So he changes *but* to *and,* and has this:

> *Man is the most intelligent of creatures, and the most perverse.*

This pleases him, but to make sure that he is not overlooking something better, he tries it as a complex sentence:

> *Though man is the most intelligent of creatures, he is the most perverse.*

Clear enough, but still rather more obvious than he wants. He tries it as a simple sentence with a participial modifier:

> *Man, having the most intelligence, is yet the most perverse of creatures.*

This seems somewhat affected, and the rhythm is clumsy. He amends the participial modifier to an appositional construction:

> *Man, the most intelligent of creatures, is yet the most perverse.*

That corrects the rhythm, but not the affectation, so he returns to his third attempt, with its brevity and easy movement; he substitutes a dash for the comma to point up the paradox slightly, and has, as a final epigrammatic result:

> *Man is the most intelligent of creatures—and the most perverse.*

This process, as we have followed it, is very laborious, and certainly one could not apply it to the writing of every sentence in a college theme! But first, it is not necessary for every sentence—only for those which, as the student revises his first draft, seem not to suit their context or his intention. And second, the actual process of revision is not as laborious as it appears in this text. The mind works rapidly, and with practice a writer sees the problem more quickly and solves it efficiently. The solution which this writer arrived at may not please everyone; such things are to some extent questions of opinion. But the important matter is that the student be aware of the variety of ways in which he may manipulate his sentences, and that he improve steadily in adapting his choice to his purpose.

So much for the positive side. On the negative, there are certain tendencies common to inexperienced writers which it would be well to be aware of and to avoid. The rest of this chapter is given to a discussion and illustration of the chief of these.

A. Correctness.

Before thinking of writing *well,* you must be sure you are writing *correctly.* In English, as in any living language, certain things are unequivocally right or wrong; certain others vary with circumstances; and a few, being in the process of change, cannot be flatly legislated about. For the latter two kinds, refer to the Glossary of Usage (Chapter IX). For the first, refer to the Grammar (Chapter VI). In English grammar there are rules of *concord:* singular subjects must be used with singular verbs, plural with plural; reference words must agree with their antecedents in certain ways. Though these things are not strictly matters of sentence writing, errors in them are so frequent that some examples may be given here:

WRONG: Peoples must learn to live in peace with other peoples whose basic philosophy of life are different from their own. —General Eisenhower.

RIGHT: . . . philosoph*ies* . . . are . . . , or philosophy . . . *is* . . .

This particular error is probably to be charged to a linotypist, rather than to the General! Yet it belongs to a common type, occurring chiefly where something intervenes between the two words that should agree and throws the inattentive writer off the track.

I. Be sure that subject and verb agree in number.

Remember that a compound subject is plural. (See pages 217–221, also.)

WRONG: Robinson's ideas on creative thinking seems to be more for the future and provides no solution for our present needs.

RIGHT: Robinson's ideas on creative thinking seem to be more for the future and provide no solution for our present needs.

WRONG: Desire for profit is one of the things that encourages economic activity.

RIGHT: Desire for profit is one of the things that encourage economic activity.

WRONG: In contrast to these fine qualities was his appearance and habits of cleanliness.

RIGHT: In contrast to these fine qualities were his appearance and habits of cleanliness.

WRONG: The international situation is one of the factors that has been engaging our attention.

RIGHT: The international situation is one of the factors that have been engaging our attention.

2. See that the antecedent of every pronoun is unmistakably clear.

(See pages 221, 222, also.) Pronouns may be made to refer most clearly to their antecedents by being placed close to them. Sometimes this will still not make a satisfactory sentence, and the whole will have to be revised so that only one noun remains as a plausible antecedent. Make sure that *former, latter, other* are unmistakable in their reference.

FAULTY: Most manufacturers put several pads of rubber on the frame where the body is bolted on, and this filters out the noises. Also to take care of vibration from the engine, it is mounted on rubber.

REVISED: To filter out noises, most manufacturers put several pads of rubber between frame and body where these are bolted together. Moreover, to eliminate vibration, they mount the engine on rubber.

FAULTY: With a policy of internationalism, it gives the United States a chance to keep abreast of other nations in scientific, commercial, and cultural advancement. Without this we would undoubtedly fall far behind in matters of this sort.

REVISED: A policy of internationalism will give the United States a chance to keep abreast of other nations in scientific, commercial, and cultural advancement. Without such a policy we would undoubtedly fall far behind.

FAULTY: Had it not been for his ability to influence the students and the other members of the faculty, his dream of a great university would never have been realized.

REVISED: Had it not been for his ability to influence the students and his colleagues on the faculty, his dream of a great university would never have been realized.

3. Avoid shifts in the person of pronouns.
(See pages 19, 20, 56, also.)

WRONG: It feels as if I have left all the things I love behind and have come to a place where no one even notices your presence.

RIGHT: It feels as if I have left behind all the things I love, and have come to a place where no one even notices my presence.

OR: You feel as if you have left behind all the things you love, and have come to a place where no one even notices your presence.

4. Avoid inconsistencies in the tenses of verbs.

The first example illustrates a frequent type of error. (See pages 57, 230–233, also.)

WRONG: If he would have known the day before, he would have been able to leave in time.

RIGHT: If he had known the day before, he would have been able to leave in time.

WRONG: If every army private stops and asks why every time an order is given him, not much would be accomplished.

RIGHT: If every army private stopped and asked why every time an order was given him, not much would be accomplished.

OR: If every army private stops to ask why every time an order is given him, not much is accomplished.

WRONG: The interests of the majority have been satisfied, or in a few cases tried to have been satisfied.

RIGHT: The interests of the majority have been satisfied or, in a few cases, the attempt has been made to satisfy them.

Similar failures of concord, occurring particularly with collective nouns, indefinite pronouns, and case forms of pronouns, are more extensively treated in Chapter VI.

B. Clear Modification.

A *modifier* is any element which, added to another word, alters its meaning somewhat without changing it basically. The term includes adjectives, adverbs, or any word, phrase, or clause that functions like an adjective or adverb.

In English sentences, phrasal and clausal modifiers (particularly adverbial ones) have a certain freedom of movement. We may say:

> A man must work *to be elected,*   or
> *To be elected,* a man must work,   or
> A man, *to be elected,* must work.

A clause (such as *wherever he may be*) may behave similarly. Which position the writer chooses for his modifier will depend on several things—clarity, emphasis, rhythm, etc.—which become ever more important for him to attend to as he puts more clauses together. The misplacing of modifiers often leads to clumsiness, even to ambiguity.

1. Wherever possible, avoid the insertion of modifiers between subject and verb, and between verb and object.

FAULTY: Lord Bryce, to describe and explain democracy, has given illustrations from six countries.

REVISED: To describe and explain democracy, Lord Bryce has selected six countries as illustrations.

FAULTY: He must decide, within a couple of weeks, on a fraternity of which all in his estimation have a great many faults.

REVISED: Within a couple of weeks he must decide on a fraternity, though every one, in his estimation, has a great many faults.

2. Place subordinate clauses as near as possible to the words they modify.

FAULTY: This does not mean that the children should be neglected and made to do everything for themselves, as many modern parents think.

REVISED: This does not mean, as many modern parents think, that the children should be neglected and made to do everything for themselves.

FAULTY: I secured an office job soon after I was out of high school, which lasted throughout the summer.

REVISED: Soon after I was out of high school, I secured an office job which lasted throughout the summer.

3. Place phrases as near as possible to the words they modify; if they are independent, place them at one of the extremities of the sentence.

FAULTY: His warmth, personality, and sincerity have made, in my opinion, Jan Sibelius the truly great man he is today.

REVISED: In my opinion, his warmth, personality, and sincerity have made Jan Sibelius the truly great man he is today.

FAULTY: In the city children frequently play ball in the streets where traffic is heavy. Records show how many children are killed each year through this practice by automobiles.

REVISED: Records show how many children are killed by automobiles each year because of this practice.

4. Place participial, gerund, and infinitive phrases where they will cause no ambiguity.

(See pages 206, 210, 211 for definitions of these terms.)

FAULTY: When visiting Mr. Thomas not long before he left us, he compared himself to "The Last Leaf" by Oliver Wendell Holmes.

In this sentence, which appeared in a current magazine, the writer intended to say:

REVISED: When I visited Mr. Thomas not long before he left us, he compared himself to "The Last Leaf" by Oliver Wendell Holmes.

FAULTY: Returning to Robinson's essay, we find that the author deplores this credulous acceptance without doubting either source or correctness.

REVISED: Returning to Robinson's essay, we find that the author deplores a credulous acceptance of ideas which questions neither their source nor their correctness.

The following observations about "dangling" or misrelated modifiers will be helpful:

a. The construction appears more frequently in speech than in writing.

b. Certain set participial phrases are used so frequently that they no longer require the presence of the noun or pronoun which they would structurally modify, because the hearer or reader automatically supplies it.

Example: Even allowing for hasty preparation, this definitely involves a contradiction of terms.

Example: Generally speaking, the election indicated widespread dissatisfaction.

In this group may be placed phrases beginning with the participles *allowing, assuming, comparing, considering, counting, failing, glancing, granting, leaving, looking, speaking, talking, turning.* This list, though not exhaustive, includes a large number of the participles employed in phrases which either refer to a topic previously discussed or express a logical qualification on the speaker's part.

c. Ambiguity seldom results when the participial construction is followed by a possessive or pronominal adjective.

Example: In learning to write, your first problem is to clarify your own ideas.

Example: Having given this warning, one's duty to the reader is done.

d. The greatest danger of ambiguity arises when the sentence contains several nouns or pronouns, any of which might govern the participial modifier.

FAULTY: Upon questioning the validity of his belief, he at once gives substantial evidence as to its correctness.

Notice that here we do not know whether *his* and *he* refer to the same person or to two people, nor whether the participial phrase modifies the antecedent of *his* or of *he*.

Since the dangling participial or gerund phrase has come to be so frequently used by writers of acceptable English, to make a blanket condemnation of it would be to deny the facts of the language. If you do use this construction in your writing, be prepared to defend it against any charge of ambiguity. Remember that the first aim in written English is to make yourself understood.

5. Avoid placing a clause, phrase, or word modifier between two parts of a sentence when it is not clear to which part the modifier is intended to apply. This is often called a "squinting construction," because it seems to look two ways at once.

FAULTY: I was told when it was noon the boat would sail.

REVISED: I was told that the boat would sail when it was noon.

OR: When it was noon, I was told the boat would sail.

FAULTY: Students who fail in nine cases out of ten have defective reading ability.

REVISED: In nine cases out of ten, students who fail have defective reading ability.

OR: Students who, in nine cases out of ten, fail, have defective reading ability.

FAULTY: The automobile involved in the accident today was found to have defective brakes.

REVISED: The automobile involved in the accident was found, today, to have defective brakes.

OR: The automobile involved in today's accident was found to have defective brakes.

6. When a single-word modifier might be understood to apply to more than one element of the sentence, place it so that no uncertainty of meaning will arise.

This situation develops with such qualifying adverbs as *merely, nearly, just, almost, hardly, even, scarcely, quite,* etc., which might modify either the verb or any secondary word or phrase in the predicate. Such adverbs commonly occur before the verb in informal or spoken language.

INFORMAL: We just had enough time to catch the train.

FORMAL: We had just enough time to catch the train.

INFORMAL: Our team did not even score once.

FORMAL: Our team did not score even once.

7. The adverb *only* is a special case.

It may often be interpreted either as an adjective, modifying the subject, or as an adverb, modifying the verb.

Example: I only had five dollars.

This sentence is, of course, never understood to mean that I and no one else had five dollars, and in the form quoted it is common both in written and spoken English.

A second type of construction occurs when *only* modifies a clause or phrase introduced by the verb.

Example: Its expression can only be caught by side glimpses.

Here *only* is frequently found in the pre-verbal position, both in spoken and written English.

When puzzled about the position of *only,* or any other adverb for that matter, the important thing is to leave no question as to the exact meaning of your sentence. You will do well to keep in mind here the differences between spoken and written English. A sentence such as *I can only believe what I have been told* could, in spoken English, clearly indicate the function of *only* through word stress:

I can only *believe* what I have been told. (*Only* modifies *believe*. I can only *believe* it; I cannot disbelieve it or put it to a test.)

I can only believe what I have been *told*. (*Only* modifies *what I have been told*. I can believe only this and nothing more.)

The writer, lacking the aid that word stress gives to meaning, compensates for it by placing the adverb where its function as a modifier will be clearly evident.

I can only believe what I have been told. (*Only* modifies *believe*.)

I can believe only what I have been told. (*Only* modifies *what I have been told*.)

EXERCISE 7. Revise the following sentences:

1. A person in a steel plant only works eight hours a day for five days a week except those who hold higher positions.

2. The Japanese have not offered to pay for the land, but have chosen to take it by force, a principle which I oppose greatly.

3. Having been raised in an atmosphere of religion, the natural trend of thought for my mind would be religious.

4. Liberty is that state in which every one is able to do as he desires with only the restraint of his own conscience.

5. The time for graduation comes, and I do not care particularly about entering the profession. I could secure a position with many companies because of my knowledge of law.

6. Looking over the past few weeks, though I know

I'm undoubtedly silly, I realize that a great many of my thoughts were centered around these lectures.

7. They have taken away the power over the tariff from the House of Representatives and the Senate, which has been surrendered to the Secretary of State.

8. Also on most campuses there are places of religious interest of almost any denomination.

9. Although in reading one of his books there may appear to be a doubtful light cast on one of the chief characters, he may be assured that it will be quite satisfactorily erased before its completion.

10. We do ever so many things as a matter of course without thinking about them just because those before us did them.

11. The treatment at the time for consumption was no air; in winter her windows were sealed with paper; and copious doses of opium.

12. Many programs on the radio this season in my opinion should be considered among the best in radio.

13. For example, when entering an elevator, the oldest graduate waiting to return on duty, though she may have only arrived like the group of others, as the elevator reaches the floor, has supreme preference, while younger graduates and students who undoubtedly have more work to accomplish may be kept waiting for ten or fifteen minutes.

14. Unlike the average young person of today, my favorite author is a non-fiction writer.

15. The player who is offside in the end harms only his own team.

C. Clear Parallelism.

When things are to be compared, contrasted, or shown as similar, the parts of the sentence should be constructed alike, so that the parallel in the grammar may make clear the parallel in the content.

1. Make certain that the parallel in correlative constructions is carried out with full consistency.

FAULTY: This starts him on a ring career, and ends up, of course, being world champion.

REVISED: This starts him on a ring career, and he ends, of course, as the world champion.

OR: This starts him on a ring career, which brings him in the end, of course, to the world championship.

FAULTY: It tries or does get people to thinking what they believe or don't believe about the government and its projects.

REVISED: It tries—and with success—to get people to think about their beliefs concerning the government and its projects.

2. When two parallel constructions govern a single sentence element, avoid placing the single element between the two that are parallel.

FAULTY: This sort of inequality cannot be abolished because of its very nature and should not be nullified by a class of false leaders.

REVISED: Because of its very nature, this sort of inequality cannot be abolished and should not be nullified by a class of false leaders.

3. Make sure that parallel connecting words in a sentence are followed by elements in the same construction.

FAULTY: When they do go to church, it is only because they have to go, and not of their own desire.

REVISED: When they do go to church, it is only because they have to go, and not because they want to.

FAULTY: The higher classes have an entirely different manner of living as the lower classes do.

REVISED: The higher classes have a manner of living entirely different from that of the lower classes.

OR: The higher classes do not live in the same manner as the lower classes.

a. Avoid the ambiguity of meaning resulting from the placing of *not only . . . but*, as in the following sentence:

FAULTY: Charles Dickens lends not only a melancholy air to his novels, but through his humorous characters brings forth some of the more likeable of human traits.

REVISED: Charles Dickens not only lends a melancholy air to his novels, but brings forth, by means of his humorous characters, some of the more likeable of human traits.

According to the strictest interpretation of the foregoing rule, the connectives *not only* and *but* should precede words of the same grammatical classification. In actual practice this is not always observed:

Not only in the verses of those who have professed their admiration of his genius, but even of those who have distinguished themselves by hostility to his theory . . .
—Coleridge.

b. The completion of statements introduced by *the reason is* with a clause introduced by *because* is repetitious, and it is usually preferable in writing to substitute for it a noun clause introduced by *that*.

EXAMPLE: The *reason* he came *was because* he wanted to see his father.

REVISED: The *reason* he came *was that* he wanted to see his father.

EXAMPLE: Just *because* you do not like him *is no reason* to condemn him.

REVISED: The fact *that* you do not like him *is no reason* to condemn him.

These constructions with *because* are so frequent in conversation that they have an informal effect. They do also occur in current writing, and with some justification, when *reason* and *because* are widely separated in the sentence: "The chief reason why it seems so dismal an absurdity is because it could only serve . . ."

4. In formal writing it is customary to repeat introductory words before parallel sentence elements.

This applies to prepositions, articles, conjunctions, *to* before the infinitive, and at times even to auxiliary verbs.

LESS FORMAL: Labor troubles were current in America and England.

MORE FORMAL: Labor troubles were current in America and in England.

LESS FORMAL: The singular and plural of the past tense were not always based on the same principal part.

MORE FORMAL: The singular and the plural of the past tense were not always based on the same principal part.

LESS FORMAL: We were allowed to remain and attend the special service.

MORE FORMAL: We were allowed to remain and to attend the special service.

LESS FORMAL: We were notified that they were ready and would enter the stage at once.

MORE FORMAL: We were notified that they were ready and that they would enter the stage at once.

EXERCISE 8.   Revise the following sentences wherever necessary.

1. We of the radio do not hope to compete with newspapers in the richness of detail which they can afford. We can only bring history as it happens—and the experience of hearing an English prime minister make history is a thrill that it can never bring.

2. Every trivial plan or trip that the President makes or does gets in the newspapers.

3. Persuasion often is as effective, sometimes more, as physical force.

4. His greatest assets and possibly the biggest reason for his popularity is his democratic ideas.

5. However, everyone has a position and is much happier than they were under the old feudal system.

6. On this day one is supposed to rest, attend services, and above all not to write.

7. Not only does it create a restful feeling, but also a carefree mood.

8. I may say that while some people deny it, the fact is that the early potato is perishable. While some people disagree with this statement, it is a fact, and they are taken off the market before your potatoes come in.

9. Every state needs prestige among other ones that compose the civilized world. Prestige is nothing more than having all the other states admiring your social system.

10. As a general rule, the program or artist with the greatest following is considered superior for no other rea-

son than that of its fan mail, while an actually better program may be held in considerably less esteem.

D. Effectiveness.

One thing every writer must learn is to put himself in the place of the reader. What is in his mind can never be understood until he expresses it. And though it may seem clear to him, who knows his own thought best, the real test lies in his making it clear to another. He should therefore remember that the *combination* of ideas and their *sequence* have a lot to do with their clarity and effectiveness.

I. Avoid a long series of co-ordinate clauses all connected by the conjunction *and*.

FAULTY: In past days aristocratic women could be recognized by their clothes, but now the great majority of women have been educated in their tastes and a great many women today dress very well and still they could not be called aristocratic.

REVISED: In past days aristocratic women could be recognized by their clothes. Today the great majority of women have become educated in their tastes, and a great many of them dress very well. Yet these women could not therefore be called aristocratic.

2. Avoid a series of involved dependent and independent clauses which confuse the reader.

FAULTY: Although I had often imagined that my work in the U. S. Forestry Service would be an aid to society, I see now the difference between aiding society and bettering society, and that I can better society only through creative thinking, which I must learn.

REVISED: Heretofore I had often imagined that by working in the U. S. Forestry Service I would be aiding society.

Now I am able to see the distinction between aiding society and bettering society. I can better society only through creative thinking, a power which I must develop.

3. Avoid compound sentences which contain clauses having little or no logical relationship with one another.

FAULTY: The Scotch are a thrifty race and they are not musically inclined.

Note that, unless you are implying that thrifty peoples are unmusical, showing some relationship between thrift and musical inclination, these ideas are not sufficiently close to be placed in a co-ordinate relationship.

REVISED: The Scotch are a thrifty race. They are not musically inclined.

FAULTY: Shelley was a poet of the Romantic School and he went to Italy for his health in 1812.

REVISED: Shelley, a Romantic poet, went to Italy for his health in 1812.

4. Use grammatical subordination to place ideas in their proper relationship.

FAULTY: Their parents have always helped them decide matters, so that the children depend upon other people too much.

Note that the second clause, containing the idea which the writer is trying to emphasize, is grammatically subordinate to the first. The sentence will be more logical if the second clause is made the chief or independent clause.
REVISED: Since their parents have always helped them decide matters, the children depend upon other people too much.

5. Unless you wish to express a rapid tempo and tense atmosphere, avoid a series of short, simple sentences, all built on the same pattern.

WEAK: These radio programs include all types of entertainment. Not all of these are serious or educational. In fact, some of them are humorous.

BETTER: All types of entertainment, humorous as well as serious or educational, are included in these radio programs.

WEAK: Of course, this question is a matter of opinion. My opinion is divided.

BETTER: Of course, this is a question (or matter) of opinion—and mine is divided.

6. A sentence may be made more effective by placing important words at the beginning.

WEAK: They now find that their early training becomes valuable to them.

BETTER: Their early training now becomes valuable to them.

OR, if the time element is the important thing:

Now it is that their early training becomes valuable to them.

Before beginning a sentence with a conjunction, you should consider whether it will weaken or strengthen your writing. At times certain conjunctions placed at the beginning of a sentence tend to make the whole statement sound like an afterthought.

WEAK: Many famous plays and motion pictures are presented on this program. Also famous people from all walks of life are interviewed between the acts.

BETTER: Many famous plays and motion pictures are presented on this program. Famous people from all walks of life are interviewed between the acts.

Some writers consciously use a conjunction at the beginning of a sentence as a strengthening device, usually to point a contrast.

EXAMPLE: And the delegation of legislative powers to be exercised by the executive department is the same delegation of congressional powers that all Democrats and leaders in Congress in 1930 condemned as vicious legislation, unwarranted, and dangerous to our form of government.

7. Items in series should be so arranged that the strongest or most important item comes at the end.

WEAK: The news which is distributed over the radio is unbiased, accurate, and up-to-date.

BETTER: The news which is distributed over the radio is up-to-date, accurate, and unbiased.

WEAK: The game was close; the weather was good; the crowd was enthusiastic.

BETTER: The weather was good; the crowd was enthusiastic; the game was close.

8. Parallelism or balance in sentence structure may aid in making a sentence more effective.

WEAK: I do say that they bring into the limelight all of the organization's numerous faults and keep the good that it has done in the background.

BETTER: I do say that they bring into the limelight all of the faults of the organization and keep in the background all the good that it has done.

9. A sentence can often be made more effective by using a periodic structure, one in which the main clause is not completed until the end.

Avoid placing a weak or inconclusive statement or word at the end of the sentence.

WEAK: A Sunday-night presentation is assured of a fair chance to gain a listening public because of all the people who congregate around their radios that evening.

BETTER: Because of all the people who congregate around their radios on Sunday evening, a program given on that night is assured of a fair chance to gain a listening public.

One final word about sentences: The student must never forget that he is writing them to fit into a context; they are not isolated units. In a successful composition, every part contributes to the whole.

REVIEW EXERCISE. Revise each of the following sentences. Be able to point out the principles of sentence structure which have been violated.

1. Madame Recamier, after years of close association, was with him, old and blind when he died.

2. The world and times are constantly changing, and with the new times comes photography.

3. Also the world as a whole should benefit by this wise teaching.

4. Children whose parents look after them and do many things for them often cannot do their own thinking.

5. Paul Muni, who portrays the role of the land-owning Chinese who is forced to vacate his property and move south because of lack of rain, is very ably assisted by Luise Rainer, his wife.

6. My last few summers have been spent working as cashier and salesgirl in a small specialty shop, which was considered a part of the necessary practical experience I

must have in order to understand the inner working of my chosen vocation.

7. If no member of the Board was heard, it was because they did not care to be heard.

8. Neither of these give a very complete nor accurate picture of the profession whose school I plan to enter and major in however.

9. If many of the citizens of the country felt as this man does, it would be relatively simple, with a lack of law and order, for someone to set up a tyranny, according to the conservatives.

10. Another program on this order is the First Nighter which presents plays.

11. This is a surrender of legislative powers no less and no more than the surrender made by the Republican administration and Congress, and which all Democrats condemned in the name of Jefferson and Jackson, as a dangerous invasion of the Constitution, and would open the way for abuse.

12. After getting up in the morning to face an hour and a half ride to work, and after this ride to endure a hot, stuffy office, isn't my idea of a life profession.

13. Each of Iago's subjects seem to be more pliable than the other, only one does it knowingly whereas the others work right into his plans unknowingly.

14. Only recently has the average student, the independent, been given a place on the class election ballot, and even at that his number has been small when compared to the ratio of independents to fraternity men.

15. The night of the formal dinners arrived. The girls made a lovely appearance in their formals, and as we gazed at them we realized we wanted to someday be a part of all these grand persons about us.

16. About our only knowledge of the Indian situation is obtained from the papers, radio, and news reels in movies.

17. What I read must be of another world than the commonplace one in which I live.

18. It was good-bye night for the boys of Alpha Zeta Psi fraternity yesterday as Tommy Welch's brothers formally dined him and sent him back to Hennepin University, an engraved studio clock to remind him of the days he spent with them.

19. In the Senate Commerce Committee, in connection with maritime affairs, we have heard of many such disputes.

20. That is a small cost, and probably that would be the kind I would suggest that they build if they are going to build these settlement projects, not like Greenbelt, where they cost $15,000 each; but they built this project at Greensburg, Pa., in a locality where there are a great many mining communities with good homes vacant, and the people have nothing to do. They built this project, and after they had it built they did not know what to do with the people that were to live in it, notwithstanding the fact, as I called attention through several other communications, that good houses were remaining vacant in that vicinity.

THE WORD

1. WORDS

*T*HROUGHOUT all history man has been prone to attach great, and sometimes even supernatural, value to words. Some early savages felt that they could work irreparable harm upon an enemy simply by writing his name on a bit of bark and then destroying it. Other partly civilized peoples hesitated to name such words as *thunder, lightning,* and *fire,* for fear the elements so uttered would appear and destroy them. This explains the development of *taboos* or restrictions against the use of certain words, and of *euphemisms* or round-about expressions, employed to indicate a thing or idea without expressly naming it.

Even in our modern civilization words have an influence more powerful than we sometimes realize. Words play a great part in prompting us to buy and sell, to vote, to go to church, to choose our friends, even to celebrate holidays. Wars are threatened and fought sometimes as a result of slogans and propaganda. For example, the Franco-Prussian War of 1870–71 was hastened by Bismarck's skillful excision of the Ems dispatch. King William of Prussia ordered one of his personal aides to send Bismarck a telegram describing an encounter which the king had had with the French ambassador. In its original form the message described a peaceful and conciliatory meeting between the French envoy and the Prussian king. After Bismarck had reduced the telegram to about one-third of its original length—although he did not change or add a single word—and had given it to the press, it seemed to the French people as if their ambassador had been insulted, while the Germans read into it an affront to their king.

The English language has a very large stock of words. The larger dictionaries generally record about 450,000, almost half a million words. Some authorities on language have expressed the opinion that perhaps our language is too richly endowed, that there are too many words that almost duplicate one another in meaning. The opposing view is that a large vocabulary makes it possible to give to words a great many shades of emotion as well as of meaning, and that individual styles may thus be developed. Your problem is to find the appropriate word for every situation, a word which expresses as exactly as possible the meaning that you wish to convey, and one which will make your reader feel that it is just the word you should have used. Joseph Conrad has said, "Give me the right word and the right accent and I will move the world."

2. OUR VARIOUS VOCABULARIES

We must first recognize the distinction between what is called a *passive recognition* vocabulary and an *active* or *use* vocabulary. The recognition vocabulary is composed of those words which you recognize when you see or hear them but which you do not employ in speaking or writing. It is, of course, larger than the active vocabulary. Mostly you come to some conclusions about the meaning of words in your recognition vocabulary from the situation or context in which you hear or see them used. For the meanings of such words you may possibly consult the dictionary, but usually you do this only when the context is so filled with unfamiliar words that a clue to meaning is wholly lacking.

If the contexts in which you meet a new word, let us say the first ten times, are fairly representative of its range of meaning, you will have formed a reasonably accurate conception of its use; if by chance these first ten instances illustrate one particular use to the exclusion of others, then your conception of that word will be one-sided. Likewise, if the first eight or ten times that you meet the word are not too widely separated in time, that word will certainly have become a part of your recognition vocabulary; if your early encounters with the word are widely separated, your chances of retaining it are considerably lessened.

It is only after a word has become firmly fixed in your *passive* or *recognition* vocabulary that you begin to use it. If it is a short word with an atmosphere of familiarity and ease about it, you will begin to employ it both in speech and in writing. If it is a long word, an unusual word, a learned word, or one which you do not use very often, it will remain passive in your mind provided you do not forget it entirely. A much smaller number of words, those used chiefly in conversation, become a part of your active vocabulary almost as soon as you hear them. Certain slang phrases are also acquired through hearing only, but if they are somewhat offensive to you, they will remain as a part of the passive vocabulary because you do not care to use them. It is estimated that the recognition vocabulary is, for most of us, about three times the size of the vocabulary which we use from day to day.

Thus the process by which we become conscious of and acquire a stock of words is a complex one. It is not so simple as depositing into a savings bank pennies which may be drawn out at will. You must increase both your active and your passive vocabularies, and especially hasten the transfer of words from the passive or recognition to the active or use vocabulary.

3. IMPROVING DICTION

"Diction" means the use of words; good diction involves the choice of the best available words for the speaker's or writer's purpose. This is not an easy task, but it often makes the difference between merely passable writing and good writing. Many a writer's style is built on his diction; and no matter how correct a writer's grammar may be he will never achieve real quality unless he attends, among other things, to diction.

As a writer, you want to take hold of your reader, to capture his interest, to make him read willingly, even with pleasure. How is this to be done? The first thing to make sure of is that you do not drive your reader away. If you bore him, annoy him, confuse or disappoint him, he will beware of you in future. Your instructor is paid to read your productions, but nobody else has this obligation. Others must be rewarded for their effort not with a salary but with the interest, the freshness, the clarity and attractiveness of your writing.

The most frequent difficulties which students have in regard to diction may be treated under three heads:

1. Students do not possess enough words.
2. Words which they do have are not always accurately employed.
3. Words are used in violation of canons of taste and style.

4. ACQUIRING MORE WORDS

The usual advice is this: look up in the dictionary all unfamiliar words encountered in reading. The student is advised to record such words in a notebook or card index; and then he is urged to put the new words to use as quickly as possible. The real difficulty here is that scarcely anyone ever follows the plan long enough.

It is all very well to say, "Look up every word you don't know," but suppose one finds in the course of his reading a passage like the following:

Yet Keats was a born genius if there ever was one. It is perhaps only additional proof of the authenticity of this genius that it ripened, did not spring spontaneously into maturity. Certainly it should be regarded as a pre-eminent quality of true genius to utilize and transform to its own purposes the rich resources of the world in which it resides, to accomplish, in the words of Coleridge, a reconciliation between the inner world of thought and feeling and the outer world of fact and substance. Precocity flames up in a brief moment, and, drawing only from within, quickly burns itself out; but genius, growing with what it feeds on, its natural powers reinforced through union with congenial elements from without, glows with increasing warmth until it reaches its full potential strength.[1]

This is a passage of about ordinary difficulty. In it you might be uncertain of six words: *authenticity, spontaneously, pre-eminent, utilize, reconciliation,* and *precocity.* If you were to follow literally and conscientiously the instructions usually given, you would have to look up all six words, a task which not only would increase the reading time of the paragraph by perhaps four minutes but would break the train of thought six times.

Yet it is evident that even if you were unfamiliar with all six words, all except *precocity* would be quite clear from context. Instead of looking up all six words, concentrate upon the one word *precocity* which does need explanation if the sentence in which it occurs is to mean anything.

Examine this one word thoroughly. Note that it is formed from the adjective *precocious,* that it comes from Latin *prae + coquere,* "to cook or ripen beforehand"; that

---

[1] John Keats, *Complete Poems and Selected Letters,* ed. C. D. Thorpe, Doubleday Doran, Introduction, p. xv. Reprinted by courtesy of the publisher.

an adverb, *precociously,* and another noun, *precociousness,* may be formed from the same stem. Notice also that the slang phrase *half baked,* used to describe a rather stupid or perhaps quixotic individual, makes use of the same figure of speech as *precocious.* If a single difficult word is thus carefully studied, there is a greater likelihood that it will remain in your memory longer than any six words hastily looked up.

Learn to recognize words from context. You will make some mistakes; everyone does. Look up only those words which are necessary to the meaning. When you do look up a word, work carefully. Get everything your dictionary offers. Interest yourself in these words. Become word-conscious in a wholesome, not in a picayunish manner.

The other usual admonition is: keep a notebook in which you list new words which swim into your consciousness. "Use a word three times and it is yours." The difficulty here is that we can't always manufacture situations in which our newly acquired words can be used. We are then in the position of Leora in Sinclair Lewis's *Arrowsmith:* after an afternoon spent reading about modern painting to impress her husband's associates, she found herself unable to maneuver the evening's conversation in that direction. Suppose we do discover for ourselves the words *atavistic, ontology,* and *recrudesce.* Finding even one normal conversation in which any of these could be used will not be easy; three situations, that the word might be "ours," would require patent manufacture!

It is here that writing comes to our aid. In writing we *can* choose the subject, as Leora could not, which will allow us to use our newly acquired words. This has to be done with caution, of course; we must be quite sure of the word and use it with reasonable ease. It must not, for example, stick out as the lone polysyllable in an otherwise plain piece of writing.

But the surest way to acquire new words is to acquire new knowledge. Expand mentally and your vocabulary will expand. Increase the range of topics on which you write, and your command of words will improve.

5. ACCURATE USE OF WORDS

Misuses of words connected with their grammar are treated in detail in Chapter VI. A few, however, also call for attention here, along with misuses connected with meaning and idiom.

A. Do not make one part of speech perform the function of another in a way which does not conform to normal usage.

FAULTY: Whenever forestry is mentioned to the average uninformed citizen, his immediate reaction is to *vision* a raging forest fire.

REVISED: Whenever forestry is mentioned to the average uninformed citizen, his immediate reaction is to *visualize* a raging forest fire.

FAULTY: To the man of today, the idea of thinking has become more and more *loathe.*

REVISED: To the man of today, the idea of thinking has become more and more *loathsome.*

Note in the first sentence that the noun *vision* has been transformed into a verb, while in the second, the verb *loathe* has been made to serve as an adjective.

It is true, of course, that many words in English often serve as any one of several parts of speech. This aspect of the language is dealt with in somewhat greater detail on p. 187. Many such words, however, were long considered incorrect or inappropriate in their newer functions before they were finally accepted. As a student rather than an authority on the use of English, it will be best for you to follow the parts-of-speech labels in your dictionary.

B. Do not use derivatives or compound words in a position or in a construction which alters their intended meaning.

FAULTY: After all the teas were over, we waited at home for the telephone to ring, and hoped it would be the rushing chairman of our *partial* sorority.

REVISED: After all the teas were over, we waited at home for the telephone to ring, and hoped it would be the rushing chairman of the sorority *to which we were partial*.

FAULTY: Along with his personality and *speaking* popularity, we also see that the president is doing his best.

REVISED: Along with his personality and his popularity *as a speaker,* we also see that the president is doing his best.

In the first sentence *partial* may mean either "an inclination to favor" or "a part." The first meaning occurs usually when the word is used as a predicate adjective after some form of the verb *to be* ("he was partial to the green"), whereas the second meaning generally occurs when the adjective directly precedes the noun it modifies ("a partial estimate"). By using the adjective *partial* before the noun *sorority* here, the writer has suggested a meaning which is wholly at odds with the context.

In the second sentence the writer has attempted to make the present participle *speaking* do the work of an adjective phrase *as a speaker*. The difficulty lies in the closer connection of *speaking* with the verb *to speak* than with the noun *speaker*.

C. Avoid words of your own invention that are not otherwise current.

The moment a word enters our active vocabulary it is no longer an isolated mental phenomenon; it is subject to all the inflectional and derivational patterns we normally employ. For example, suppose we have just become actively aware of the words *precocious* and *precocity*. If there should arise a situation in which more than one *precocity* was involved, it would not be necessary for us to have learned the plural, *precocities*, as a separate fact. We would automatically form the plural of this word by fitting it to the general pattern of all the regularly formed plurals that we already know.

This tendency goes farther than mere inflection. If we know the adjective *precocious* and a situation arises which calls for the use of an adverb with this meaning, we again automatically apply the *-ly* adverb pattern to the adjective, thus creating what is for us a new word, *precociously*. All languages grow and adapt themselves to new situations through the employment of such inflectional and word-forming patterns. But at times our creative instincts do betray us, and we form non-existent words. This is often the result of putting together word-forming elements in a unique combination:

FAULTY: From the tone of this paper one is apt to believe me critical of these tendencies of *undemocracy*.

REVISED: From the tone of this paper one is apt to believe me critical of these *undemocratic* tendencies.

FAULTY: The best way to distinguish rationalized thinking from *irrationalized* thinking is simply to question statements made in defense of a particular idea.

REVISED: The best way to distinguish rational thinking from *irrational* thinking (or rationalized thinking from

that which is not rationalized) is simply to question statements made in defense of a particular idea.

It is interesting to see how these unique words came to
be formed. Beginning with the word *democrat,* one may
form from it the adjectives *democratic* and *undemocratic*
and then proceed to an abstract noun which is the an-
tithesis or opposite of *democracy* by forming it on the pattern of the adjective *undemocratic.* The attempt is laudable enough; the only difficulty is that the word *undemocracy* just doesn't exist. In the same manner *irrationalized*
results from a blending of the *rational:rationalize* and the
rational:irrational patterns.

It is true, of course, that words are frequently coined to
meet special or unusual situations. President Harding, during his campaign for election, coined the word *normalcy,*
presumably because it could be made to fit the rhythmic
swing of a slogan more readily than *normality,* which contains an extra syllable. During the prohibition period, the
word *scofflaw* was created to apply to those who disobeyed
the prohibition law. Almost every new invention requires
a noun to name it and frequently a verb to describe its
operation. For example, what verb shall we employ to
describe the operation of television? Usage now seems to
be divided between *televise* and *telecast,* and there are
proponents of *video.* Yet, our present large stock of words
will undoubtedly meet any needs which you will encounter.
Better leave the coining of new words to the experienced
writer.

D. Do not add superfluous prefixes and suffixes when the simple word is sufficient to give the desired meaning.

FAULTY: Reverie is a pleasant *pre-occupation* and is also
conducive to progress.

REVISED: Reverie is a pleasant *occupation* and is also conducive to progress.

FAULTY: Moreover, this idea is so firmly *affixed* in our minds that probably nine out of ten persons would refuse to accept the scientist's findings.

REVISED: Moreover, this idea is so firmly *fixed* in our minds that probably nine out of ten persons would refuse to accept the scientist's findings.

FAULTY: It was a very plain door, with few *ornamentations* on it.

REVISED: It was a very plain door, with few *ornaments* on it.

Attaching word-forming elements (prefixes and suffixes) is such a common phenomenon that it tends to become a habit with us. It is true that the words *affix* and *ornamentation* do exist. In the sentences given, the simple words are more economical and in better taste.

Quite frequently clumsiness in diction results from the addition of noun suffixes to words that already have corresponding abstract nouns. Avoid *virtuousness, cruelness, annoyingness, summarization;* use *virtue, cruelty, annoyance, summary.*

As you become more familiar with the meaning and uses of prefixes and suffixes, and with the derivations of the words you use, you will develop a feeling for the right word.

EXERCISE I.

  1*a*. Examine the list of prefixes and suffixes below and form all the words you can from each.
  b. What does each of these contribute to the meaning of the word to which it is added?
  c. Observe to what part or parts of speech each is added and what part of speech the result is.

To illustrate, let us examine the suffix *-ness,* in such derivative formations as *blackness, holiness, coldness, hardness.* Note that this suffix is added to adjectives, and converts them into abstract nouns. It means "state or condition of being"; e.g., *hardness*—state or condition of being hard.

Suffixes

-aceous, acious	-fy	-let	-tude
-craft	-ish	-ment	-ward
-dom	-ile	-ory	-wise

Prefixes

amphi-	dia-	multi-	retro-
bene-	homo-	neo-	sur-
cath-	hyper-	ob-	under-
contra-	mal-	pseudo-	with-

2. By adding prefixes and suffixes, form as many derived words as you can from each of the following simple words. Include also all the compound words in which the given word is an element, e.g., *stand: understand, withstand, standby.*

anima, Latin, "soul"	*philos,* Greek, "friend"
crux, Latin, "cross, torture"	*pipe*
duc-, Latin, "to lead, draw"	*sand*
good	*take*
ora-, Latin, "to speak, pray"	*water*

3. Improve the diction of the following sentences by selecting another word for the one italicized. Explain why each italicized word is open to criticism.

a. He did everything possible to prevent a *dissolvement* of the company.

b. The type of movie varies in accord with the changes in world *happens*.

c. These changes have taken place because of the public's *non-acceptance* of certain types of pictures and its overwhelming interest in other types.

d. This class *predominates* our society by virtue of its economic power.

e. Thinking for yourself develops *independability*.

f. In *refute* to the argument that the state should be the chief end, many people believe that individuality will be destroyed.

g. If he feels *unjustice* has been done, he has a right to appeal to the State Tenure Commission.

h. This shows how popular and *wanted* the radio is.

i. I, too, have been one to look very *disgustingly* at the clock at that early hour in the morning.

j. When I asked several of my close associates what they were really thinking about, they confessed that they were just *reverieing*.

k. He has lost a certain quality which to me makes life more *cherishable*.

l. Whenever a nation keeps a large standing army, it is clearly demonstrating an *unpeacelike* spirit.

m. The plan to recognize this little nation was put into writing and *initialized* by the President.

n. John's greatest fault is his *cowardness*.

o. The store was robbed last week, but the owner *suspicions* the janitor.

p. The Congress is seeking *finalization* of several of the wartime agencies.

q. History and its *relating* subjects have always interested me.

r. In this manner the frequent strikes tied up the operaation of the entire factory and, in some cases, of an entire industry by stopping the output of some vital *manufacturing* necessity.

s. A strike is usually the fault of some one individual who spreads the feeling of *uncontentedness* among the workers.

t. The words "co-operative" always has a great *connoting* effect on me, arousing my sympathy, support, and approbation.

E. Do not confuse words that are more or less alike in sound but have a different meaning or use.

The following list contains some of the more frequent confusions of this nature.

> *accept,* to receive.
> *except,* to leave out, reject.
>
> *affect,* to act or produce an effect upon, to influence.
> *effect,* verb—to bring to pass, execute, accomplish.
>
> *allusion,* an indirect reference.
> *illusion,* an unreal or misleading image, a deceptive appearance.
>
> *already,* an adverb: They had *already* gone.
> *all ready,* separate words, a pronoun and an adjective: They were *all ready* to go.
>
> *altogether,* an adverb: They lost *altogether* too many sales.
> *all together,* separate words, a pronoun and an adjective: Our seats are *all together* in the first row.
>
> *censor,* as a noun: an overseer of morals and conduct, sometimes official; as a verb: to subject to the act of a censor.
> *censure,* verb: to blame, condemn.
>
> *compose,* to form by putting together, to constitute, to dispose in proper form.

comprise, to comprehend or include.

contemptible, worthy of contempt.
contemptuous, expressing contempt.

continual, a close or unceasing succession or recurrence, e.g. *continual* interruptions.
continuous, an uninterrupted continuity, e.g. a *continuous* murmur.

council, an assembly summoned for consultation, or the deliberation itself.
counsel, the advice given as a result of deliberation, or one who gives advice.

credible, worthy of belief, capable of being credited.
creditable, praiseworthy.

decided, unquestionable, clear cut, free from doubt, e.g. a *decided* change.
decisive, having the power of deciding or terminating a controversy, e.g. *decisive* proofs.

effective, impressive, striking; emphasizing the actual production of an effect, e.g. an *effective* manner.
effectual, fulfilling an intended purpose; looking backward to a purpose having been fulfilled, e.g. an *effectual* retort.

emigrate, to leave a place or country.
immigrate, to come to a country to take up residence there.

founded, placed or based on something for support.
foundered, to fall or sink down, fail, miscarry, dumbfound.

human, belonging or relating to man, characteristic of man.
humane, kind, benevolent, having feelings and inclinations creditable to man.

imply, to express indirectly, to hint at: He *implied* that he did not favor the measure.

infer, to derive by reasoning or implication: From the substance of his speech we *inferred* that he was displeased.

indefinite, having no prescribed or known limits or reference.

infinite, without limits.

later, opposed to *earlier,* referring primarily to time.

latter, opposed to *former,* referring primarily to order, in which one of two things is mentioned.

livid, discolored, as bruised flesh; ashy gray.

vivid, bright in color.

loose, to unbind, untie, undo.

lose, to fail to keep, maintain, or sustain something.

luxuriant, exuberant or profuse in growth or display, e.g. *luxuriant* whiskers.

luxurious, pertaining or ministering to luxury, e.g. *luxurious* upholstery.

malicious, proceeding from ill will, dictated by malice.

malignant, having an evil influence, characterized by intense and active ill will.

manly, having qualities pertaining or becoming to a man.

manual, of or pertaining to the hands.

observance, act or practice of observing a rule or custom, or the customary act itself.

observation, the act or result of considering or marking attentively a fact or occurrence.

practicable, capable of being put into practice or action.

practical, pertaining to or manifested in practice; opposed to *theoretical, ideal,* or *speculative.*

propose, to offer for consideration or adoption.
purpose, to intend.

statue, a likeness of a person or animal, sculptured in solid substance.
stature, height.
statute, a law or act of a government or corporate body.

transfer, to convey from one place, person, or thing to another.
transform, to change the form, shape, appearance of.

venal, capable of being bought or obtained for money or other valuable considerations.
venial, capable of being forgiven.

Other pairs of words, confused because of similarity in spelling rather than through likeness of pronunciation, are treated on pages 321, 322.

F. Discriminate carefully between synonyms.

Many pairs of words are synonymous in some, but not in all, of their senses.

The meaning of words is based upon human experience. Such a common word as *dog* will call up one mental picture and set of emotions in someone fond, say, of Irish terriers, whereas a person, bitten as a child by a police dog, who has avoided dogs ever since, will have a quite different set of mental and emotional reactions to the word. Because of this variability of experience, no one word means exactly the same to all people, nor is it likely that there are any absolutely identical synonyms. Words overlap in meaning, but they do not coincide.

Though synonyms may lend variety and novelty, they are not always used exactly:

FAULTY: The tribute paid to the heroes was an excellent piece of *penmanship*.
REVISED: The tribute paid to the heroes was an excellent piece of *writing*.

It is clear that the student meant to say that this tribute was an excellent piece of *writing,* using the word *writing* in a sense synonymous with *composition. Writing,* in another of its meanings, is synonymous with *penmanship,* but that does not make *penmanship* synonymous with *composition,* as the student consciously or sub-consciously assumed.

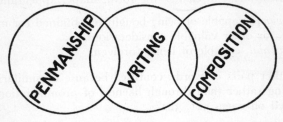

FAULTY: Colleges and universities *take up* a part of the graduates of our high schools.
REVISED: Colleges and universities *absorb* a part of the graduates of our high schools.

Here the synonyms have even less in common. Of the five meanings of *absorb* given in the *Oxford Dictionary,* two might be represented satisfactorily by *take up;* of the twenty-six meanings of *take up* given in the same dictionary, again only two could be represented by *absorb* as a synonym.

To help avoid tiresome repetition in your themes, consult the dictionary for synonyms or use a thesaurus. If you have a sufficiently complete dictionary, it will discriminate at some length between synonyms; and if you take the trouble to read these detailed treatments, you will be helped by such advice. But if your dictionary is small and merely lists synonyms, or if you do not trouble to read the explanatory material, you may make mistakes such as those cited. If, after an honest search, you cannot find a good synonym, it is better to repeat the first word than to mislead the reader with a bad synonym.

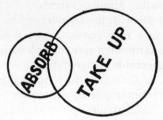

EXERCISE 2. 1. Consult your dictionary for the distinction in meaning between each of the following pairs of frequently confused words, and be able to use each word in a sentence:

ability—capacity	contemptible—contemptuous
addicted to—subject to	exceptional—exceptionable
allude—refer	definite—definitive
anxious—eager	ingenious—ingenuous
avenge—revenge	noted—notorious
avocation—vocation	noteworthy—notable
climactic—climatic	proposition—proposal

respectful—respectable—respective

2. Fill in the blanks with the words most appropriate to the context:

a. The doctor was certain that a long vacation would ——————— a cure. (affect, effect)

b. We had to admit that Peter's explanation of his laziness was entirely ——————, even if we didn't approve. (credible, creditable)

c. Although the invitation was very urgent, Elizabeth was not prepared to ———————— it. (accept, except) *d.* The lecturer was exasperated by the _____ interruptions. (continual, ~~continuous~~)

e. The speaker made an _____ to the Twenty-Third Psalm. (allusion, ~~illusion~~)

f. |John seemed to _____ that his brother was not telling the truth. (imply, infer)

g. According to the will, the property of the _____ was divided into four parts. (deceased, ~~diseased~~)

h. All the contestants then returned to their _____ schools. (~~respectable~~, respective)

i. It was a _____ effort, indicating a mean and petty spirit. (contemptible, contemptuous)

j. The _____ made by the visiting expert were of considerable help to us in our work. (observances, observations)

3. Improve the wording of each of the following sentences by making substitutions for the italicized words:

a. We must recognize the difference between common and *statue* law.

b. The author of the article was severely *censored* for overlooking many of the essential facts.

c. The sky at sunset was *livid* with many rich colors.

d. It is said that habits make our lives and *wield* us to our destiny.

e. It was *all ready* six o'clock and the train had not yet arrived at the station.

f. Clear enunciation, a fine choice of words, excellent grammar, and a complete and thorough knowledge of the topic chosen for discussion *compose* the qualities of a good news commentator.

g. It was an *ingenuous* device for removing the impurities from crankcase oil.

h. He has retired now, but *formally* he was the president of a large manufacturing company and director of a bank.

i. Practical thinking was the kind of mental activity that was *cultured* most during my high-school course.

j. The concluding speech was very *forcible* and aroused a great deal of enthusiasm.

G. Do not employ words which are not in logical agreement with other terms which they govern or are dependent upon.

Inconsistencies of this nature occur most frequently in the following grammatical situations:

1. Noun-verb relationships, chiefly subject-verb, and verb-object.

FAULTY: I shall try in every way to *carry out* the *statements* I have previously set forth.

REVISED: I shall try in every way to *carry out* the *resolutions* I have previously set forth.

OR: I shall try in every way to *explain* the *statements* I have previously made.

Notice that the meaning of the original sentence is not wholly clear as a *statement* is not *carried out.* Substitute for *statement* something which can be *carried out;* replace the verb *carry out* by some other verb which can logically govern the object *statement.*

FAULTY: Americanism is the *act* of *being* a good citizen who obeys the laws of the land, and who defends his country in times of invasion.

REVISED: Americanism is the *state* of *being* a good citizen who obeys the laws of the land, and who defends his country in times of invasion.

OR: Americanism includes such *acts* of good citizenship as *obeying* the laws of the land and *defending* the country in times of invasion.

The noun *act* implies that some activity is to follow.

whereas the participle *being* which it governs suggests a passive condition. We may change *act* to *state*, a word logically compatible with *being*, or we may omit the *being* and use the less neutral verbs *obey* and *defend*.

2. Adjective-noun relationships.

FAULTY: The masses of American citizens have shown an *irrefutable* loyalty to him.
REVISED: The masses of American citizens have shown an *unquestionable* (*undeniable*) loyalty to him.

An adjective not logically appropriate to the noun it modified was chosen. A loyalty may be *denied* or *questioned;* it is not *refuted*.

3. Adverb-verb relationships.

FAULTY: During the past few months his popularity has *increasingly* diminished.
REVISED: During the past few months his popularity has *rapidly* (*progressively*) diminished.

4. Verb-verb relationships.

FAULTY: If war propaganda can maintain the spirit, so can the spirit of making a new and better society *hold* the people *to agree* with the centralized authority.
REVISED: If war propaganda can maintain the spirit, so can the spirit of making a new and better society *lead* the people *to agree* with the centralized authority.

We cannot be *held* to agree with something; we can be led or induced to agree with it—or we can be held *to obey* or *in obedience to* something.

5. Parallel situations involving any parts of speech.

FAULTY: It would be foolish for the employers to *lower* the very standard of labor they have helped to *increase*.

REVISED: It would be foolish for the employers to *lower* the very standard of labor they have helped to *raise*.

FAULTY: He kills the man and goes on trial for his life, *outwardly* calm, *inside* sad and discouraged.
REVISED: He kills the man and goes on trial for his life, *outwardly* calm, *inwardly* sad and discouraged.

H. Do not omit words necessary for the completion of a suggested relationship.

FAULTY: In Mexico especially, the young people are no longer *moved* by their *country*.
REVISED: In Mexico especially, the young people are no longer *moved* by *love* for their *country*.

Speaking strictly, a physical entity or thing does not *move* us; an emotion, feeling, or idea does.

FAULTY: The present administration has poured millions of dollars into the spoils system for political *cohorts*.
REVISED: The present administration has poured millions of dollars into the spoils system for political *patronage*.
OR: The present administration has poured millions of dollars into the spoils system for the *benefit of its cohorts*.

I. Use the preposition appropriate to each word or situation.

(See pages 214, 215, also.)

The correct use of prepositions is one of the most difficult aspects of almost any language. This is especially true of English, where we say, for example, *at noon, in the evening, on Wednesday, in July, on July first*. You have already mastered hundreds of prepositional phrases such as those mentioned, which you write or speak with absolute ease and without even thinking about them. There are others, however, which are likely to give you trouble.

Observe the prepositions used with the following words. In no instance do they represent all the possible prepositional constructions which may follow the word in question, but rather those which will be of greatest use to the student. When in doubt about other similar expressions, consult your dictionary.

accord with
accordance with
according to

accuse of
accused by (a person)
accused of (a deed)

agree in (an opinion, a characteristic)
agree on (a plan, a matter)
agree to (a proposal)
agree with (a person)
agreeable to

angry at, about (a thing, an occasion)
angry with, at (a person)

argue against, for (a measure, a policy)
argue with (a person)

authority on (a topic, subject)
authority of (doing or acting in a certain way)

comply with

conform to
conformity with

contend against (an obstacle)
contend for (a principle)
contend with (a person)

correspond to (things)
correspond with (persons)

desire for
desirous of

differ about (a question)
differ from (something else)
differ with (a person)

disagree with
dissent from

identical with
independent of

inferior to

in search of

jealous of

listen to

part from (a person)
part with (property, possession)

prior to

profit by

repent of

sensitive to

separate from

stay at home

superior to

treat of (a subject)
treat with (to negotiate)

unmindful of

wait at (a place)
wait for (a person)
wait on (a customer)

EXERCISE 3. 1. Consult your dictionary for the preposition or prepositions which may be appropriately used with the following words, and be able to use each expression in a sentence:

abhorrent	compare	oblivious
absolve	desist	preferable
acquiesce	inseparable	reconcile
acquit	mastery	repugnant
collide	meddle	subscribe

2. Improve the wording of each of the following sentences by making substitutions for the italicized words. Be able to explain what principle has been violated in each instance:

a. The industrial equality to which I refer hinges directly *with* several conditions.

b. One can concentrate on helping his own kind or country *much easier* and with better results than upon improving the state of the world in general.

c. There is also the *point* of self-satisfaction which cannot be overlooked.

d. Although our Constitution guarantees us life, liberty and the pursuit of happiness, it does not *ascertain* to us the privileges of a college education.

e. The *world* is becoming more and more *specialized*.

f. My first job was that of assistant sweeper, that is, assistant to the lowest form of *life* in a foundry.

g. Herein has education been *lacking* in that it has too frequently approached the subject without going beneath the surface.

h. Some sort of work is almost always done, whether it be in the *form* of a job, school, or something different.

i. It is believed that the serum, rushed from Chicago by army plane and *instituted* at once, was the saving factor.

j. Almost never does idle speculation lead to any practical *phase* because it revolves about the ego.

k. His speaking voice and his pleasing personality *lead* a pathway to millions of people in this country.

l. If a teacher has the *good will of prestige,* he need not be particularly well trained in his subject.

m. He kidnapped the other members *of* the airplane.

n. It is usually very restful to drop *on* a large, comfortable chair.

o. One of the greatest secrets behind his efficiency is his mastery *over detail.*

6. EFFECTIVE USE OF WORDS

Beyond fullness and accuracy in the use of words there are efficiency and effectiveness. You want your words to count: you *do not* want to waste them, to repeat yourself, to use vague expressions which require further explanation; you *do not* want your words to be flat, threadbare or faded; and you *do* want them to be appropriate to the kind of writing you are attempting.

The things to avoid will be dealt with in detail in the following pages; the things to seek are, of course, their opposites. The positive side of good diction, however, may be summed up in a single word: appropriateness. Every word is used in a context, grammatical, stylistic, even physical. The author, if he knows what he is about, is seeking to produce a certain effect upon a certain kind of reader. What words will produce this effect? Is he trying to be familiar, literary, chatty, impressive? He must choose his diction accordingly.

Consider the following:

> The poor fish. fell for that stale gag.
> The silly fellow was fooled by that old trick.
> Simpletons are deceived by outworn devices.
> Springes to catch woodcocks!

All four expressions say virtually the same thing—but with what a difference! The first is altogether slangy; the second, informal and conversational; the third, literary and sententious; the fourth, highly connotative to those who catch the allusion and recall Polonius's advice to his daughter given in his characteristic manner.[1] In each case the diction makes each phrase appropriate to a very different situation. The student must consciously make himself aware of such differences and suit his own words to his purpose.

A. Use nouns and verbs concretely and specifically. Avoid hazy or general terms.

Be especially careful in your use of the following general or classifying terms:

aspect	instance	question
case	manner	situation
factor	matter	style
fashion	phase	thing
feature	point	type
field	problem	way

FAULTY: Questions which they have never before had to face will arise, and they must know how to combat these *things*.

REVISED: Questions which they have never before had to face will arise, and they must know how to solve such *problems*.

FAULTY: Another *phase* of writing studied in fourth-year English was poetry.

REVISED: Another *form* of literature studied in fourth year English was poetry.

FAULTY: Therefore, to create a community which will satisfy each of its members, certain set rules cannot be put down and religiously carried out, for they would be sure to *go against* someone.

[1] *Hamlet*, Act I, scene iii, line 115.

REVISED: Therefore, to create a community which will satisfy each of its members, certain set rules cannot be put down and religiously carried out, for they would be sure to *harm* or *dissatisfy* someone.

B. Avoid unnecessary repetition of the same word within a small compass of your writing. Use synonyms where possible, making sure that they are accurate ones.

FAULTY: There was also, at this time, a great *deal* of unscrupulous business *deals,* mortgage foreclosures, trusts, and monopolies.

REVISED: There were also, at this time, a great *many* unscrupulous business transactions, mortgage foreclosures, trusts, and monopolies.

FAULTY: Because I am a graduate nurse, a *highly* enthusiastic Public Health follower, I realize that to become *highly* efficient in that *field* I must complete my education, not only in the *field* of Public Health, but in the Literary College as well.

REVISED: Because I am a graduate nurse, a *most* enthusiastic Public Health advocate, I realize that to become highly efficient in that *vocation,* I must complete my education not only in the field of Public Health, but in the Literary College as well.

C. Avoid the use of co-ordinate synonyms which merely repeat one another.

FAULTY: With the *deeds* and *doings* of these pioneers of science still retained firmly in my mind, I have decided to enter the field of medicine.

REVISED: With the *accomplishments* of these pioneers of

science still retained firmly in my mind, I have decided to enter the field of medicine.

FAULTY: Therefore we must differentiate *definitely* and *distinctly* between amateurs and semi-professionals.

REVISED: Therefore we must differentiate *clearly* between amateurs and semi-professionals.

D. Avoid the use of modifiers which repeat an idea already implicit or present in the word modified.

FAULTY: In the last decade movie production has advanced *forward* with great strides.

REVISED: In the last decade movie production has advanced with great strides.

FAULTY: Her civilian population is shot at daily in the most *un*merciless fashion.

REVISED: Her civilian population is shot at daily in the most merciless fashion.

E. Avoid the use of qualifying adjectives and adverbs which contribute little to the meaning intended and detract from the strength of the expression.

FAULTY: My station is a *rather* typical *one,* consisting of a low-powered transmitter and a seven-tube receiver.

REVISED: My station is typical; it consists of a low-powered transmitter and a seven-tube receiver.

FAULTY: Why is it that poems always have to be enriched by *such* colorful adjectives and phrases?

REVISED: Why is it that poems always have to be enriched by colorful adjectives and phrases?

Such implies, of course, that certain specific illustrations have already been cited; in this case there were none.

F. Avoid the use of overemphatic words.

In the first example, the adjective and adverb are almost contradictory, which gives a ludicrous effect.

FAULTY: In the world of today the superstitions of yesterday are *somewhat extinct*.
REVISED: In the world of today the superstitions of yesterday are *no longer active*.

FAULTY: One example will *prove* my point.
REVISED: One example will *illustrate* my point.

FAULTY: A person with a truly open mind has an attribute that will be of *eternal* use to him.
REVISED: A person with true open-mindedness has an attribute that will be of *lifelong* use to him.

A common occurrence in almost all languages is the constant weakening of words. The word *nice* at one time in its history meant "foolish"; then it came to be used to indicate a minute degree of discrimination. *Fine* originally meant "finished," then "brought to perfection," "free from impurity," and finally "superior." Now both of these words are used to indicate varying degrees of general approval: a *fine* day, a *nice* book, a *fine* performance, a *nice* garden, etc. Obviously no amount of emphasis upon word history could restore these to their original meanings, nor is it particularly desirable that they be restored. The language needs some very general words of approval. They are necessary to the informality of conversation.

A number of other words, however, are undergoing the same processes to which *nice* and *fine* were subjected, but they have not yet gone the whole way. Exercise discretion in using them. Particularly are they out of place in formal or serious writing, because they suggest a certain poverty in the diction of the writer. The reader is likely to think that he has no more precise or exact terms at his command.

Avoid the use of the following in your writing:

amazing	magnificent
awful, -ly	mighty
dreadful	phenomenal
elegant	splendid
fierce	terrible, -ly
grand	tremendous
horrid	weird
lovely	wonderful

G. Avoid mixed or inappropriate figures of speech.

We are all familiar with the man who smelled a rat, saw it floating in the air, and felt that he must nip it in the bud. Be careful also not to slip from figurative language to literal language before the figure has been carried out to its logical conclusion.

Examples:

> A foothold seems to have been established in the minds of many of our people, and that foothold seems to hang upon one word—growth.

> Yet they knew that there would be hurdles ahead as the spirit of Americanism passed from one hand to another. If a man is to open his mind to other people, he must first unlock the barriers of prejudice.

The *New Yorker* magazine regularly reprints mixed figures of speech as one source of their incongruous and inadvertent humor. An example:

BLOCK THAT METAPHOR!

[*Virgil Thomson in the* Herald Tribune]

The tempos were all correct and the balances proper, but the work tended to tread water for lack of a plain emotional trajectory.   (January 4, 1947)

H. Avoid trite or hackneyed expressions.

You may have just discovered *acid test* and *aching void* but they have long been hackneyed through overuse. Avoid these clichés:

abreast of the times	green with envy
bathed in tears	Hand of Justice
bitter end	in the last analysis
breakneck speed	mantle of snow
budding genius	motley throng
captain of industry	nipped in the bud
checkered career	paramount issue
Dame Fortune	psychological moment
dazed condition	replete with interest
depths of despair	simple life
epic struggle	soul of honor
ere long	thereby hangs a tale
filthy lucre	words fail to express
ghastly corruption	wreak havoc

Avoid such trite expressions as the following:

He is a person of *high ideals*.

I came to college to *broaden* myself.

The greatest boon that college can give you is to *develop your personality*.

This teacher constantly held up before his pupils the *finer side of life*.

EXERCISE 4.   1. Improve the wording of the following sentences:

1. I studied early and late but still lacked the seed for any brilliant advance in the course.

2. He tries to find points that will carry out or continue his ideas.

3. This epidemic of non-thinkers has been present as long as man.

4. Naturally and inevitably, it is necessary that she take every other subject that is in any way connected with her major field of specialization.

5. When the cooler weather had come, and the epidemic was at its worst, I took to my home to rest up for more hard labor of the coming fall.

6. Ere long there came a swarm of locusts which devoured all the crops.

7. It may be of greater advantage to the sorority to "rush" the first three weeks of school, but it is a decided disadvantage to the freshmen to have to make such an important decision in such a short time.

8. Some student, perhaps, through the study of literature will open up that spark of genius which we all hear so much about.

9. I do feel, however, that future years must bring a complete reversal of our present economic system so that the mass of people will become much happier and have better means of existence.

10. The ironical part of the entire situation is that parents and relatives who had grieved for loved ones lost in the wars were once more bearing their kin to the grim and gray business of war.

11. It is conceivable that mankind has failed to unite into a friendly brotherhood.

12. The prime requisite to my personal well-being is that necessary requirement which consumes, or should consume, at least eight hours of our daily living—namely, sleep.

13. When the President was inaugurated, his whole heart was seemingly out for the mass majority, the laborer.

14. Each of the two boys was so inseparably suited for the throne that even the prince's father didn't recognize the difference between his own son and the pauper lad.

15. She did all her tasks with tender care, especially that of tending the garden.

2. The following passage, by using vague, superfluous and hackneyed expressions, becomes much longer than need be for what it has to say (95 words). How far can you condense it without loss of meaning? "Blue-pencil" it as an editor might, then rewrite it. How many words have you used?

The question is as to whether or not it will be possible or feasible to do this. It has been doubted by those most intimately concerned in the matter. Because of the fact that these experts, who in the nature of things ought to have worth-while opinions on the subject, are uncertain about the probable outcome themselves, we must proceed with caution. We must not undertake to do that which may, for all we know to the contrary, have disastrous results and lead in the final analysis to unforeseen consequences of a most undesirable nature.

I. Avoid the use of trade jargon.

The term *trade jargon* (sometimes called *shop talk*) is to be understood here as "the technical vocabulary of a science, art, trade, sect, profession, or other special group." All such groups—radio technicians, gamblers, printers, evangelists, circus men—have their special vocabularies, and from time to time words stray from these vocabularies into current English. Some of the words are incomprehensible to the person without a special knowledge, but a good proportion of them are generally understood. Few of us would need a glossary to explain *flunk, layout, reaction, turn on the heat, screwball, kibitzer,* all originally part of the technical vocabulary of students, advertising men, psychologists, criminals, baseball players, and card players, respectively.

Trade jargon enters formal literary English more slowly than it enters conversation or informal writing. If you employ trade jargon at all, make certain that you use it competently. Incompetently used:

FAULTY: The types of pictures the public enjoys are widely distributed, and *those to which it has no reflex* are taken off the market.

FAULTY: He whizzed into the stadium in a long, low, convertible Lincoln, with Secret Service men on all sides, and cordons of police *before and aft*.

Notice the writer has confused *reflex* with *reaction,* although he means a negative reaction rather than *no* reaction. In the second sentence the expression should be *fore and aft*; the writer also has failed to note that this is always used in respect to parts *of* a ship and that it can scarcely be applied to a part *outside* the automobile itself.

Legal language must employ such terms of reference as *above, above-mentioned, below, said, same.* They are out of place in writing that is at all dignified and imaginative. For *above* it is well to substitute *preceding* or *foregoing* and to use these words adjectivally, not pronominally. For *below,* substitute *following;* for *said* and *same,* use the personal and demonstrative pronouns.

FAULTY: For the *above* reasons, Bulgaria has shown herself to be the aggressor.
REVISED: For the *foregoing* reasons, Bulgaria has shown herself to be the aggressor.

FAULTY: In order to understand the term "democracy," let us examine the definition of *the same* advanced by Bryce.
REVISED: In order to understand the term "democracy," let us examine Bryce's definition of *it*.

Other terms common in commercial usage which may arouse antagonism are: *contact* used as a verb; *line,* meaning a field of endeavor or occupation; *balance* for remainder *favor* for letter or communication.

FAULTY: It seems to me that there is no greater field in the teaching *line* than that of English.
REVISED: It seems to me that there is no more promising field in the teaching *profession* than English.

J. Avoid the inappropriate use of slang.

Slang is not jargon, it is not profanity, it is not provincial language, nor does it consist of violations of the rules of grammar. That is to say, *flunk, damn, reckon,* and *hain't* are not slang.

Much of it is metaphor heightened to the point of grotesqueness. *Gilt-edged* for "valuable" is basically a metaphor derived from the appearance of negotiable securities. *Pass* (or *cash*) *in your checks* for "to die" is a figure derived from a poker game.

Another form of slang occurs by shortening or clipping words. *Bus* for "omnibus," *cab* for "cabriolet," *mob* for "mobile vulgus" all started out in this fashion, but in the course of time became wholly accepted in standard formal usage, as they are today. Such words as *ad, auto, phone, photo, exam, gent, gym, prof,* and *taxi* are more recent shortenings, and have acquired varying degrees of respectability. Still other forms taken by slang include intentional mispronunciations such as *wiff* for "wife" and the intentional addition of endings as in *kiddo.* Even this is by no means a complete account, for it has omitted the so-called "counter-words" such as *swell* and *elegant,* which develop from a desire for emphasis, but soon wear thin from frequent use.

Much slang, particularly of the metaphorical kind, arises from the praiseworthy desire for effectiveness. But because it is exaggerated it soon loses its freshness and spontaneity.

Avoid slang in your written compositions: much of it s ephemeral; it acquires and then loses its currency so quickly that in a very short space of time much of it is no longer understood; the rest of it becomes a part of the standard language and ceases to be recognized as particularly strange, emphatic, or effective. Again, slang is out of keeping with serious thought or formal writing. Born of a desire for very strong emphasis, it suggests a lack of reasoned restraint, flippancy at the expense of good manners.

Examples:

The judgment of the members of the Supreme Court is by no means infallible. Many of the justices were appointed not because of their legal knowledge or experience but because of political pull.

Undoubtedly the chief reason for the conversational effectiveness of many individuals is their inherent ability to sling it.

Shall he endure four years of a tough premedical course only to be refused permission to enter the overcrowded medical schools?

When slang is deliberately used, it should be put in quotation marks.

K. Avoid a mixture of colloquial and formal literary language.

In the chapter on the dictionary, page 169, dictionary definitions are cited to show that the term *colloquial* means "pertaining to conversation," and that, properly used, it is in no sense a term of condemnation.

The relationship between literary and colloquial English is frequently likened to that between formal evening wear and business clothes. A business suit with turn-down collar and four-in-hand tie would be out of place at a formal reception, just as a white tie and tails would inspire comment in a business office. This figure is satisfactory, but it does not go far enough. First of all, it should be pointed out that of the two garments, the business suit is undoubtedly the more useful—it is worn every day, while formal evening wear is reserved for special occasions. In the same way, more of our writing and speaking is informal and colloquial rather than formal and literary. Recall that the wing collar, now one of the distinguishing marks of formal attire, was once worn with a business suit; and that styles in both tail coats and business suits vary from year to year. So, too, words which are now considered limited to one level of language can change their status.

What the student must guard against most is an incongruous mixture of the two styles. A white dress vest would be out of place with tweeds, as would a flowery necktie with a dinner coat.

Examples:

As far as I can *figure out,* Freshman Week was designed by the authorities to be hurried and confusing, half fun and half work.

They were well informed on *most* any topic that came up for discussion.

When he was in high school, he spent his after-school hours and his evenings *doing* the advertising for his father's theatre.

Once we *suspicion* another of reading our minds, we immediately assume the defensive.

EXERCISE 5. The following sentences contain violations of the principles of diction which have been discussed in various parts of the chapter. Revise each of the sentences.

1. The majority of people feel that the profits that are secured by the few should be curtailed and divided more evenly among the people who do the manly labor.

2. It hasn't gone far enough underneath the surface; it hasn't snatched the fundamentals, and it has not brought them to the light of a blinded people.

3. If this be the purpose of an education, an education seems to be a way of becoming above the average man.

4. Another influential feature in the building up of stories on false foundations was the feudal system.

5. If a certain actor can play a particular part well, he is typed as that particular kind until he finds himself actually enjoying his screen roles.

6. Disregard all signs of good or bad luck, and do not let them make a particle bit of difference in the planning of your life.

7. This time, though, there was no great responsibility, there was no rush, there were no new people to meet, and then too, the weather was swell.

8. If the people of a nation or state do not believe in the system, they are going to try to agitate reform.

9. I have found working very helpful to me, however, in understanding the value of money-taking to put me through school, and hope to take all the advantages set before me.

10. The answer to the question of defining a highbrow person, group, or place, is one which requires considerable distinction, separation, and investigation.

11. After many weeks of hardships on location or filming of said picture, the actors usually return to Hollywood for a period.

12. Localization of concentration is one way of securing satisfactory results.

13. More and more parents have been considering it important to send their children to college, so that they may become not only cultured but specialized as well.

14. It might seem that Dickens exaggerated his malicious characters, and this may be true, but he has not failed in his errand.

15. I vigorously believe that the movies of today, and even those of yesterday, were produced to fulfill a public desire.

16. If troops are sent, a great number will be needed to guard the immense holds of some of our American companies which have property all over China.

17. Although this hatred is most pronounced in Germany, in certain other countries people are sort of antagonistic against foreigners.

18. In other words, you must be eligible in your studies to be able to partake in any activities.

19. If one contrasts other forms of government with democracy, he will find that property rights have a dominant place in a democracy.

20. I will be better able to uphold a better position when I go forth with the knowledge I have gained.

21. To err is human, but I will put the question plainly. "Can you name anyone who could steer us through this difficulty any better?" True enough, some snags were struck, but we managed to eke by.

22. The result of this unity of people, all united by a sense of duty toward the church, is an organization that has endured through the ages, and has never been disbanded, even through the most trialing conditions.

23. It is truly a crime how low the intelligence of the average voter is about democracy.

24. He too has certain prerequisites in choosing his friends.

25. This fellow wrote of his travels and his accomplishments so vividly that you could imagine yourself on the trip with him.

26. There is so much that should not be known that I censure my letters very carefully.

27. Journalism then is a powerful agency with ability to do great good or even greater harm.

28. During a revolution on one of the rich houses in the North his wife found a bag of jewels.

29. From the beginning of their childhood, the poor class of people has few chances of acquiring courage and intelligence, because of their environment and their parental standing.

30. Now I realize that receiving a letter from friends at home seems to comfort you and soothen your feelings.

31. As for his personal life, he is probably well fixed and can live as he usually does.

32. I read all of Haliburton's books with a fiendish delight.

33. This is true of most all athletics that involve a team.

34. When it first came into general use, the radio could not offer such a wide variety of programs as is now presented for an ever-enlarging audience.

35. The reaction of a person after having seen this picture is very depressing.

36. This type of thinking is more or less of a habit, and since habits can be broken, this can also be substituted by an open-minded mind.

37. The Fascist doctrines were origined by the industrialists.

38. Labor in summer time is always hard, but yet last summer the weather was passable. It was plenty cool, and only once or twice did it really boil.

39. The poor boy was not much different from the rich, and he adjusted himself to his new environment with the same speed that the rich boy was forced to assume his new environment.

40. During the war we either did not take part in many important traditions or did away with them altogether.

PART II

Standards of Modern Writing

*E*FFECTIVENESS in writing is not easily reduced to a set of rules. The features and devices of language which make for effectiveness may vary considerably, depending upon the effect which the writer wishes to produce and the audience he has in mind. The writer has all the resources of the English language at his command. From among these he chooses the particular words, the groupings of words, and the organization of ideas which he believes will produce the effect that he is seeking.

The English language itself, however, has its own patterns of structure, its own conventions which underlie the various resources available to the skilled writer. If he does not observe certain of these patterns, confusion will result and no one will understand what he is trying to say. If the writer or speaker violates certain of the conventions of the language, he runs the risk of being marked as ignorant or uncultivated by his audience, and his language detracts attention from the material that he wishes to communicate.

The first part of this book was concerned with the basic questions of composition: the planning of the whole and the effective command of the various kinds of units or parts. This portion of the text will deal with the more mechanical and conventional considerations. Fortunately, these can be reduced to rather definite rules. When you have mastered these rules so thoroughly that they have become a part of your unconscious speech and writing habits, you will have acquired a mastery of the standard forms of present-day English.

CHAPTER V

THE DICTIONARY

*W*E HAVE now considered the larger units of language and communication: the whole composition, the paragraph, and the sentence. But themes, paragraphs, and sentences are composed of individual words. Consequently, the word in itself is an important aspect of language.

As we shall see, no one person knows everything there is to be known about all the words in the English language or in any language. Therefore dictionaries have been compiled for most of the modern languages as a help and a convenience. The English language is particularly fortunate in that several excellent and complete dictionaries of it have been put together.

In order to deal with words competently, you must learn how to use a dictionary intelligently. It is your responsibility to learn how to use a dictionary, to get everything out of it which it has to give, to interpret its information correctly, and above all not to misunderstand or misinterpret what is there.

1. KINDS OF DICTIONARIES

Dictionaries may be divided into two classes: the extensive unabridged works, usually found in schoolrooms and libraries, and the condensed treatments which are easily within the means of the average student. In the condensed versions the rare uses of a word are frequently omitted and the definitions are not so fully illustrated, but these smaller works will satisfy a large portion of your needs. Here are two definitions of the word *facility,* one from an abridged dictionary and one from an unabridged version. They illustrate the difference in fullness of treatment found in the two types of dictionaries.

ABRIDGED [1]

fa·cil'i·ty (-tǐ), *n.*; *pl.* **-ties** (-tǐz). **1.** Quality of being easily performed; ease. **2.** Readiness from skill or use; dexterity. **3.** Easiness to be persuaded; — usually in a bad sense; pliancy. **4.** A thing that promotes the ease of any action, operation, or course of conduct; — usually in *pl.*; as, *facilities* for study.

UNABRIDGED [2]

fa·cil'i·ty (fà·sǐl'ǐ·tǐ), *n.*; *pl.* **-ties** (-tǐz). [F. *facilité*, fr. L. *facilitas*, fr. *facilis* easy. See FACILE.] **1.** Quality of being easily performed; freedom from difficulty; ease.
2. Ease in performance; readiness proceeding from skill or use; dexterity; as, practice gives a wonderful *facility*.
3. Easiness to be persuaded; readiness or compliance; — usually in a bad sense; pliancy.
    It is a great error to take *facility* for good nature.   *L'Estrange.*
4. Easiness of access; complaisance; affability. *Obs.*
5. A thing that promotes the ease of any action, operation, transaction, or course of conduct; advantage; opportunity; — usually in *pl.*; as, special *facilities* for study.
6. *Scots Law.* Compliancy such that legal measures for protection are justified.
Syn. — Easiness; adroitness, address, expertness, skill; pliability; help, furtherance. FACILITY, EASE, READINESS agree in the idea of freedom from effort. FACILITY, though sometimes used in a derogatory sense (as, fatal *facility* in composition; "His *facility* in language has been fatal only too often to his logic and philosophy"), more frequently than EASE expresses the power, proceeding from practice and use, of performing an act or dispatching a task with lightness and address. But *facility* and *ease* are often interchanged. READINESS lays stress on the quickness or promptitude with which anything is done; as, his *readiness* in repartee. Cf. SKILLFUL, DEXTEROUS.
Ant. — Difficulty; awkwardness; hesitancy.

A. Unabridged Dictionaries.

Of the unabridged dictionaries, those furnishing the most accurate and recent information are:

The Oxford English Dictionary, 10 vols. and Supplement, Clarendon Press, Oxford, 1888–1933. A corrected

[1] Reproduced by permission of the publishers of *Webster's Collegiate Dictionary,* Fifth Edition, copyright, 1936, by G. & C. Merriam Co.

[2] Reproduced by permission of the publishers of *Webster's New International Dictionary,* Second Edition, copyright, 1934, 1939, by G. & C. Merriam Co.

reissue appeared in 1933. The original issue bears the title *A New English Dictionary.*

The Shorter Oxford English Dictionary, 2 vols., Clarendon Press, Oxford, 1933.

Webster's New International Dictionary of the English Language, G. & C. Merriam Co., Springfield, Mass., 1934.

The Universal Dictionary of the English Language, edited by H. C. Wyld, George Routledge and Sons, London, 1932.

New Century Dictionary of the English Language, 2 vols., D. Appleton-Century Company, New York, 1927.

New Standard Dictionary of the English Language, Funk & Wagnalls, New York and London, 1913.

Of these more extensive works, the most important is the *Oxford English Dictionary.* It is the product of more than fifty years of research. Particularly valuable are the illustrative citations which are given for every meaning of every word.

B. Abridged Dictionaries.

Here is a list of the abridged or condensed dictionaries:

Webster's Collegiate Dictionary, Fifth Edition, G. & C. Merriam Co., Springfield, Mass., 1936.

Winston Simplified Dictionary, Advanced Edition, John C. Winston Company, Chicago, 1926.

Macmillan's Modern Dictionary, Macmillan Company, New York, 1938.

New College Standard Dictionary, Funk & Wagnalls, New York and London, 1947.

American College Dictionary, Random House, New York, 1947; Harper and Brothers, New York, 1948.

2. *DATES OF EDITING AND OF PUBLICATION*

In these two lists of dictionaries, care has been taken to name the publisher, the date of publication, and in some instances the number of the edition. The particular edition is important because you will want to refer only to the current or most recent edition of the unabridged works. For example, the unabridged Webster's of 1934 is a completely new dictionary. The definitions have been rewritten, new pronunciations and new meanings have been recorded.

If the Webster's you consult has, let us say, the date 1928 on its title page, that particular volume is based on the edition of 1909 and differs from it chiefly in that some new sections have been added. It is a *reprinting* of the 1909 edition, rather than a new edition, and its treatment of any word may not always reflect the changes in meaning or new developments in pronunciation which have taken place in the last thirty years. Always look for the date of publication on the title page of any unabridged dictionary you use, and determine, if possible, when that particular edition was compiled.

The same caution must be exercised with the abridged dictionaries. You should notice particularly that the *fifth* edition of *Webster's Collegiate Dictionary* is the one based upon the 1934 or *second* edition of the unabridged Webster's; any edition of the *Collegiate* earlier than the fifth is based upon the 1909 edition of the unabridged. It is safest not to buy an abridged dictionary whose title, publisher, and date do not correspond to those given in the list.

3. MEANING

This function of the dictionary requires little comment. One word of caution must be given. When you consult the dictionary for the meaning of a word, it is necessary to read *all* the definitions. Do not stop with the first definition; it may not be the one you want or need.

The following illustration shows how misleading such a practice may be: In an old play, written more than three hundred years ago, there is the following line: "Such a crafty spy I have caught. . . . Brought him to the court and in the porter's lodge *dispatched* him." The word *dispatched* is not wholly clear and we consult one of the unabridged dictionaries to get help. The first meaning given is "to send off or away." Certainly this meaning does not make sense in the context we have. A second meaning is "to put to death." This is a plausible interpretation, but we see that on the next page or so this same character bobs up again, and evidently he was not killed; we have not yet found the right meaning. A number of other definitions such as "to settle a piece of business quickly," "to consume or devour," "to start promptly for a place," are all out of the question. Finally we come to one which reads "to put out of the way, to stow away." This, from all appearances, fits the case. The spy had been placed in the porter's lodge for safekeeping.

Remember that the other definitions are just as important as the first, and that you must keep on applying the various definitions until you find one that exactly fits the context.

EXERCISE I. 1. Find, in your abridged dictionary, the definition which properly applies to the italicized word in each of the following sentences:

1. Mr. Lockhart's own writing is generally so good, so clear, direct and *nervous*.

2. In many of its relations, hydrogen *demeans* itself much like a metal.

3. My watch is *fast*. She was *fast* asleep.

4. Everyone is familiar with the common *phenomenon* of a piece of metal being eaten away by rust.

5. If the Admiral had small vessels, he could not venture to *unman* his fleet.

2. How many definitions can you think of for the word *pipe,* both noun and verb? Write as many as you can, then look up the word in an unabridged dictionary, comparing your list of definitions with those you find in the dictionary.

A. Order of Definitions.

Did it occur to you when you were writing your definitions of the word *pipe,* that, if you were compiling a dictionary, you would have to decide which of your several definitions you would place at the beginning of your treatment of the word, which would come second, and so on? This problem faces the compiler of every dictionary. Can you find, by consulting the preface of your dictionary, upon what basis the order of definitions was determined? The *Webster's Collegiate Dictionary,* for example, says on page xxiii of the Preface, "So far as possible the order of definitions is that of the historical order of development of the meanings of a word."

B. Changes in Meaning.

The dictionary can trace for us the changes in meaning which words undergo over a long period of time. If we look up the word *deer,* we find as the earliest meaning (one which is no longer current), "Any animal, especially a wild animal." In the course of centuries the word has become more particular or specialized in its meaning. Conversely, the first recorded meaning of the word *frock* is, "A coarse gown or habit worn by monks or friars." Now it is applied to any dress or gown. This word has developed in a direction opposite to that taken by *deer*; it has become more general in meaning.

EXERCISE 2. Trace the changes in meaning that have taken place in the following words, and in the case of each, determine whether the development has been in the direction of generalization or specialization. Use an unabridged dictionary in preparing this exercise.

| business | ordeal | starve | wade |
| butler | quarantine | undertaker | zest |

Changes in meaning are not limited to those proceeding from a specific meaning to a more general, or from a general meaning to a more specific. Certain words which, at the outset of their history, denote thoroughly respectable ideas in the course of time acquire disreputable meanings and finally come to stand for an unpleasant or not wholly respectable thing or idea. The word *villain* originally meant a farm laborer, a person of ignoble birth. By gradual stages the word came to signify ignobility of character instead of occupation.

Other words have changed in the opposite direction. The word *marshal* meant originally a groom or stable servant; today it may be used to denote an officer in a royal household or one of high rank in the army. Still other words which originally referred to specific, concrete objects are now used as names for abstractions. Our modern word *dreary* once meant "bloody." The opposite change, from abstract to concrete, has also occurred in many words.

EXERCISE 3. Trace the changes in meaning that have taken place in the following words, and in each instance point out what the direction of the change has been, in the light of the discussion given in the preceding paragraphs.

| boor | doom | humor | pioneer |
| - counterfeit | fame | imp | steward |

4. SYNONYMS AND ANTONYMS

We often find that we are using a certain word so frequently that it becomes monotonous. If you have used the word *advance* four or five times in one paragraph, you will want to find a word such as *proceed* or *progress* to substitute for it. Such substitute words are called *synonyms*, and in most dictionaries they appear after the definition of each word.

Two words rarely have exactly the same meaning. An accurate reader and writer differentiates carefully between nearly synonymous pairs of words. The unabridged dictionaries and the better abridged dictionaries usually point out such differences with great care.

EXERCISE 4. 1. Consult the Preface of your own dictionary and read the section on synonymy. Note particularly what is said about the order in which the synonyms are given, the punctuation within the synonymy, the typefaces used in this section and their significance, and any system of cross references which is employed.

2. Find suitable synonyms for the following words:

| discern | peremptory | praise (verb) |
| empty | soar | praise (noun) |

3. These pairs of words are at times interchanged in use. Be able to point out the distinction in meaning between the two members of each pair, and use each word correctly in a sentence.

gift . . . . present	serene . . . . tranquil
mortal . . . . fatal	expand . . . . distend
exemption . . . . . . immunity	inert . . . . sluggish
observation . . . . observance	elevate . . . . exalt
arrest . . . . check	grotesque . . . . bizarre

4. What is an *antonym*? Find suitable antonyms for the following words:

| facility | countenance (verb) |
| parsimonious | impromptu |

5. *LABELS*

Immediately preceding the definition of many words is found what dictionary makers call a *label*. This indicates that such a word or a particular meaning of it is somewhat restricted in actual use. There are three kinds of labels: subject labels, geographical labels, and usage labels.

Subject labels are generally applied to technical words or to technical meanings of a word, and show the department of knowledge to which it is confined. The noun *stop* has special meanings in the fields of machinery, music, phonetics, finance, and sailing, and each of its definitions peculiar to these fields is prefixed with the appropriate label.

The geographical labels show the particular region where a word, a meaning, or a pronunciation occurs most frequently. Words such as *floorwalker,* which is used chiefly in the United States, *dogie,* which is used only in the Western United States, or *petrol,* confined to British use, are so labeled in an accurate dictionary.

The usage labels are often misunderstood. The one most frequently misinterpreted is the label *colloquial.* If you will consult any dictionary for the meaning of this word, you will find *colloquial* means simply "pertaining to, or characteristic of, conversation." The unabridged Webster is careful to add to its definition, "Colloquial speech may be as correct as formal speech." If a word or a particular meaning of a word is marked *colloquial* in a dictionary, this label means merely that the word is used in informal conversation rather than in formal writing, and you may feel perfectly free to use it in conversation.

Another common usage label is *dial.* for *dialect* or *dialectal.* This is applied when a word is used in several localities, so many, in fact, that it would be awkward to assign it to any particular one. Again this label is not necessarily a condemnation. It merely states that a word or meaning not characteristic of the whole English-speaking world is used in a particular manner in certain regions. Notice also such labels as *illiterate, slang, obsolete,* and *archaic.* If you are uncertain of the meaning of any of these, look them up.

6. DERIVATION

The English language is derived from a number of different sources. Many of our common words were in the language when the invading Anglo-Saxon tribes made their homes on the island of Britain. But the English-speaking people have always been great word borrowers; consequently Latin, French, Scandinavian, Italian, German, Dutch, Greek, and almost every other known language, have contributed something to our word stock.

That branch of language study which concerns itself with the origin and derivation of words is known as *etymology*; the *etymology* of any particular word shows the elements of its formation and the origin and derivation of these elements. If we look up the word *draw* (verb) in the dictionary, we shall find its etymology given as AS *dragan*. This means that *draw* is a native or Anglo-Saxon word, that it was in the language spoken by the Anglo-Saxon tribes that came to England in the fifth and sixth centuries. The Anglo-Saxon word is recorded without comment, so we may assume that the meaning of *dragan* in Anglo-Saxon was about the same as its modern descendant.

A longer and more complicated history is illustrated by the word *energy*. The dictionary shows that it is derived from Late Latin *energia* which in turn came from the Greek *energia,* a noun made from the adjective *energos,* "active"; finally, *energos* was composed of the prefix *en-,* "in," and *ergon,* "work."

At times two or more elements coming from different languages have combined to make a single English word. In the word *eatable,* the French suffix *-able* has been added to the Anglo-Saxon verb *eat*. English and Latin are combined in *speedometer*. Even such a strange combination as Persian and Latin is to be found in the word *asafetida*.

EXERCISE 5. 1. Look up the following words in your dictionary. What limitations does the dictionary place upon their usage in the English language?

flunk	glare (noun)	hoosegow	petrol
gadget	goober	movie	swell (adjective)

2. Turn to page xciv in the Preface of Webster's *New International Dictionary* and read everything that is said about the way in which the etymologies are presented. Where, in respect to the complete word treatment, do they appear? Are there any situations where the word itself is not given in the etymology, but only the language from which it is derived? Familiarize yourself with the abbreviations used to indicate the various source languages, and find out where these abbreviations are listed.

3. Consult your dictionary for the origin of the following words. Be able to tell from which language they are derived, what they meant when they were taken into the English language, and what change in meaning they have since undergone.

adobe	flank	landscape	quartz
asterisk	flannel	moose	skin
finger	junk	peninsula	umbrella

7. WORD FORMATION

When we looked up the etymology of the word *energy* we found that this word was put together centuries ago by the Greeks, who placed the syllable *en*, meaning "in," before *ergon*, their word for "work." They made a word where none had existed before.

In our present-day language we still do the same thing. As soon as the term *New Deal* had acquired definite political meaning, we began to characterize the opposite political group as *anti-New Deal.* Syllables at the end of a word may be used in a similar fashion. In 1945, when the atomic bomb was first used, the word *atomize* became current in a new meaning, its root alluding to the bomb and the suffix forming a verb. Hundreds of new words were formed similarly during the war period—for example, *anti-tank, pre-flight, sub-stratosphere, super-fort.* By means of these word-forming prefixes and suffixes, we often make a single word answer the purpose of a whole clause or phrase.

The extent to which word derivation (the combination of word-forming elements) has taken place in the English language is ably illustrated by A. G. Kennedy in *Current English.* From such a familiar root word as *bear,* he shows that at least thirty-six other words have been formed, ranging all the way from *barrow* to *birth* to *overburdensome.* The Latin root *ced,* "go from," with its participial form *cess-,* and the related French form *cease,* have been even more prolific, resulting in eighty modern English words.

Some dictionaries will not give separate definitions for all words so formed, but expect the user to look up the prefix or suffix and then the main word, that he may put together his own definition.

Note: The student should be cautious about coining words for himself, for he may not follow the accepted patterns. At best, the novelty of such coinages will be their striking feature, and they will give a journalistic flavor where it may not be desirable.

EXERCISE 6.   1. Consult your dictionary to determine how each of the italicized prefixes in the following list modifies the meaning of the word to which it had been attached.

*ante*room	*extra*legal	*semi*solid	*trans*oceanic
*dis*able	*omni*potent	*super*human	*ultra*violet

2. Consult your dictionary to determine how each of the italicized suffixes in the list below modifies the meaning and changes the grammatical function of the word to which it has been attached. Look for the treatment of the suffix as a whole rather than for the individual word; that is, look up -*able* as a separate entry rather than in connection with *perishable*. Do likewise with the others.

perish*able*	bak*er*	sterili*ze*
marri*age*	botan*ist*	amaze*ment*

8. PRONUNCIATION

Second only to the service performed by the dictionary in supplying meaning, is the information given about pronunciation. This is difficult to convey accurately in print and is frequently misunderstood.

Our pronunciation of many words varies with the situations in which we use them. A public speaker or actor may pronounce *evil* from the lecture platform or stage with two distinct syllables, being very careful to give the second vowel the sound of *i* in *bit*. The same speaker, in ordinary informal conversation, may pronounce the same word and omit the second vowel completely. There is nothing wrong or incorrect about this second pronunciation of *evil*. It is just as appropriate to the situation in which it is used as is the first. Moreover, it would be quite as inappropriate for any speaker to pronounce all of his words in a familiar conversation in the manner of a formal speech, as it would be unsatisfactory for a public speaker to assume that he would be heard or understood if he spoke from the platform with the same rapidity, tone of voice, and obscuration of certain vowels that he uses at the dinner table.

A dictionary tells in its preface what kind of pronunciations it records. The Preface to the unabridged Webster's states:

> The style adopted for representation is that of formal platform speech—and this must be clearly remembered by consultants of the pronunciations here given. . . . The pronunciations contained in this Dictionary . . . represent . . . the speech of cultivated users of English, speaking formally with a view to being completely understood by their hearers.

After you do know what style of pronunciation is recorded, it is then possible to make adjustments of the information given about particular words which will apply to other kinds of speech.

Next you must understand clearly what is meant by each of the symbols employed to indicate pronunciation. It is often not enough to refer to the running key, found at the top or bottom of each page. Suppose you are confused about the pronunciation of the *a* vowel in the word *master*. If you consult any of the Webster dictionaries for its pronunciation, you discover the symbol à is given for the sound. The key at the bottom of the page shows that à has the sound of the vowel in *ask*. Now, one speaker may use the sound of the *a* vowel in *hat* in his pronunciation of *ask*, while another may employ the sound of the vowel *a* in *father*. Thus far, we have learned only that the *a* in *ask* and in *master* are pronounced alike; we have not yet learned how they are pronounced. It is not until we turn to that portion of the Preface (Par. 9, p. x in *Webster's Collegiate*) where this symbol is discussed in detail that we discover that à has in reality three different values all of which are in current use by cultivated speakers.

EXERCISE 7. 1. Consult the Preface of *Webster's New International Dictionary*, Second Edition, for the values of the following symbols. Make certain that you find all the values each symbol may have.

â	ĭ	ô̊
ŏ	û	tû̂

2. In how many ways might you expect to hear each of the following words correctly pronounced?

bog	half	offer
dreary	learn	sorry
grandeur	nature	vary

3. Compare the values given in the Preface of the unabridged Webster's for the symbols ă, ĕ, ŏ, ŭ. Read also paragraph 72 in this Preface. How much difference would you ordinarily expect in the unaccented vowels of the following words?

vacant	connect
angel	circus

A. Stress.

In addition to the exact quality of the sounds which make up a word, we also need to know the amount of stress which the various syllables of a word normally receive. Stress is quite as important as sound quality in our scheme of pronunciation; this is illustrated by a word such as *increase*. If the first syllable is accented (**in′crease**) the word is a noun; if the second syllable receives the stress (**increase′**), we interpret the word as a verb.

In many words accent is variable, dependent either upon the rhythm of the other syllables in the phrase or upon the amount of emphasis. We might say *The up′stairs room*, yet in *The room upstairs′* the accent would be reversed. *Necessarily* is often pronounced with the primary accent on the first syllable (**nec′essar″ily**), but when spoken with more than usual emphasis, the accent shifts to the third (**nec"essar'ily**). In this connection, read carefully the Preface to *Webster's New International Dictionary,* paragraphs 64–67. A good dictionary will always recognize the variability of accent, where it occurs, by special reference marks.

EXERCISE 8.   1. Consult your dictionary to discover how many degrees of accent are marked and whether the accent marks precede or follow the syllables to which they apply.

2. How does your dictionary mark the accent of the following words? When the word in question is used as both noun and verb, note the position of the stress in both functions.

accent	detour	finance	prospector
address	dictator	irrefutable	recall
ally	discourse	perfume	resource
defect	divan	pretense	robust

3. What change in grammatical function occurs in the following words when the accent changes?

adept	frequent	refuse
convert	progress	subject

B. First Pronunciations.

There is a widespread belief that when a number of pronunciations are given for any word, the first of these pronunciations is to be greatly preferred over the others, that it is more correct than those which follow. If the first pronunciation is so much more correct than those which follow it, why should the dictionary even take the trouble to record a second and at times a third pronunciation?

In the first place, the editors of dictionaries do not give the first pronunciation nearly so much preference as is commonly believed. The Preface of *Webster's Collegiate Dictionary* (p. xxii) states:

> When two or more pronunciations are recorded the general rule has been to place first the one that has been selected as preferable. *Each form entered, however, has the support of good usage,* and in some cases *this usage is nearly or quite equally divided.*[3]

In the second place, no really scientific and accurate dictionary claims to set up a single standard of correct pronunciation for all the words in the English language. The Webster dictionaries admit that there can be no *single* standard of correctness in present-day pronunciation.

> When the essential facts are considered, "correctness of pronunciation" must be a flexible term. It is perhaps as accurate a definition as can be made to say that *a pronunciation is correct when it is in actual use by a sufficient number of cultivated speakers.*[3] This is obviously elastic, depending both on knowledge—not always obtainable—of the number of users, and on judgment as to the cultivation of the speakers.
>
> The standard of English pronunciation, so far as a standard may be said to exist, is the usage that now prevails among the educated and cultured people to whom the language is vernacular; but, since somewhat different pronunciations are used by the cultivated in different regions too large to be ignored, we must frankly admit the fact that, at present, uniformity of pronunciation is not to be found throughout the English-speaking world, though there is a very large percentage of practical uniformity.[4]

[3] Italics ours.
[4] *Webster's Collegiate Dictionary,* 5th Edition, p. ix. For a more extended statement reflecting the point of view of the dictionary editors, see *Webster's New International Dictionary,* Second Edition, paragraph 5, p. xxvi.

The editors further state that:

The function of a pronouncing dictionary is to record as far as possible the pronunciations prevailing in the best present usage, rather than to attempt to dictate what that usage should be. In so far as a dictionary may be known and acknowledged as a faithful recorder and interpreter of such usage, so far and no farther may it be appealed to as an authority.[5]

It is now plain that where two pronunciations of a word exist it is the duty of the dictionary to record both of them. Naturally, the dictionary editor is compelled to place one of them first, and he will undoubtedly put that one first for which he has the most evidence. You can be very certain that if a pronunciation is recorded in the dictionary at all, there is sufficient justification for its use.

EXERCISE 9. 1. There is frequently some disagreement about the proper pronunciation of the following words. Look them up in *Webster's New International Dictionary*, Second Edition, and find out what pronunciations are recorded. Remember that there is no disapproval attached to the word *colloquial*. Remember also that the dictionary cannot always keep abreast of current usage.

abdomen	clematis	hygienic
acclimate	creek	indisputable
advertisement	decadence	inquiry
alien	decorous	interesting
apparatus	discern	isolate
apricot	drama	lever
biography	either	literature
bouquet	gape	mobile
calf	granary	mustache
centenary	harass	nascent

[5] *Webster's Collegiate Dictionary*, 5th Edition, p. ix. See also *Webster's New International Dictionary*, Second Edition, paragraphs 6 and 7, p. xxvi.

new	ration	tomato
obesity	robot	version
often	romance	yolk
patronage	route	zenith
pumpkin	student	
quintuplet	tissue	

2. Consult a trustworthy dictionary for the pronunciation of the following words. See whether your pronunciation is included among those given.

blatant	impious	perforate
cavalry	incognito	respite
chasm	incisive	sagacious
eccentric	irrelevant	schism
exigency	indict	status
garrulous	Italian	superfluous
heinous	orchid	victuals

3. Most dictionaries devote special sections to the pronunciation of foreign personal and place names. Consult the preface of yours and familiarize yourself with any symbols representing non-English sounds. Practice making such sounds until you can produce them with some degree of ease. Then determine the pronunciation of the following words:

Casals	Padraic Colum	Boulogne
Gauguin	Novgorod	Popocatepetl
Genghis Khan	Majorca	Versailles
Récamier	Gari Melchers	Pago Pago

9. SPELLING

(See also Chapter VIII)

The dictionary is our guide also in matters of spelling. Everyone knows that if he doesn't know how to spell a certain word, he can from the pronunciation guess at various spellings and look through the dictionary to see which of them is recorded. This is a hit-and-miss method and an impractical one. We shall be spared many trips to the dictionary if we learn and apply the general rules for spelling. Most dictionaries give a series of such rules in their prefaces (see pp. xx and xxi of *Webster's Collegiate* and pp. lxxviii-lxxx of *Webster's New International Dictionary*).

It is desirable to use accepted American rather than British spellings where the conventions of the two countries are not the same. The dictionary enables you to distinguish between them. There may be a section on the differences between British and American spelling in the preface. In the body of the dictionary, the British variant may be given under the American spelling. The British spelling may have a cross reference to the treatment of the word under its American spelling. There may be a special section of each page devoted to spelling variants. Examine your dictionary carefully and find out how such differences in spelling convention are indicated.

We have all seen such spellings as *thru, tho',* and *nite.* Some of these, such as *thru,* may appear in formal writing; others, such as *nite,* are found only in advertisements and in informal use. In general the condensed dictionaries do not treat simplified spellings; consult the unabridged works for a treatment of them.

Remember that when two spellings are given for any word, you must interpret the dictionary treatment just as you did in the case of two pronunciations. One form must appear first in the treatment; the editor places first that form for which he has the most evidence. The second spelling would not be there at all if it did not have the support of good usage. Look in the preface of your dictionary to see how it indicates preferred spellings. In *Webster's Collegiate* this information is given on page xxii, paragraph 1.

SPELLING

EXERCISE 10. What is the preferred spelling of the following words? In each case state whether the alternate spelling is British, reformed, or exactly what its status is.

aeon	eon	husht	hushed
caliber	calibre	inflexion	inflection
civilize	civilise	judgement	judgment
cyanid	cyanide	mold	mould
defence	defense	right	rite
enclose	inclose	staunch	stanch
hidn	hidden	vapour	vapor

A. Word Division.

When one is writing in longhand, it is a common practice to spread or crowd letters along toward the end of a line in order that the ends of words may form a comparatively straight margin down the page. In typewriting this is not so easily accomplished. The dictionary tells us how words are usually divided. The more complete dictionaries generally include a discussion of this problem in their prefaces (see p. lviii, *Webster's New International Dictionary*), and most dictionaries indicate word division in the spelling of their headwords.

EXERCISE 11. Find out how syllabic division is indicated in your dictionary, and whether there is any discussion of the problem in the preface. Without first looking up the words in the following list, indicate what seems to be the proper division; then look them up in your dictionary. In how many instances do your divisions correspond to those in the dictionary?

bookmark	feeble	oblige
chasm	formulate	pressure
dabble	hearty	situation
exasperate	magic	telegraph
favor	multiply	transact

10. GRAMMAR

The dictionary offers three kinds of grammatical information:

1. Immediately after the pronunciation of any word, the dictionary tells you what part of speech that word is. Learn the symbols and abbreviations your dictionary employs in indicating the parts of speech. If any word may perform the function of more than one part of speech, this is also indicated in its treatment. Verbs are also labeled *transitive* or *intransitive* in most dictionaries.

2. After the part-of-speech entry, irregularities in inflectional forms are noted: Irregular plurals such as *mice,* irregular past tenses such as *went,* irregular comparatives such as *better.* If there are alternate forms for any word, such as the plural of *formula,* which may be either *formulas* or *formulae,* this is also indicated.

3. When there is uncertainty about the use of a word, the dictionary often makes a definite statement about it. For example, in connection with the troublesome use of the pronoun *none,* the Webster dictionaries say, "As subject, *none* with a plural verb is the commoner construction."

EXERCISE 12. By reference to an unabridged dictionary, answer the following questions dealing with problems of grammar. Note any differences between colloquial and formal English which you may find and remember that the term *colloquial* is not used in a derogatory sense.

1. What is the plural of *stigma?*
2. Is the verb *try* ever used with *and* followed by the infinitive (*Try and get it*)?
3. What is the past tense of *sing?*
4. May one say "In hopes of seeing you"?
5. What part or parts of speech is the word *like?*

6. Some writers insist that there is no such word as *enthuse*. Are they justified in this?

7. What is the past tense of the verb *light*? of the verb *plead*?

8. May one say "I have got" for "I have"?

9. Is *gladiola* singular or plural? What is the plural of *gladiolus*?

10. Does *whoever* occur as the object of a verb as well as the subject?

11. What are the principal parts of the verb *strive*?

12. Is *neither* ever used with a plural verb?

13. What is the plural of *partridge*?

14. Can *go* be used as a transitive verb?

15. How do you spell the plural of *bus*?

16. Is *loan* used as a verb?

17. What is the past participle of *hide*?

18. Is the verb *can* used to indicate permission?

19. Is *where* ever used as a pronoun?

20. What is the past tense of *dive*?

GRAMMAR

L IKE THE dictionary maker of today, the grammarian is a scientist. First, he observes the language under study to see how it behaves; he gathers facts about it. Then he classifies the results of his observations just as the botanist sorts out his plants, or the geologist his rocks. Finally, from his classifications he draws certain general conclusions, which we call *laws* or *rules*. Grammar, then, is a descriptive statement of the way a language works.

1. PARTS OF SPEECH

Perhaps the best way to approach the grammar of your own language is to look at it as if it were a foreign language, entirely new to you, about which you were trying to learn something. During the war in the Pacific many an American soldier was suddenly faced with this kind of problem. A pilot might parachute to safety on an unknown island, and have to depend on the natives for his existence. To communicate with them, he would have to learn their language. If you had to do this, how would you go about it?

Undoubtedly, you would begin by pointing to certain objects, and by means of signs indicate that you wanted to know the names for these objects. You would point to a tree, a table, a hut, and so on. After a while you would begin to include two or more of the same objects within the scope of your questions. You might even put your hat on your head, take off your coat, light a fire, to find out what names were given to these various actions.

Through such a procedure you would, either consciously or unconsciously, have begun to probe into the noun and verb systems of this unfamiliar language. By comparing the word for one hat with that for many hats you would begin to find just how the idea of number or the function of plurality was indicated. By putting first a hat on your head, then a hat on a native's head, then motioning to him to put a hat on his own head, and then on yours, you would be learning something about the functions of person, subject, and object in relation to certain verbs.

After each conversation with the islanders you would look through the material you had collected, and attempt to put together into a single class those words which behaved fundamentally in the same way, took the same or similar endings, affected other words within the sentence in a similar fashion, or perhaps indicated the same general kinds of ideas. The classes or classifications which you formed as a result of this comparative process might well be called parts of speech.

The parts of speech, then, are classes of words in any given language which have been sorted out on the basis (1) of certain changes that take place in their form, such as the addition of certain endings; on the basis (2) of certain functions they perform, such as that of description or the indication of *who* might be acting; and on the basis (3) of certain modifications in meaning.

For the English language, such attempts at classification have given us eight parts of speech: noun, pronoun, adjective, verb, adverb, preposition, conjunction, and interjection. Since these parts of speech represent merely human endeavors toward a satisfactory classification, you will not be surprised to learn that we have not always recognized the same number of classes, nor have we always given these classes the same names. For example, grammars of the sixteenth century did not recognize the adjective as distinct from the noun. At various other times articles, infinitives, participles, and expletives have all been recognized as separate classifications.

Nor are all present-day authorities on the English language in complete agreement about the number of parts of speech we should recognize. One recent grammar proposes a reduction from eight to six parts of speech. Another scholar goes even further, suggesting a reduction to three, along with an elimination of such terms as *noun, adjective,* and *verb.* The dissatisfaction of these and other scholars with our conventional system of parts of speech arises primarily from the fact that the present system does not employ a consistent basis of classification.

All this is mentioned, not to make the ability to identify the parts of speech seem less important, but rather to suggest that English grammar is not the dead, cut-and-dried subject many students suppose it to be. Nor is any system which is set up and employed today guaranteed to be in use fifty years hence. Yet we need to master a terminology which will enable us to discuss the various ways in which speech is put together, just as we learn the terminology pertaining to an automobile. You would not be content to say, "The thing that I work with my foot and that connects the motor with the rear wheels," instead of *clutch.* If you are to deal with problems of language, you must distinguish a noun from an adjective as readily as you would distinguish the clutch from the transmission. Remember, also, that in dealing with parts of speech you are dealing with intellectual abstractions which are not final or utterly definite categories. They are subject to change, because our way of looking at language changes.

The traditional definitions for the various parts of speech are as follows:

1. A **noun** is the name of a person, place, thing, quality, collection, or action.

2. A **pronoun** is a word used in place of a noun.

3. An **adjective** is a word used to modify (*i.e.* describe, limit, or qualify) a noun or pronoun.

4. A **verb** is a word that asserts action, state, or being.

5. An **adverb** is a word that is used to modify a verb, adjective, or other adverb.

6. A **preposition** is a word showing the relationship of its object (usually a noun or pronoun) and some other word in the sentence.

7. A **conjunction** connects words, phrases, or clauses.

8. An **interjection** expresses strong feeling or emotion.

The	old	horse	ambled	up	the	street.
Adjective or Article	*Adjective*	*Noun*	*Verb*	*Preposition*	*Adjective or Article*	*Noun*

The	captain	quickly	ordered	him	from	the	room.
Adjective or Article	*Noun*	*Adverb*	*Verb*	*Pronoun*	*Preposition*	*Adjective or Article*	*Noun*

We	came	early	but	did	not	mind	waiting.
Pronoun	*Verb*	*Adverb*	*Conjunction*	*Verb*	*Adverb*	*Verb*	*Noun*

Oh,	is	that	you?
Interjection	*Verb*	*Pronoun*	*Pronoun*

Observe that in English words that are spelled and pronounced alike frequently function as any one of several parts of speech. Where this is possible, the way in which the word is used, i.e. its *function,* determines its classification. In the following sentences the word *down* is used in five different functions, and consequently it is classified as a different part of speech in each instance.

1. It was second *down* and five yards to go. (Noun)
2. The *down* grade was very steep. (Adjective)
3. He will *down* the ball on the goal line. (Verb)
4. The runner was knocked *down*. (Adverb)
5. The team marched *down* the field. (Preposition)

EXERCISE 1. What part of speech is each word in the following sentences?

1. We need to oil the car.
2. The snow drove by in sheets.
3. Do you plan to buy it tomorrow?
4. This oil will stand about in pools for weeks.
5. Because of the cost of the material, she had to alter the pattern.
6. You must eagerly help her in buying whatever she wants.
7. Oh, how can one ever forget!
8. The company was composed of relatives, neighbors, and a few strangers.
9. Such conditions are worse and more common than we realize.
10. I prefer the green hat to the yellow.

2. NOUNS

The grammatical properties of a noun are gender, number, and case.

A. Gender. Gender is that property of a noun which states the sex of the object.

English recognizes three genders: masculine (male), feminine (female), and neuter (without special sex-defining characteristics). *Boy* is a masculine noun, *cow* is feminine, and *table* is neuter.

In the English language the problem of gender is not very troublesome—we need only to make sure that any pronoun which we use will agree in gender with its noun antecedent (the noun to which it refers); that is, we must refer to a table as *it,* not as *he* or *she*.

B. Number. Number is that property in a noun by means of which we indicate whether one thing or more than one thing is named.

English has two numbers, singular and plural. In general, the plural number of a noun is indicated by the addition of *-s* or *-es* to the singular. Small groups of nouns form their plurals in other ways, e.g. *oxen, leaves, geese, sheep.*

When we must form the plurals of nouns taken from other languages, notably those which have been borrowed from Latin and Greek, we are faced with this question: Shall the noun retain its foreign plural suffix (*-i, -a, -ae,* etc.), or shall the English plural suffix be adopted? Our practice in this matter is not consistent; some nouns such as *spatula* take only the native English suffix (*spatulas*); others, such as *stimulus,* retain only the ending appropriate to the language from which they were adopted (*stimuli*); a third group, illustrated by *formula,* may employ either ending (*formulas, formulae*). If you are in doubt about any particular word, consult your dictionary.

Observe that our practice in forming the plural of compound nouns is also not consistent, for example: *fountain pens, aides de camp, passers-by, menservants, brothers-in-law, stepbrothers.* Note that in the case of compound nouns ending in *-ful, three bags full* and *three bagfuls* may mean something quite different. The first form calls up a picture of three bags simultaneously filled, whereas the second centers the attention upon the amount that would fill the bags, though it may not actually be in them. Both derivation and frequency of use affect our practice here.

A special group known as *collective nouns* is composed of those words, singular in form, which are the names of a group or class. *Family, government, crowd* are collective nouns. (For their use, see below, p. 218.)

C. Case. Case is that property of a noun by means of which its functional relation to other words in a sentence is indicated.

In certain languages, such as Greek and Latin, this relationship is indicated primarily by means of inflectional endings placed on the noun. To illustrate: if in a Latin sentence we come upon the word *puellam,* we know immediately by the *-am* ending or inflection, which has been attached to the stem *puell* (*puell+am*) that it must be in the accusative or objective singular case. Then we begin to look for some relationship in meaning that necessitated this case form.

With English nouns the situation is different. There are no case endings or inflections, except for the so-called possessive or genitive case—*John's book*. In the absence of inflectional endings, we have come to depend upon word order to indicate certain relationships in meaning.

John	hit	the ball.
Subject	*Verb*	*Object*

The ball	hit	John.
Subject	*Verb*	*Object*

Sentences such as these derive their meaning from the position of the noun in respect to the verb. Except in questions, the subject-verb-object pattern of word order is the standard one in English; the noun or pronoun which precedes the verb is thereby known to be its subject, and that which follows the verb, its object (if it can take one). Thus the form of a noun does not change with its function as subject or object; only its position changes.

One other way of indicating case relationship is employed in English. For example, it is possible to show a connection between *warrior* and *weapons* through the inflection -'s (*warrior's weapons*), or the same relationship may be indicated by the prepositional construction *the weapons of the warrior*. Here *of* is roughly equivalent in functional and meaning value to *-'s*. Therefore *of* in this use is called a *function word* and the whole construction is spoken of as a *periphrastic genitive,* i.e. "a roundabout genitive, or one formed by means of a phrase."

Likewise the indirect object relationship may be indicated either by means of word order (subject-verb-indirect object-object) or by using the preposition *to.*

I	gave	Tom	the book.
Subject	*Verb*	*Indirect Object*	*Direct Object*

I	gave	the book	to Tom.
Subject	*Verb*	*Direct Object*	*Object of the Preposition*
			(Periphrastic Indirect Object)

Certain other relationships can be shown only by prepositions or function words, and the noun following or governed by the preposition is called *the object of the preposition.*

I went *with* the man.
We came *into* the room.
They stayed *in* the room.

I. How many English cases shall we recognize? What names shall we give to the cases?

The number of cases to be recognized in Latin or Greek is automatically settled for us by the number of distinctive endings the nouns can acquire. In English the noun has only two such forms: one without ending and one with a distinctive ending (*-'s*). Consequently if we were to use the same scheme as for Greek or Latin, the English noun could be said to have only two cases. Since we want to recognize more than two distinctions, however, it is more useful in English to pay attention to functions rather than forms. Thus if we limit ourselves to the terms *subject, predicate noun, direct object, indirect object, object of the preposition,* and *genitive,* that is, if we speak of nouns in terms of these functional relationships, we shall find them adequate.[1] This is not an exhaustive list of all the noun functions, but it does include those occurring most frequently. Certain others are given in the Grammatical Glossary, pages 254–265. The following sentences illustrate various functions just named:

The bird	flew.	
Subject	*Verb*	
George	was	a carpenter.
Subject	*Verb*	*Predicate Noun*
The bird	swallowed	the worm.
Subject	*Verb*	*Direct Object*

The horse's	head	was	white.
Genitive	*Subject*	*Verb*	*Predicate Adjective*

The head	of the horse	was	white.
Subject	*Object of the Preposition*	*Verb*	*Predicate Adjective*
	(Periphrastic Genitive)		

I	sold	him	a book.
Subject	*Verb*	*Indirect Object*	*Direct Object*

I	sold	the book	to him.
Subject	*Verb*	*Direct Object*	*Object of the Preposition*
			(Periphrastic Indirect Object)

[1] For those who wish to use case names rather than functional names, the following terms are given:

a. The subject of a verb is in the *nominative* case, so called because it names or identifies the author of the action.

b. A predicate noun is in the nominative case.

c. The direct object of a verb, the indirect object, and the object of a preposition are said to be in the *objective* case.

d. A noun with the inflection -'s in the singular or plural or with the inflection -s' in the plural is in the *genitive* case. The stem of this word, *gen-,* implies origin (compare *genus, generate*) and is employed as the name for this case because it fits such relationships as *world's fair, duty's call, Garfield's assassin,* as well as the more familiar function of possession, *John's book.*

EXERCISE 2. 1. Consult your dictionary for the feminine forms corresponding to the following nouns of masculine gender: *emperor, Joseph, administrator, earl, fox, hero, host, alumnus.*

2. What are the plurals of the following nouns? If in doubt, consult your dictionary: *piano, potato, tooth, child, brother, knife, antelope, vertex, plateau, seraph, nucleus, nebula, grouse, synthesis, apparatus.*

3. What is the case function of each of the nouns in the following sentences:

> *a.* James made one comment concerning Ruskin's book.
> *b.* The book was a large volume.
> *c.* God's mercy prolongs the life of man.
> *d.* With the talents of an angel, a man may be a fool.
> *e.* Sidney gave the soldier some water to drink.
> *f.* The Temple of Victory stands upon a hill.

3. PRONOUNS: CLASSES

The pronouns are divided into a number of different classes, depending partly upon the nature of their antecedents and more particularly upon the functions performed by the pronouns themselves. The classes of pronouns are: personal, relative, interrogative, demonstrative, indefinite, reflexive, intensive, and reciprocal.

A. Personal Pronouns. *Person* is the property which indicates to whom reference is being made, the speaker (*I, we*), the person addressed (*you*), or some third person or thing (*he, she, it, they*). Personal pronouns are so called because they have different forms for the various persons.

They also have distinctive forms for each of the three genders in the third person singular, and, with two exceptions, the form used for the various subject (or nominative) case functions is different from that used for the several object functions.

The personal pronoun declension is as follows:

	SINGULAR			PLURAL		
	Subj.	*Gen.*	*Obj.*	*Subj.*	*Gen.*	*Obj.*
1st Per.	I	my, mine	me	we	our, ours	us
2nd Per.	you	your, yours	you	you	your, yours	you
3rd Per.						
masc.	he	his	him			
fem.	she	her, hers	her	they	their, theirs	them
neut.	it	its	it			
					all genders	

B. Relative Pronouns. A relative pronoun, as its name indicates, is used to relate or connect the different clauses of a sentence to one another.

Did you see the man *who* came yesterday?

There are three relative pronouns, *who, which,* and *that,* and certain compound forms based upon the pronoun *who: whoever, whosoever.* Likewise, *what, where, as, but* sometimes serve in relative functions. None of the relative pronouns has forms distinctive either of number or gender. What changes in form do occur, serve only to indicate case relationships, and the relative pronoun *that* does not even show these. The remaining two pronouns are declined as follows:

Subject	who	which
Genitive	whose, of whom	whose, of which
Object	whom	which

Although it has been said that the relative pronouns have no gender inflection, it is true that the choice of pronoun is determined in part by the nature of the antecedent. The relative pronoun *who* is used only to refer to persons, the pronoun *which* to animals and inanimate objects, and the pronoun *that* may refer to any of these.

C. Interrogative Pronouns. The interrogative pronouns are used in asking questions.

The interrogative pronouns are *who, which, what,* and compound forms based upon them (*whoever, whichever, whatever,* etc.). The declensional forms of interrogative *who* and *which* are the same as for relative *who* and *which. What,* like the relative pronoun *that,* is not declined in present-day English.

D. Demonstrative Pronouns. The demonstrative pronouns, *this* and *that*, indicate or point out.

They are declined for number (*these* and *those*) but neither for gender nor case.

E. Indefinite Pronouns. The term *indefinite* applies to meaning rather than function.

This class of pronouns includes *one, none, any, some, anyone, someone, no one, everyone, everybody, nobody, all,* etc. The pronoun *one* and the compound forms built upon it and upon the element *-body* assume the genitive case inflection just as the nouns (*one's, someone's, everybody's*), and *one* may be pluralized when it is used in an expression such as *the worst ones.* The number of *none* is discussed in the Glossary, Chapter IX; certain problems of number affecting other indefinite pronouns will be considered later in this chapter, pages 218, 219.

F. Reflexive Pronouns. A reflexive pronoun is generally the direct object of a verb, and has as its antecedent the subject of that verb.

> John hurt *himself*.

The forms of the reflexive pronoun are as follows:

myself	ourselves
yourself	yourselves
himself, herself, itself	themselves

G. Intensive Pronouns. The same pronouns which perform the reflexive functions serve also as intensives.

An intensive pronoun, as its name indicates, serves to intensify or emphasize its antecedents. It is not limited to any single function in respect to the verb; it may act as subject, object, or prepositional object, but it is in the same construction as its antecedent.

> I broke it *myself*.
> I gave it to John, *himself*.
> We saw the king, *himself*.

For a more complete discussion of situations in which intensive pronouns are used, see Chapter IX, s.v. *-self*.

H. Reciprocal Pronouns. A reciprocal pronoun denotes interchange of the action indicated by the verb.

> The two brothers saw *each other*.
> The members of the company shouted at *one another*.

For further comment on the use of *each other* and *one another* see Chapter IX, s.v. *each other*.

EXERCISE 3.   Classify and give the construction of each of the pronouns in the following sentences:

1. I spoke to Mr. Jones, who is the manager.
2. Are you looking for someone?
3. What are the various opinions about this?
4. She cut herself with the knife that you gave her.
5. Anybody can do that.
6. Many like to play the violin because they think it has the sweetest tone of all instruments.
7. He lost it himself, but blames no one.
8. The jury, which was confused, asked them for instructions.
9. She will have none of this.
10. We lost each other in the woods.

4. ADJECTIVES

The adjective occupies a unique position among the four major parts of speech (*i.e.* noun, pronoun, verb, and adjective) in that inflections for person, number, and case are altogether lacking.

A. Comparison (see page 235, also). The adjective is regularly inflected only to indicate the degrees of comparison:

positive	warm	comfortable	happy
comparative	warmer	more comfortable	happier, more happy
superlative	warmest	most comfortable	happiest, most happy

[Notice that in place of the *-er* and *-est* inflections attached to *warm*, we use the function words *more* and *most* when comparing the adjective *comfortable*. This is called *periphrastic* comparison. We are seldom at a loss to decide whether to use the inflections or the function words. Although an accurate statement of our prac-

tice in this respect would require a great many qualifica-
tions, it is safe to say that short words assume the
inflectional ending and long words require periphrastic
comparison.]

Comparison is a device used to indicate degrees of superiority in quality, quantity, or intensity. The positive
degree merely denotes the quality named by the adjective
without implying a comparison with anything:

Florida is warm.

An increase in the quality named by the adjective may
be viewed or expressed in two different ways.

a. Florida is *warmer* than Missouri or Minnesota.
b. Florida is the *warmest* of the three states (Missouri,
Minnesota, Florida).

In the first sentence, where the comparative degree is
employed, Florida is being compared *with* certain other
states but is *not* included within the group with which it is
being compared.

In the second sentence, where the superlative degree is
employed, Florida *is* included within the group from which
it is selected. The important thing to notice is that, since
sentences *a* and *b* say the same thing, the difference between the comparative and superlative degrees is not so
much one of quality or intensity, but rather one of point of
view.

B. Position. Usually adjectives either precede the noun they modify, or appear in the predicate after such verbs as *be, seem, appear:*

The *red* rose   Pre-substantive adjective, *i.e.* occurring
                     before the noun.
The rose is *red*   Predicate adjective

Certain adjectives are limited to one of these two positions. The demonstratives *this* and *that* do not appear as predicate adjectives, nor do such words as *former, latter, inner, outer, utter, upper.* Certain other adjectives such as *alive, asleep, awake, afloat, alone, content* may not be used in a pre-substantive position (although they do appear at times after the noun though not necessarily in the predicate, i.e. *the man asleep*). This difference is a matter of idiom or the custom of the language.

An application of this principle of adjective position clears up very neatly the question of such pairs as *your, yours, my, mine,* whose proper classification (pronoun or adjective) often gives trouble.

> *a.* This is your (my) book.
> *b.* This book is yours (mine).

From their position in the sentence, it is immediately clear that *my* and *your* (sentence *a*) are pre-substantive modifiers, and that *mine* and *yours* (sentence *b*) are predicate modifiers. The important question is not whether they are pronouns or adjectives. Because our present system of classification into parts of speech admits of some overlapping, it happens that these words satisfy both the definition of pronoun (they do "stand" for a noun) and of adjective (they do modify a noun). The real difference between them is that of position; their form varies according to where they come in the sentence.

The words *a, an,* and *the* perform limiting or specifying functions of the adjective and are known as articles. *A* and *an* are called indefinite articles; *the* is the definite article.

5. VERBS

(See pages 230–235, also.)

The properties of the verb are person, number, tense, mood, and voice. The first two of these need little com-

ment, since they are qualities or properties which have to
do with the subject rather than with the verb itself. In
certain languages the verb ending does reflect these qualities of the subject. In English only the third person singular
form of the verb (in the present indicative tense) is distinct
from all the others; it is characterized by the ending *-s* or
-es (*I go, you go, he goes*). Observe that the frequently
used auxiliary or helping verbs, *shall, will, can, may, must,*
do not follow this pattern (*I, you, he* can).

A. Tense.

It is customary to recognize six tenses of the verb in
English. They are: present, past, future, present perfect,
past perfect, and future perfect. These are formed as
follows:

Present	I see
Past	I saw
Future	I will see, I shall see
Present Perfect	I have seen
Past Perfect	I had seen
Future Perfect	I will (shall) have seen

The first two tenses, since they are formed only from the
principal parts of the verbs themselves, are called *simple
tenses*. The last four, since they require an auxiliary along
with some one of the parts of the main verb, are known as
compound tenses.

I. The Future.

There is little variation in the practice of forming the
various tenses except for the future, where the speaker or
writer is forced to choose between two possible auxiliaries,
shall and *will*. Moreover, there appears to be a difference
between American and British practice in this respect, and
there is the further problem of the contracted colloquial

forms, *I'll, you'll,* etc. American practice recognizes two kinds of future, the informal or simple future and the formal or emphatic.

a. The informal or simple future is formed by using the auxiliary *will* and represents the subject as a free agent.

I will go	We will go
You will go	You will go
He, She, It will go	They will go

The contracted forms *I'll, you'll, he'll* are more informal and less emphatic.

b. The formal or emphatic future is formed by using the auxiliary *shall*, which retains much of its original force of obligation or necessity, and which represents the subject as under constraint, especially in the second and third persons.

It is used chiefly to express a prophecy, to express determination or dominant authority on the part of the speaker,[2] and in legal enactments, judicial decisions, commands.

I shall go	We shall go
You shall go	You shall go
He, She, It shall go	They shall go

For a discussion of the use of the auxiliaries *should* and *would,* see Chapter IX, s.v. *should.*

[2] Note that *I will' go, you will,'* etc., with heavier stress upon the auxiliary *will* than upon the main verb, is also used to express determination or authority on the part of the speaker. This discussion of the future owes much to an article by Professor Amos J. Herold, "The Future Tense in Modern English," *English Journal* (College Edition), 25. 670–677.

2. Time.

Since the terms *present tense, past tense,* and *future tense* are regularly used in speaking of the verb, there is danger of concluding that the grammatical function of tense corresponds point by point to the idea of time. This is not correct. Note these three points:

a. A single tense may represent varying times of action:

1. *Present tense—present time:* I take off my hat.
2. *Present tense—past time:* Then he comes in and tells me what I am supposed to do. (In narrative, the so-called historical present.)
3. *Present tense—future time:* I leave for Boston this evening.
4. *Present tense—no stated time but repetitive action:* I eat cereal every day.

b. A single time of action may be represented by more than one tense.

5. *Past time—past tense:* Then he came in and told me what I was supposed to do.
6. *Past time—present tense*—see *2* in the preceding division.
7. *Past time—present perfect tense:* I have already told you what to do.

c. Certain times of action may be represented by verb constructions not always included in the regular verb conjugation:

8. *Past time:*   I used to take off my hat.

9. *Future time:*   I am going to take off my hat.
    I am to go to the theatre.
    I am about to write a letter.

When we use the simple present tense, moreover, scarcely ever do we have reference to an action which is actually taking place here and now. Suppose one says:

> I *eat* cereal in the morning.
> Of course I *wear* a necktie.
> I *drive* from my home to the campus in seven minutes.

It is obvious that I am neither *eating* nor *driving* as I speak, and although I may be wearing a necktie, it is clear that my reference is to a much larger block of time than merely the present moment. If I were to refer to present action, I would be much more likely to say:

> I *am eating* cereal.
> I *am wearing* a necktie.
> I *am driving* from my home to the campus.

In other words, the simple present tense is used to indicate eternal or habitual action without reference to any precise time. To indicate what is happening here and now, I am obliged to use a tense form which is expanded. This expanded present (*I am driving*), composed of the present tense of the verb *to be* and the present participle of the verb, is usually called the *progressive present,* because it refers to action progressing or going on.

The third possibility, *I do eat,* the emphatic present, is generally felt to be more emphatic than either of the preceding forms. It may refer either to a specific action or to a habitual or an eternal one.

The conjugation of the present tense may then be represented as follows:

Simple Present	Progressive Present	Emphatic Present
I eat	I am eating	I do eat
You eat	You are eating	You do eat
He eats	He is eating	He does eat

Notice also the corresponding past tense forms: *I ate, I was eating, I did eat.*

When we turn from the simple declarative statement to questions and denials, instead of having three possible forms of the present tense, we now have only two: *am I eating, do I eat, I am not eating, I do not eat.* Notice that *do I eat* and *I do not eat* must now perform the interrogative and negative function for both the simple and the emphatic present, and *am I eating, I am not eating* are the interrogative and negative forms for the progressive present.

3. The Perfect Tenses

In general the term *perfect* means that an action has been completed or perfected. In actual practice, the three perfect tenses are most often used to indicate completed action but usually with reference to some other time, either mentioned or implied in the rest of the sentence.

To illustrate, let us begin with a sentence having the verb in the simple past tense: *I saw him.* If we wish to indicate that something else was finished and done with in reference to this first statement, we would use the past perfect tense:

I had been in Omaha ten days before I saw him.
Past Perfect   *Past*

Our practice in respect to the future is exactly the same. We may begin with such a future statement as: *This will occur.* A second expression of time made with reference to the first, in other words a "before-future" action would be expressed as:

I shall have gone before this will occur.
Future Perfect   *Future*

I shall have gone before this occurs.
Future Perfect   *Present used as Future*

Finally, we come to the third of the perfect tenses, the present perfect. Just as the past perfect indicates a before-past action or one made with reference to the past, and the future perfect indicates a before-future action, so the present perfect indicates a before-present action:

> I have come to Hollywood to see a picture made.
> *Present Perfect*

The past tense, "I came to Hollywood, etc.," also indicates an action prior to the present. Notice that the present perfect is used only when there is a specific or implied reference to the present; when a definite time in the past is given, then the past tense is always used.

I came to Hollywood (*yesterday*) (*last month*) (*last year*) to visit a studio.

I have (*just*) (*now*) come to Hollywood to visit a studio.

Such a sentence as "I have come to the United States last year," frequently spoken by foreigners who have not an idiomatic command of the English tense system, violates the general practice of not using the perfect with a definitely marked past event.

B. Mood.

(See pages 234, 235, also.)

Mood (or *mode*, as it was formerly called) shows how an act is conceived, whether as a fact, a possibility, a desirability, or a command. Mood is indicated either by certain changes in verb form or through the employment of function words.

The number of moods recognized by grammarians has varied from time to time; the maximum number is generally four: imperative, infinitive, indicative, subjunctive.

I. Imperative. The imperative mood expresses a command, suggestion, request, or entreaty:

Come here! Be careful. Don't bump your head.

The imperative consists of the uninflected present stem of the verb (*Come!*) and is held to be in the second person, singular or plural, in terms of the person or persons addressed. There is no difference in form between a singular and a plural imperative.

2. Infinitive. The infinitive (no longer generally recognized as a mood) was so named because the action indicated is not limited by definite notions of time, nor of persons acting or involved in the action.

It seems, rather, to occupy a place in infinity. *To come* says nothing about who is coming, how many are coming, when the coming is to occur; it is the action of coming in a timeless, personless sphere. The infinitive in English has developed a variety of uses:

> *To hesitate* is to be wise. (Substantive or noun use, subject of verb.)
>
> I like *to eat* candy. (Substantive use, object of verb. Verbal use, governing *candy*, which in turn is the object of the infinitive.)
>
> He had a question *to ask*. (Adjective use, modifies *question*. Notice that this is not equivalent either in structure or meaning to "He had to ask a question.")
>
> The task is not easy *to perform*. (Adverbial use, modifies *easy*.)
>
> I may *go*. (Verbal use with *may*.)
>
> They allowed her *to sing*. (Objective complement; *her* functions as the subject of the infinitive and is in the objective case.)
>
> Notice that the infinitive may appear either with or without *to*. Usually it is with *to;* but when used with any of the auxiliaries *can* (and *could*), *do, may* (and *might*), *must, shall* (and *should*), *will*

(and *would*) it is without *to*; when used with *dare* or *need* it may be with or without *to*; when used with *ought* it is seldom without *to*.

3. Indicative. From the name given to this mood, we understand that it refers to an action or state conceived as a fact; it *indicates*.

It is the mood to which all the verbal examples given on pages 200–204 belong.

I drive a car.
We buy groceries.

4. Subjunctive. Since we have called the indicative the "fact" mood, it would be equally appropriate to call the subjunctive the contrary-to-fact, the hypothetical, or the imaginative mood. It is used to express the following attitudes:

Wish: If I *were* only on time. Long *live* the king.
Exhortation: Heaven *forbid*.
Reporting of motions and resolutions: I move that Joe *be* sent as a delegate to the convention.
Concession: Be it ever so humble, there's no place like home.
Condition contrary to fact: If it *were* later, I would expect him. If he *had been* here, this would not have happened.
Improbability: If this report *be* (*is*) true, anything can happen.
Supposition: We shall start if the weather *permit*(*s*).

Observe that in the last two sentences most speakers would use the indicative form of the verb (that enclosed in parentheses) rather than the subjunctive form; the subjunctive is reserved for the most formal usage.

Differences in form between the indicative and the subjunctive:

LOOK

Present Indicative		*Present Subjunctive*	
I look	We look	I look	We look
You look	You look	You look	You look
He looks	They look	*He look*	They look

Past Indicative	*Past Subjunctive*
I, you, he, we, they looked	I, you, he, we, they looked

BE

Present Indicative		*Present Subjunctive*	
I am	*We are*	*I be*	*We be*
You are	*You are*	*You be*	*You be*
He is	*They are*	*He be*	*They be*

Past Indicative		*Past Subjunctive*	
I was	We were	*I were*	We were
You were	You were	You were	You were
He was	They were	*He were*	They were

A glance at the conjugation of the verb *look,* typical of all ordinary English verbs, shows just one difference between indicative and subjunctive in the present tense, namely in the third person singular, and none in the past tense. In the verb *to be,* the present subjunctive is wholly different from the present indicative, but in the past tense there are only two points of difference.

Earlier in the history of our language the subjunctive and the indicative differed in five of the six present tense forms of all verbs. At that time the subjunctive was a strong, vigorous part of the verb conjugation. Today we often hear that the subjunctive is being largely replaced by the indicative. Very probably such a development has taken place because the two moods came to be identical in form in eleven of the twelve possible places in the conjugation.

Note also that the expressions of possibility, permission, power, or obligation to perform an action are not the same as expressing the action itself. Shall we include as subjunctives such expressions as:

I can work	I could work	I must work
I may work	I might work	I should work

Observe that these modifications of attitude are expressed by auxiliary verbs rather than by inflections. For this reason such expressions are sometimes classified separately as the *potential* mood. Yet certain of these expressions once did employ the inflected subjunctive, and some of them are still interchangeable with that form of the verb: [3]

If the account *be* true—If the account *should be* true.
Were I only at home—If I *might* (*could*) only be at home.
He acts as though he *were* ill—He acts as though he *might be* ill.

C. Voice.

English has two voices, *active* and *passive,* which represent the subject either as acting or acted upon. The pas-

[3] This illustrates a development in the verb which we have seen paralleled in the nouns and adjectives. In the noun, the periphrastic genitive (*the side of the mountain*) has assumed many of the functions of the old inflected genitive (*the mountain's side*). In the adjective, periphrastic comparison (*more judicious*) has often replaced the inflected form (*judiciouser*). So, too, periphrastic verbal constructions are performing many of the functions formerly indicated by inflectional endings.

sive voice is formed by using the auxiliary *be* in combination with the past participle of the verb. All the forms of the English passive are compound or periphrastic in form.

Note that *book,* which functions as the object of the verb in the active voice in the illustrations which follow, becomes the subject of the verb in the passive sentences.

	ACTIVE	PASSIVE
Present:	I take the book (subject acting)	The book is taken (subject acted upon)
Progressive Present:	I am taking the book	The book is being taken
Past:	I took the book	The book was taken
Future:	I will (shall) take the book	The book will be taken
Present Perfect:	I have taken the book	The book has been taken
Past Perfect:	I had taken the book	The book had been taken
Future Perfect:	I will (shall) have taken the book	The book will have been taken

D. Other Parts of the Verb.

These are: the participles, present and past, and the gerund, sometimes called *verbals.*

I. A participle is a word partaking of the nature of both a verb and an adjective.

Rowing is the present participle derived from *row; rowed* is the past participle. A participle may take either a direct or both direct and indirect objects, thus functioning as a verb. Like an adjective, it may be modified by an adverb.

> I was *rowing*. (Participle used in verb phrase, but it may also be regarded as a predicate adjective.)
>
> The *straining* runner overtook him at last. (Participle used as pre-substantive adjective.)
>
> *Giving* us a worried look, he began to speak. (*Giving* is a participle modifying *he*. At the same time it governs the direct object *look* and the indirect object *us*.)
>
> The boat was swiftly *rowed*. (The past participle *rowed* is modified by the adverb *swiftly*.)

2. The gerund or verbal noun is a verb form ending in *-ing*, used as a noun.

Like any other noun, the gerund may be modified by an adjective. It resembles a verb in that it may take an object and may be modified by an adverb.

> *Rowing* is *exercising*. (Two gerunds, the first acting as subject, and the second as predicate noun.)
>
> I hate *rowing*. (Object of a verb.)
>
> Good *rowing* takes practice. (Gerund modified by an adjective.)
>
> We are in favor of *leaving* early. (Considered as a noun, *leaving* is the object of the preposition *of;* because of its verbal quality, it is also modified by the adverb *early*.)

E. Principal Parts.

Most of us *do* use hundreds of verbs in our daily conversation, and rarely do we give conscious attention to their formation, for the reason that the great majority of English verbs are regular. They form their past tense and their past participle simply by adding the ending *-ed*, and make no alteration in the chief vowel, i.e. *look, looked, looked; row, rowed, rowed.* Such verbs as *look* and *row* are called regular.

Certain verbs, instead of adding endings to form the past tense and past participle, change the vowel (*begin, began,* past tense, *begun*, past participle); certain others not only change the vowel, but add an ending as well (*ride, rode, ridden; bring, brought, brought*). Though verbs which do make such internal changes are few in number, it is important to recognize that, in some cases, there are alternate forms for one or more of the principal parts. Webster's dictionary shows that either *sang* or *sung* may be used as the past tense of *sing*. Whenever in doubt about the acceptable form of any verb, use your dictionary.

F. Transitive and Intransitive Verbs.

Those verbs which can take a direct object to complete their meaning are *transitive* verbs.

He *reads* the book.

Verbs which by virtue of their meaning do not permit a direct object are called *intransitive*.

He *stands*.

Notice, however, that the verb *stand* in the sense of "endure," "tolerate," does take an object and is transitive in those meanings.

I can't *stand* it.

Confusion sometimes arises when transitive and intransitive verbs are similar in sound and meaning, as is the case with *sit* and *set, lie* and *lay*. These particular verbs, in fact, are so often confused that their correct use is usually taken as a sign of literacy. See the Glossary, Chapter IX.

EXERCISE 4. 1. Indicate the person, number, tense, mood, and voice of each of the verbs in the following sentences:

1. The house was struck by lightning.
2. If the baby does not thrive on raw milk, boil the milk.
3. That will do.
4. He is not listening, for he has fallen asleep.
5. It was moved that the minutes be approved.
6. My father convinced me that nothing was useful which was not honest.
7. I am pleased that you should have remembered my birthday.
8. Will you give me a light?
8. Eating is a pleasure.
10. If you should miss the train, you will have to wait an hour.

2. Consult an unabridged dictionary for the principal parts of the following verbs. Remember, if two forms are given for the same principal part, both are acceptable. Remember also the label *colloquial* is not a condemnation of any form.

dive	bite	awake
spring	beat	strive
hang	get	break
show	light	dream

3. Write the complete conjugation (*i.e.* all persons, numbers, tenses, moods, and both voices) of the verbs *shake* and *look*.

6. ADVERBS

The adverb has already been defined in terms of function as modifying verbs, adjectives, or other adverbs. In terms of meaning we recognize the following classes:

Adverbs of time: *then, quickly, suddenly, early*
Adverbs of place: *there, here, yonder, over, up*
Adverbs of manner: *sweetly, badly, brightly*
Adverbs of degree: *very, quite, not, rather*

Other classifications are, of course, possible. The adverbs given in the foregoing list will show how much the ending *-ly* has become associated with the adverbial function.

Remember that not all adverbs have the *-ly* ending. For example, although *rapidly* is found only with the *-ly* form, the adverb *fast* has not adopted it. Certain English adverbs have two forms, one identical with the corresponding adjective (*loud, soft, quick, slow*) and the other formed with the *-ly* suffix (*loudly, softly, quickly, slowly*). Either form is grammatically correct; we usually choose the form that sounds better. In an imperative sentence, *go slow, come quick*, the shorter form is generally used; in longer and more leisurely sentences, the longer form is employed. Always consult your dictionary to find the acceptable forms.

The adverbs are subject to comparison just as are the adjectives.

7. PREPOSITIONS (See also pp. 139–141)

The notion that a sentence should never end with a preposition has been current for over two hundred years. It arose in part from the rhetorical theory that a sentence must always end with a strong word (noun, pronoun, verb, adjective, adverb). Moreover, from its etymology (*pre,* "before" + *position*), the word *preposition* was held to mean "that which comes before." Therefore it was concluded that something must always come *after* the preposition.

Whatever the reasons for the belief, it clearly does not apply to the English language, nor has it ever been observed in general practice. Two things should be pointed out here:

A. In many sentences the relative construction necessary to avoid ending the sentence with the preposition is unnatural and lacks force.

NATURAL: We had interesting things to talk *of*.
CLUMSY: We had interesting things *of which* to talk.

NATURAL: It is not a good gymnasium to play basketball *in*.
CLUMSY: It is not a good gymnasium *in which* to play basketball.

NATURAL: What a foolish thing to think *about*.
CLUMSY: What a foolish thing *about which* to think.

B. In many instances the function of adverb and preposition cannot be clearly separated, and the so-called preposition is really a verbal particle which cannot be displaced without altering the meaning of the sentence.

> This is the bill I ran *up*.
> Here is the quotation he brought *in*.
> Did he break the teapot when he knocked it *over?*

8. CONJUNCTIONS

Conjunctions or connecting words may be divided into two classes according to the kind of elements they connect.

1. Co-ordinating conjunctions connect words, phrases, or clauses of equal rank: *and, or, but*.

2. Subordinating conjunctions introduce clauses subordinate to the rest of the sentence: *as, since, because, for, so, unless*, etc.

> *Since* I know he is in earnest, I believe he will succeed.

3. There is also a group of adverbial connectives, including the words *however, moreover, nevertheless, also, therefore, consequently,* etc., which may be used to link the independent clauses, in which they occur, to the preceding clause. They differ from the true co-ordinating conjunctions in that they introduce a clause which, though *grammatically* independent, is *logically* subordinate to or dependent upon what has gone before.

I know he is in earnest; *therefore,* I believe he will succeed.

EXERCISE 5. Select and classify the conjunctions in the following sentences:

1. He lost the race although he made a good run.
2. I missed the target because I was excited.
3. He likes to visit libraries and wander about them for hours.
4. It seems that he ought to go at once.
5. He finally arrived, but it was too late.
6. I will not write unless I hear from you.
7. Because I am over twenty-one, I am ineligible.
8. I know it is true, for he told me so.
9. She was quite disturbed when I told her about it.
10. If you hear from them, let me know at once.

SYNTAX

We have now studied the forms and functions of the various parts of speech, and have interpreted them in terms of meaning. For the most part, nouns, pronouns, verbs, and adjectives have been treated as if they were quite separate and unrelated, as if they had little to do with one another. This, of course, is but a small part of the study of the English language, for in it nouns, verbs, pronouns, and the rest of the parts of speech rarely occur in isolation, but constantly act and re-act upon one another to form a unified whole.

The study of the patterns of relationship of the various parts of speech to one another is called *syntax*. As a result of careful observation of the behavior of the various parts of speech with one another, grammarians have formulated certain laws or rules. With some of these you are familiar, as, for example, "A subject agrees in number with the verb that it governs." Such rules are often helpful, but at times they are so very general that they do not help us in particular problems.

9. PROBLEMS OF NUMBER

A. Subject and Verb. A subject agrees in number with the verb that it governs.

(See pages 95, 96, also.)

Few of us would be likely to say, "The sidewalk are covered with snow" or "The men has come." Subject and verb are side by side, and the relation is obvious. When some phrase or clause of a different number comes between them, however, an inattentive speaker or writer may be thrown off the track. Such errors as "The sidewalk between the armory and the stadium are covered with snow" or "The men you sent for to repair the furnace has come" may result. If the subject is clearly held in mind and the rule applied, such errors may easily be avoided.

On the other hand, occasional confusion may arise over the application of the rule. We may begin a sentence with such a noun as *family, committee,* or *board* and hesitate just a moment, wondering whether to use the singular or plural form of the verb. Or we may puzzle over such a sentence as, "The wages of sin (is) (are) death." Note the following exceptions to the general rule: [4]

1. A collective noun takes a singular verb when the group is thought of as a unit, and a plural verb when the individual members of the group are thought of separately.

By ten o'clock the family *were* all here. (Considering them as having arrived separately.)

The family *goes* to church at ten o'clock. (Thinking of going to church at a definite time as a group action.)

This applies also to such nouns as *number, part, rest, remainder.*

A number of tickets *were* sold but not called for.
The greatest part of his youth *was* spent in study.
The greatest part of his days *were* spent in study.

a. The pronouns *none* and *any* may be in either number, according as the singular or plural idea is uppermost in the speaker's mind.

None of us *seem* to have thought of it.
None but the brave *deserves* the fair.

b. Though the pronouns *either* and *neither*[5] (like *none* and *any*) have for centuries been singular or plural according to the conception of the speaker,

---

[4] Observe, however, that except for the verb *to be,* a distinction between singular and plural number in the verb is apparent only in the present tense, third person.

[5] The *Oxford Dictionary* shows that *neither* has been used with a plural verb when the occasion demanded since 1611. Among the authors cited to illustrate this use are Shakespeare, Dryden, Newman, and Ruskin.

the present tendency, particularly in the United States, is to make them singular.

Formerly acceptable:

> Neither of your heads *are* safe.
> *Are* either of you going to the fair?

Today, *is* would replace *are* in formal and careful usage.

2. The verb is generally singular if a singular subject is associated with other words (*with, together with, as well as, no less than, in addition to,* etc.) which logically, though not formally, are part of the subject.

Examples:

> The captain with his soldiers *makes* the charge.
> The mayor, as well as the members of the council, *was* re-elected.

In sentences like these there is a conflict between the *grammar* (since the subject is singular) and the broader *meaning* (since we are really talking about a number of things or people). Such sentences may therefore seem clumsy. If they do, avoid them in the interests of style.

3. Two or more subjects joined by *and*, or several subjects without a connecting conjunction, require a plural verb.

> The students and faculty *join* in the chorus.
> A boat, a book, a shady nook, *are* better to me than gold.

a. When several co-ordinate subjects represent the same person, or when they are felt as forming

a distinct collective idea, the verb is in the singular.

> Your guide and mentor *tells* me of your progress.
> The sum and substance of the argument *is* this.
> The tumult and the shouting *dies*. (Kipling)

b. When each of a number of singular subjects is considered separately, the verb is in the singular.

> At the camp every boy and girl *is* taught to swim.

4. Two or more singular subjects separated by such disjunctives as *not only . . . but, either . . . or, neither . . . nor* are generally followed by a singular verb.

> Either a cow or a horse *was* in the field.
> Not only the father but the mother also *refuses* to give permission.

5. When one of two subjects separated by a disjunctive is singular and the other is plural, the verb agrees with the nearer.

> Either the governor or his advisers *are* responsible.
> Not only the actors but the playwright *was* disappointed.

6. When a subject and a predicate, connected by some form of the verb *to be*, differ in number, the verb generally agrees with the subject.

> Books *are* his only concern.
> His only concern *is* his studies.

a. Here it is sometimes difficult to determine which is the subject and which is the predicate. If

the noun following the verb is unquestionably more specific in meaning than the noun preceding the verb, it may be considered as the subject and the verb made to agree with it.

The wages of sin *is* death.

7. Introductory *there* and *here* are generally followed by a singular verb if the subject is singular, and by a plural verb if the subject is plural.

There *are* many things to think about.
Here *is* one thing to remember.

a. When a compound subject, the first member of which is singular, is introduced by *there* or *here*, a singular verb may be used.

There *was* a bed, a dresser, and two chairs in the room. (Rated as "established" by *Current English Usage*.)
Here *comes* an old man and his three sons. (Shakespeare)

8. In mathematical calculations either the singular or the plural of the verb may be used.

Two times three (*is*) (*are*) six.
Eight and six (*makes*) (*make*) fourteen.

B. Pronoun and Antecedent. The general rule is that a pronoun agrees in number with its antecedent (see p. 56, also).

The boys gave *their* skates to the poor children.
Someone has left *his* books in my room.

1. A collective noun demands a singular pronoun of reference when the group is thought of as a unit and a plural pronoun when the individual members of the group are thought of separately.

> The army guards *its* plans carefully.
> The mob threw up *their* caps and cheered.

2. In formal, literary English it is now customary to use a singular pronoun in referring to the indefinite pronouns *each, every, everyone, everybody, someone, somebody, anyone, anybody.*

> Each is anxious to do *his* part.
> Everyone should guard *his* health carefully.

a. In colloquial speech and informal writing, as in older literary English, the plural pronoun is often used where a plural meaning is definitely implied:

> It is desirable in times like this that everyone should be careful of what *they* say.—Prime Minister Chamberlain, as reported by Associated Press, April 5, 1939.
> Neither of *us* had broken *our* word.

3. For the use of the singular demonstratives with *kind, sort,* see Chapter IX, s.v. *kind,* p. 347.

In conclusion it may well be pointed out that all the special problems considered in Section 9 (Problems of Number) come about as a result of a conflict between form and meaning. Usually such a conflict arises when a form, singular in number, conveys a plural idea (the reverse situation does occur, but less often) and we are uncertain whether the other words in the sentence should agree with the form or with the essential nature of the idea. It is interesting to note that in situations where there is such a conflict, meaning generally prevails over form.

EXERCISE 6. Decide whether the singular or the plural form should be used in the following sentences:

1. A number of us (goes) (go) to the concerts regularly.
2. Everybody is happy because (he) (they) (has) (have) been excused from classes.
3. Neither Duke nor Pitt (is) (are) likely to win the title.
4. The value of these houses (varies) (vary) from six to ten thousand dollars.
5. All that we can promise (is) (are) reasonably good results.
6. The golf team, which (has) (have) five members, (wins) (win) the tournament every year.
7. My friend and colleague (does) (do) me great honor.
8. Everybody was here, but (he) (they) all went home early.
9. There (has) (have) been many attacks against the share-the-wealth plan.
10. This is a matter of importance to every man and woman who (owns) (own) property.

10. PROBLEMS OF CASE

Most of the problems of case need only to be considered in relation to the pronouns we use, as the noun forms are alike for all cases except the genitive.

A. Case forms of the personal pronoun.

I. In formal literary English the subjective case form of the personal pronoun is generally demanded in the predicate after forms of the verb *to be*.

> If it were *he,* I could not say.
> It is *they* who have deceived us.

Note that this rule can apply only to the pronouns of the first and third persons, since *you* is both the subjective and objective form.

a. In informal, colloquial language the objective case forms of the personal pronoun are considered acceptable when used predicatively after forms of the verb *to be*.

FORMAL: It is *I*. That is *he*.
INFORMAL: It is *me*. That's *him*.

Although the *Oxford Dictionary* sanctions *him, us* and *them* in such a situation quite as readily as *me*, there is evidence of considerably more prejudice in American usage against *it is* (*them*) (*him*) than against *it is me*. Therefore, *it is him* (*them*) should be used with caution, if at all.

It is me and similar uses of the personal pronouns seem to have arisen from the strong tendency to place the objective case form of the pronoun *after* a verb, regardless of what the verb might be. For a discussion of the importance of word order in connection with matters of case, see page 191.

2. The words *than* and *as* in formal literary English are considered as conjunctions and do not affect the case of the following pronoun.

You are stronger than *I*.
He skates as well as *they*.

3. The object of a preposition and the direct and indirect objects of the verb require the objective case form of the pronoun.

He gave it to John and *me*.
They notified *us* boys immediately.

Because so much stress is laid upon the form of the pronoun in expressions like *John and I decided to go, we boys are going,* one sometimes gets the notion that *John and me* and *us boys* are incorrect in all situations. Remember that the form of the pronoun is always determined by its function in the sentence.

CORRECT: He gave it to John and *me.* (*Me* is part of the object of the preposition *to.*)

INCORRECT: John and *me* are going to the circus. (Since the pronoun here is part of the subject of the verb, *I* should be used.)

4. The subject of an infinitive is in the objective case.

> John wanted *him* to go.
> Tom ordered *them* to let him know at once.

a. The objective case form of the pronoun is employed after the infinitive *to be* when the infinitive has a subject

> They took him to be *me.*
> Harry imagined the culprit to be *him.*

Here the infinitive acts merely as a connecting link or equals sign (=) joining the subject of the infinitive to the pronoun which follows. Since the subject of the infinitive is already in the objective case (see rule 4), the pronoun following the infinitive also takes the objective case form.

5. An appositive should be in the same case as the substantive with which it is in apposition.

> He nodded to both of us, Jane and *me.*
> All the family, Mother, Father and *I,* will be at home.

B. Interrogative and Relative Pronouns.

Only the pronoun *who* and compound forms built upon it have different forms for the subjective and objective cases.

1. In formal literary English, interrogative *whom* regularly appears as the direct or indirect object of a verb or the object of a preposition.

> *Whom* is he choosing for the part?
> To *whom* was the part given?

In colloquial English, the use of interrogative *who* as direct object is common when it is in a pre-verbal position, or when the preposition governing the pronoun does not precede it.

> *Who* are you looking for?
> *Who* did they find?

In a sentence employing an interrogative pronoun, the normal sentence order (subject-verb-object) is so altered that the object appears *before* the active verb. The strong sense of a pattern calling for the subjective case form of a pronoun in a pre-verbal position, here gives rise to the use of *who*.

2. Avoid the use of relative *whom* for *who* in the following situations:

When a parenthetic expression like *I think, I consider, he says* intervenes between the relative pronoun and the verb it governs:

DOUBTFUL: We feed children *whom* we think are hungry.
REVISED: We feed children *wko* we think are hungry.

When the pronoun is the subject of a clause which in its entirety functions as the verbal object.

WRONG: Determine *whom* are the guilty ones.
RIGHT: Determine *who* are the guilty ones.

The complete clause, not the pronoun *who,* is the object of the verb *determine.*

C. The Genitive Case.

1. The inflected genitive of nouns is chiefly used with animate objects and less frequently with nouns that denote lifeless things.

RARE: the table's leg, the mountain's foot, the room's door.
COMMON: the leg of the table, the foot of the mountain, the door of the room.

When the inflected genitive is used with the names of things, they are usually thought of as having life, e.g. *duty's call, the ocean's roar.* There are also a number of fixed combinations employing the inflected form: *heart's content, week's pay, money's worth, boat's length.* Notice that we frequently convert the noun into an adjective: *table leg, mountain top.*

2. The genitive pronoun *whose* is frequently used to refer to neuter antecedents when the periphrastic *of which* would result in an awkward construction.

In actual practice the use of *whose* has never been confined to persons.

> This is the chapter *whose* contents cause much discussion.
> Soon we came to a river on *whose* bank stood a deserted factory.

Note that when *of* is already a part of the construction, the insertion of *of which* would be exceedingly clumsy.

FAULTY: This is a book of the contents of which he was quite ignorant.
REVISED: This is a book of whose contents he was quite ignorant.

3. A noun or pronoun preceding and governing a gerund is usually in the genitive case.

What was the reason for *John's* leaving so soon?
What was the reason for *their* leaving so soon?

a. With nouns, the use of the common or uninflected case form preceding the gerund is not unusual; it may occur in both formal and informal English.

What was the reason for *John* leaving so soon?

b. With personal pronouns, however, the use of the objective case form preceding the gerund is limited to informal speech and writing.

FORMAL: What are the chances of *my* being discovered?
INFORMAL: What are the chances of *me* being discovered?

c. In certain instances the choice of the case form is a useful guide to the emphasis which the writer or speaker wishes to give the construction.

Imagine *him* dancing.

If in this sentence *him* is interpreted as the object of *imagine,* and *dancing* is therefore construed as a present participle modifying *him,* the meaning or emphasis suggested is, "Imagine him' dancing," i.e. the very idea that *he* should dance, or "Imagine him dancing'," i.e. not walking, running, or some other activity.

Imagine *his* dancing.

If in this sentence *dancing* is interpreted as a gerund, the object of *imagine,* and *his* is therefore construed as a pronoun modifier of the gerund, the meaning suggested is, "Imagine what his dancing, not his walking or running, would be like," or "Imagine his, not John's or Mary's, dancing."

EXERCISE 7.   Assume you are writing formally. Select the appropriate case form in each of the following sentences. Explain your choice.

1. He sat down beside Jane and (she) (her).
2. She approved of (me) (my) doing the work.
3. The police are not certain as to (who) (whom) was the culprit.
4. (Who) (Whom) have you selected for class president?
5. There is some talk of the (governor) (governor's) running for re-election.
6. (Who) (Whom) do you think is the sports editor?
7. The committee and (we) (us) counted all the votes.
8. The man (who) (whom) they believed set the fire had suddenly disappeared.
9. John is more ambitious than (she) (her).
10. Everybody expected you and (I) (me) to come late.

11. PROBLEMS OF PERSON

The general rule is: A subject agrees in person with the verb it governs. (See page 200, also.)

Substitute *you were* for *you was* on all occasions.

Substitute *he, she, it* (or any noun), *does not* (*doesn't*) for *he, she, it*, etc. *don't*.

12. PROBLEMS OF TENSE

(See pp. 97, 98, also.)

A. The tense of verbs in co-ordinate constructions within a single sentence or unit of writing should be consistently maintained.

WRONG: The ghosts *decide* to accomplish their good deed by changing the dull life of the bank president to a gay one, and they *proceeded* to do so.

RIGHT: The ghosts *decide(d)* to accomplish their good deed by changing the dull life of the bank president to a gay one, and they *proceed(ed)* to do so.

WRONG: By cutting classes in order to enjoy a more extended Christmas vacation they *missed* work and thus *lose* out in the end.

RIGHT: By cutting classes in order to enjoy a more extended Christmas vacation they *miss* work and thus *lose* out in the end.

B. The tense of the verb in a subordinate clause should be in *logical agreement* (not necessarily the same tense) with the verb in the main clause. Do not shift about in time among past, present, and future.

WRONG: As time *rolls* on and on, the common people *began to demand* and *secure* a few of the rights that *belonged* to them.

RIGHT: As time *rolled* on, the common people *began to demand* and *to secure* a few of the rights that *belong(ed)* to them.

For the tense of *belong*, see paragraphs E and F in this section.

WRONG: Enough people *were* so opposed to this that they *rise* up and *overthrow* the king and *establish* their own religion.
RIGHT: Enough people *were* so opposed to this that they *rose* up and *overthrew* the king and *established* their own religion.

WRONG: If I *were* there, I *would have disagreed*.
RIGHT: If I *had been* there, I *would have disagreed*.

Notice that the auxiliary verbs *must* and *ought* require expanded forms in situations where they must be put into the past tense.

WRONG: She *held* no jurisdiction over the children and *must* have a guardian for them.
RIGHT: She *held* no jurisdiction over the children and *had to have* a guardian for them.

C. Guard against an unnecessary use of the conditional auxiliary *would* in the following:

Where the condition has already been suggested by some other word or construction.

FAULTY: If the great inventors *would have* stopped to daydream, they could have accomplished little.
REVISED: If the great inventors *had* stopped to daydream, they could have accomplished little.

FAULTY: By observing the reveries of our neighbors, we *would be* able to judge their character.
REVISED: By observing the reveries of our neighbors, we *are* able to judge their character.

Where the intended meaning is wholly indicative and not conditional.

FAULTY: Something happened which again *would* focus the eyes of the people upon this extraordinary person.
REVISED: Something happened which again *focused* the eyes of the people upon this extraordinary person.

Where *would* appears as the result of attraction to another verb in the sentence.

FAULTY: If they had been born three thousand years ago under the same financial circumstances, they would still have been as unequal as they *would be* today.
REVISED: If they had been born three thousand years ago under the same financial circumstances, they would still have been as unequal as they *are* today.

D. Do not use the present perfect tense to indicate an action completed in some remote past. It suggests the recent past.

FAULTY: She *has made* so much progress under the first five-year plan that she *has* now *undertaken* a second five-year plan.
REVISED: She *made* so much progress under the first five-year plan that she *has* now *undertaken* a second five-year plan.

E. Use the simple present to indicate actions or conditions unlimited by definite time boundaries.

FAULTY: We *had* no better example of these conditions than the United States as it was one hundred years ago.
REVISED: We *have* no better example of these conditions than the United States as it was one hundred years ago.

F. Occasionally the "eternal present" is attracted into some other tense by another verb in the sentence.

"Galileo discovered that the earth *moved*," is undoubtedly satisfactory, although a severe critic might insist that *moves* be substituted.

EXERCISE 8.   Improve the following sentences by altering the tense of the verbs whenever it seems necessary:

1. Always being somewhat serious-minded, I have done very well in high school.

2. The youth of today are of an inquisitive nature and thus decided to delve into the past to discover the causes of the misfortunes current today.

3. If there is to be censorship of thought at universities, the word *university* would become a misnomer.

4. As far back as 1900 world citizenship has been stressed.

5. A democratic government does provoke a restless energy in its citizens, but this energy might not be of benefit to democracy.

6. If the two opponents had campaigned on the same platform, the result would be doubtful.

7. He will be on hand every time a person of note will talk upon politics.

8. Van Johnson and Betty Grable carry off the leading parts very well and the supporting cast also contributed toward the success of the picture.

9. Throughout one's high school career there are, without a doubt, many times when the subject being studied required more thought than it got.

10. The *Survey Graphic* impressed me as being a magazine which would interest anyone who was concerned with the affairs of the world today.

13. PROBLEMS OF MOOD

(See pp. 205–209, also.)

Condition. In the expression of a condition, the indicative form is present so markedly in literary English that it must be considered acceptable.

So far as colloquial English is concerned, *were* in the singular survives chiefly in the fixed formula, "If I *were* you."

> If it (*wasn't*) (*weren't*) for football, school life would be dull.

Either form is acceptable.

Wish. Literary usage in the expression of a wish also varies between indicative and subjunctive.

It is possible to find instances where both forms occur in the same sentence.

> The captain says he wishes I *were* black; I wish I *was*.
> (Marryat)

In colloquial English *was* is the common form.

After *as if* and *as though* both forms occur, but the indicative occurs more frequently when the verb is in the negative.

NEGATIVE: As if I *wasn't* old enough!
DECLARATIVE: I feel as if I *were* coming down with a cold.

Note that in all these choices *were* is the more distinctive, since it occurs only on the formal level while *was* occurs on both formal and informal levels.

In the reporting of motions and resolutions and in the indirect imperative, the subjunctive is the *only* form employed.

Resolved, that the secretary *be* instructed to deliver the following communications to the trustees.

The terms of the treaty provide that each nation *pay* its contractual obligations.

14. PROBLEMS OF DEGREE

A. The comparative degree of an adjective or adverb is used when speaking of two things, and the superlative degree when speaking of three or more.

See p. 198, also.

For example:

John is *taller* than Henry.
John is the *taller* of the two boys.
John is the *tallest* of the boys in his class.

From the very earliest period of our language the desire for emphasis has led to the use of the superlative with two, and it may be found frequently in literary English.

We must consider whether Homer was not the *greatest* poet, though Virgil may have produced the *finest* poem. (Johnson)

Feeling against the superlative with two is strong, however, and seems to be increasing. Cautious writers had better use the comparative with two and reserve the superlative for more than two.

The superlative for the comparative is very common in

colloquial English, but **neither in speech nor in writing does this construction occur before** *than.*

> She was the *most* popular of the girls.
> She was *more* popular than I.

B. According to strict logic, those adjectives and adverbs which indicate absolute qualities or conditions are incapable of comparison.

I.e., if a thing is *unique* or *round,* nothing else can be *more* unique or *more* round.

It is a recognized fact that, in the course of time, many of these absolute words tend to become weaker in meaning, and to lose their absolute character, chiefly because of a desire on the part of speakers and writers to give emphasis to their language. One needs only to cite the Preamble to the United States Constitution, "in order to form a more perfect union," to show that this may happen in serious writing as well as in speech. It is a tendency which is often criticized. It will be the better plan for you to choose the word which indicates exactly the quality you have in mind.

LOGICAL: It was a *unique* experience (the only one of its kind).

ILLOGICAL: The material for her dress was *most unique.*

LOGICAL: The material for her dress was *most unusual.*

15. THE SPLIT INFINITIVE

Avoid split infinitive constructions when they result in awkwardness or incoherence.

AWKWARD: It would be inappropriate *to* in any way, shape, or manner *question* the remarks of the previous speaker.

BETTER: It would be inappropriate *to question* in any way the remarks of the previous speaker.

There are circumstances when the split infinitive is necessary, if the meaning is to be clear. This is particularly true when the infinitive follows another verbal construction. Suppose we begin with a sentence such as, "He wished to forget his past," and decide that we must modify the infinitive *to forget* with the adverb *utterly*.

If the adverb is placed before the infinitive, "He wished utterly to forget his past," we have a squinting construction; the adverb *utterly* looks both ways, and the sentence is not immediately clear.

If *utterly* is placed immediately after the infinitive, "He wished to forget utterly his past," it intrudes between verb and object and produces a clumsy rhythm.

If *utterly* is placed after the verbal object, "He wished to forget his past utterly," it loses force because of its distance from the verb, and sounds like an afterthought.

In this instance the best solution is, "He wished to utterly forget his past."

The split infinitive has been used steadily (though not frequently) by English and American authors since the fourteenth century. To mention only a few, Goldsmith, Coleridge, Irving, Hawthorne, Dickens, Arnold, Whittier, Lowell, Browning, George Eliot, Theodore Roosevelt, Woodrow Wilson, all have used it.

Our purpose is not to give a blanket approval of the split infinitive construction. As the historical and logical facts show us, however, the blanket condemnation of the split infinitive construction which is so often met with is ridiculous. In practice, each individual case must be decided upon its own merits. Before committing thoughts to paper, you should put the adverbial modifier in all the possible places—before, after, and within the infinitive. If the split infinitive is the least ambiguous of all the possible

constructions, and if in only that position does the adverbial modifier seem to have the proper emphasis, then it
should be used. Sentence rhythm may sometimes affect
your decision.

Note that the passive and perfect infinitives regularly
permit the insertion of adverbs between the infinitive of
the auxiliary and the past participle of the main verb.

> *Passive infinitive:* He deserves to be *well* treated.
> *Perfect infinitive:* He appears to have *just* arrived.

16. DIAGRAMMING

One way of clarifying the relationship of the various
elements of a sentence to each other is to diagram the
sentence. Sentences are often so long and involved that it
is difficult to analyze them in the abstract; a diagram can
be of immense help.

In general, the method of all diagramming is to place
each word in the sentence along a horizontal, vertical, or
diagonal line, depending upon its function in the sentence,
and to place all words near those which they govern or
are governed by, regardless of what their position in the
sentence itself may be.

**A. Subject and Verb. The simple subject and
the verb or verb phrase are placed on a horizontal
line, and they are separated by a vertical line which
intersects the horizontal line.**

Birds fly.   Spring has come.   I have been eating.

| Birds | fly. | | Spring | has come. | | I | have been eating. |

Observe the treatment here of the compound subject and predicate.

Boys and girls run, play, and sing.

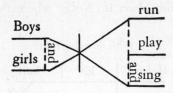

A question is diagrammed in exactly the same manner as a declarative statement.

Do birds fly?

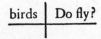

EXERCISE 9.   1. Diagram the following:

1. He disagrees.
2. Planes are flying.
3. Is he going?
4. Flowers and leaves blew and swirled.

2. Select from the following sentences the subject and verb or verb phrase, and diagram them.

1. The ground was carefully prepared.
2. The good things of this world have come my way.
3. What exactly was the nature of this doctrine?
4. To England my father returned for further triumphs.
5. May you never be crossed in love.

B. Complements.

1. The direct object is placed on a horizontal line with
the subject and verb, but is separated from the verb by a
vertical line which merely comes down to the horizontal
line but does not bisect it. Notice where the article *the* is
placed.

John hit the ball.

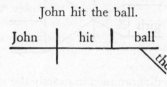

The ball hit John.

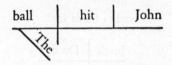

The ball hit John and James.

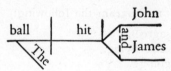

2. A predicate noun or predicate adjective is placed on
the same line with the subject and verb, and is preceded by
a line running diagonally toward the subject to indicate
the relationship.

George is president.

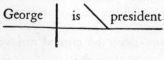

Grass is green.

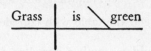

3. **An objective complement or cognate object is placed on the same line with subject, verb, and direct object, and is preceded by a line running diagonally toward the object to indicate the relationship.** Always place the cognate object before the direct object.

We made John treasurer.

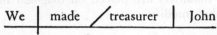

4. **The indirect object is placed on a horizontal line between verb and object, and above the main line of the sentence.**

Father gave me a dollar.

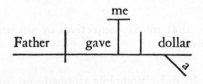

EXERCISE 10. 1. Diagram the following sentences:

1. I sent Father a letter.
2. The orchard was green.
3. I wanted my dinner and a nap.
4. The President appointed Mr. Bowers ambassador.

2. Select from the following sentences the subject, verb, and complements of each, and diagram them.

1. He arranged the table with considerable pains and care.
2. Why should we bother ourselves about them?
3. The frightened maid soon brought back the astonishing news.
4. My ideas on the subject were by no means profound.
5. The occasional visitors all adored the young artists and writers.

C. Modifiers.

1. Word modifiers are placed on diagonal lines under the words they modify.

The red automobile stopped quickly.

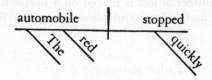

2. Adverbs that modify adjectives or adverbs are indicated as follows:

The bright red automobile stopped very quickly.

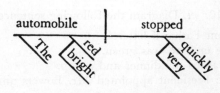

3. An appositive is placed in brackets after the word it explains.

Mr. Jones, the grocer, hurriedly sold his business.

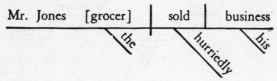

EXERCISE II. Diagram the following sentences:

1. An old, disreputable vendor sold me some black laces.
2. A wood fire glowed cheerily and heated the large room.
3. My good friend moved cautiously.
4. I could justly be called his best friend.
5. Many foreign and English dignitaries were assembled there.

4. A phrase modifier is placed on two joining lines ⟍＿, the preposition on the diagonal line, and the noun on the horizontal line under the word it modifies.

He was a man of action.

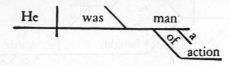

We walked for miles.

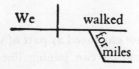

243

At the top of the hill we came to a grove of trees.

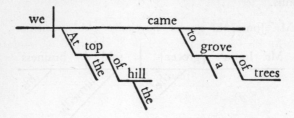

A bushel of apples sold for a dollar.

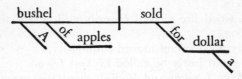

The farmer from New York sold a bushel of apples for a dollar and bought three yards of cloth.

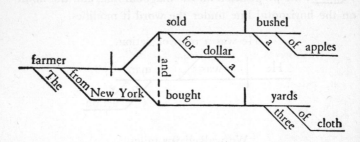

D. Verbals.

1. A participle not employed as part of the main verb or verb phrase is placed on two joining lines ＼＿＿, under

the word it modifies. Note that the object of a participle is indicated just like any other direct object.

Believing his story, we wrote the desired recommendation.

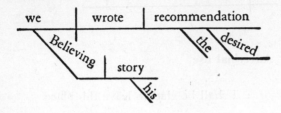

Scowling faces appeared at the closed window.

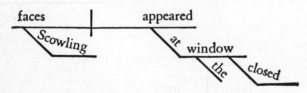

2. **Infinitives are diagrammed as follows:**

a. **Substantive use.**

I wanted to go at noon.

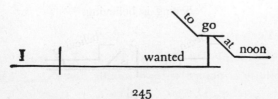

245

I told him to take the book.

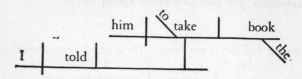

b. **Adverbial use.**

I shall be glad to leave this place.

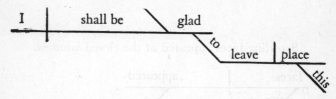

John went to call his father.

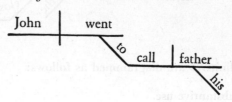

3. **The gerund is placed on a stepped line.**

Seeing is believing.

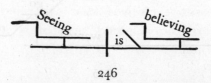

246

Rowing a boat is exercise.

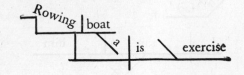

Imagine his leaving so soon.

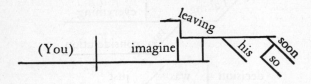

EXERCISE 12. Diagram the following sentences:

1. We shall also be glad to mail you a copy of this book.
2. To row is to exercise.
3. Believing this to be the best plan, I decided to go.
4. This is my correct mailing address.
5. This diversity of natural attractions is reflected in a similar diversity of living and playing.

E. Independent Elements. Nouns of address, absolute phrases, expletives, and other independent elements are diagrammed separately above the main sentence.

In fact, I saw him today.

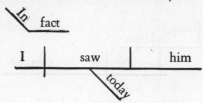

Taking everything into consideration, the decision was just.

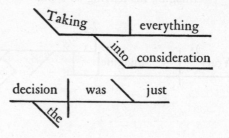

James, close the door.

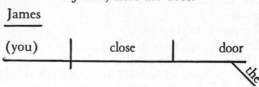

F. Clause Modifiers; Complex Sentences. In general, clauses are diagrammed as if they were separate sentences. The subordinate clause is placed below the main clause and is connected with it by a dotted line projecting from the word it modifies.

248

1. **Adjective clauses.**

I saw an automobile which I liked.

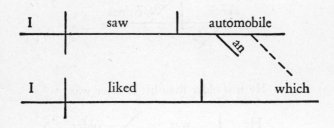

The man who came to the door was my uncle.

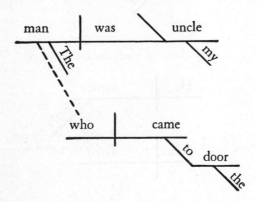

2. **Adverbial clauses.** When diagramming adverbial clauses, connect the verb of the adverbial clause with the word which it modifies in the independent clause, and write the connecting word along the dotted line.

I will leave Boston when my check comes.

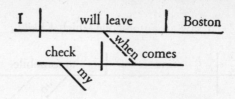

He was older than his brother was.

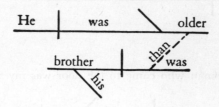

He came as early as he dared.

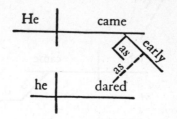

3. **Noun clauses.** Since a noun clause frequently has no conjunction which connects it with the rest of the sentence, it is diagrammed as a separate clause but is connected with a dotted line to the proper place in the diagram of the main clause.

250

I know he is a thief.

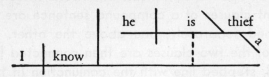

I know that he is a thief.

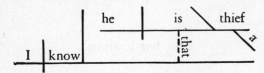

That he was a thief was never doubted.

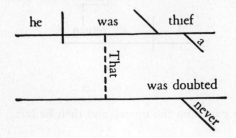

We asked for whoever might be there.

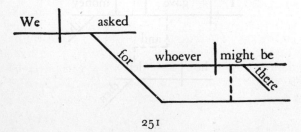

G. Compound Sentences. The two or more independent clauses of a compound sentence are diagrammed separately, one above the other. The verbs of the two clauses are then connected by a dotted, stepped line with the conjunction (if there is one) placed on the horizontal portion of this line.

I go, but I return.

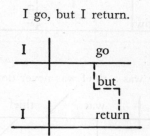

I gave him the money and then he left.

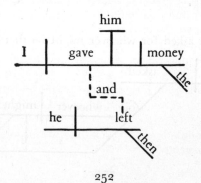

I called, and the man who heard the cry
replied immediately.

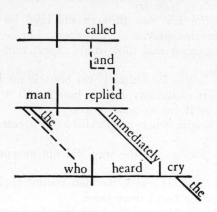

EXERCISE 13.   Diagram the following sentences:

1. John bought a coat.
2. John and Mary bought a cloth coat and a straw hat.
3. Mr. Jones, the banker, found a badly battered hat in the garden.
4. Finding the hat was clearly an accident.
5. The hat that was found belonged to my older brother.
6. Mr. Jones decided to return the hat after he discovered its owner.
7. Many thousands of acres are devoted to the production of fruit.
8. To those who seek a home in the industrial centers or in the rural communities, Jackson County offers a rare opportunity.
9. The railroads and truck lines transport the fruits, grains, and vegetables.

10. The great cement plants manufacture a highly necessary product, and hundreds are afforded employment in this outstanding industry.

11. Plowing his way through the line, he gained six yards on the first play.

12. His parents said they would expect him in the evening.

13. The house in which I was born is no longer in a desirable part of the city, but we hate to sell it because we have lived in it for so many years.

14. His bright blue eyes sparkled as he greeted his guests with a smile.

15. The Joneses, by the way, did not accept your invitation.

16. After a short recess, the class resume their activities, and the teacher keeps them busy.

17. Will you buy me the book that I saw on the shelf yesterday?

18. He said that concrete is the best material for highways in countries where the temperature does not vary.

19. Many of us left before the performance was over.

20. The guests having departed, we went to the kitchen and washed the dishes.

17. GLOSSARY OF GRAMMATICAL TERMS

Absolute. A construction, frequently composed of a noun or pronoun governing a participle, which is grammatically independent of the rest of the sentence. Because of the case form demanded by the pronouns the construction is considered in the nominative case and often called the *nominative absolute*.

> Taking everything into consideration, the decision was just.
>
> He having gone, the party proceeded merrily on.

Abstract Noun. A noun denoting a quality, a general idea, or something that cannot be perceived by any one of the senses: affection, courage, weakness, justice. See also Common Noun.

Accusative Case. The name sometimes given to the direct object construction.

Active Voice. The construction of the verb that indicates that the subject is acting, rather than being acted upon. See page 210.

Adjective. A word used to describe, limit, or qualify a noun or pronoun. See pages 197–199, also Descriptive Adjective, Limiting Adjective.

Adjective Clause. A clause that modifies a substantive. I saw an automobile *which I liked.* See page 80.

Adverb. A word used to modify (*i.e.,* describe, limit, or qualify) a verb, an adjective, or another adverb. See page 214.

Adverbial Clause. A clause that modifies a verb, an adjective, or an adverb. See page 80.

> I will leave Boston *when my check comes.* (Modifies verb *will leave.*)
> He was older *than his brother was.* (Modifies adjective *older.*)
> We are working harder *than they are.* (Modifies adverb *harder.*)

Adverbial Noun. A noun used adverbially: He went *home.*

Agreement. A functional or formal correspondence between two parts of speech, *e.g.,* a verb and its subject agree in number, when both of them are singular or both are plural.

Antecedent. Literally, "that which goes before." It is the name given to the word or group of words to which a pronoun refers.

> While *John* was running, he slipped and fell. (*John* is the antecedent of *he*.)
>
> This is the *farm* which we saw in the distance. (*Farm* is the antecedent of *which*.)

Antonym. See page 168.

Apposition. When one substantive is in co-ordinate relation to another and denotes the same person or thing, the second noun is said to be in apposition to the first.

> Mr. Jones, the *grocer,* has sold his business. (*Grocer* is in apposition with *Mr. Jones.*)

Appositive. That which is in apposition.

Archaism. A word, expression, or construction which is still in occasional use but recognized as belonging to an older period of the language.

Article. The definite article is the word *the.* The indefinite article has the forms *a* and *an.* The articles may also be classified as adjectives.

Auxiliary Verb. The name given to the active verb of a verb phrase, since it *helps* the infinitive or participial form of the main verb. *Be, do, have, shall, will, can, may, must, ought,* and sometimes *dare* and *need* act as auxiliaries.

Case. That property of a substantive by means of which its relationship to other words in a sentence is indicated. See pages 190–192.

Citation. A quotation from literature or the spoken language employed to illustrate the meaning or use of a particular word.

Clause. A single subject-predicate sequence which may be all or part of a complete sentence. See page 80. Clauses are classified as independent and subordinate, and as substantive, adjective, and adverbial.

Cognate Object. An object (of an otherwise intransitive verb) which has the same sense as the verb. He dreamed a *dream*.

Collective Noun. The name of a group or class. See page 218.

Colloquial. Pertaining to spoken and informal rather than to written and formal language. See page 169.

Common Noun. A name which may refer in common to any one or all the members of a group of persons, places, or things: *city, dogs, newspaper,* etc. See also Proper Noun.

Comparative Degree. See pages 197, 198.

Comparison. That function of an adjective or adverb used to indicate degrees of superiority in quality, quantity, or intensity. See page 198. Usually three degrees of comparison are recognized: positive, comparative, and superlative.

Complement. The name given to that part of the sentence which completes the thought and gives meaning to the verb. See also Subjective Complement, Objective Complement, page 76.

Jane was *a good student*. (Subjective complement.)

Complex Sentence. A sentence consisting of one independent clause and one or more subordinate clauses. See page 80.

The dogs bark when a stranger comes.

Compound Sentence. A sentence consisting of two or more independent clauses joined by a co-ordinating conjunction. See pages 77, 78.

Dogs bark and cats run.

Concrete Noun. The name of a person, place, or thing that can be perceived by any one of the senses: *flower, glass, whisper, iron,* etc. See also Abstract Noun.

Conjunction. A part of speech which connects or joins words, phrases, or clauses. See pages 215, 216.

Conjunctive Adverb. An adverbial connective which may be used to link the clauses of a sentence. See page 216.

Co-ordinate. Gramatically equal, in the same rank or order, as, for example, the two independent clauses of a compound sentence.

Co-ordinating Conjunction. A conjunction used to connect grammatical elements of equal rank. See page 215, also Subordinating Conjunction.

Copula. A term sometimes applied to such verbs as *be, seem, appear,* etc., viewing their function primarily as a connecting link between subject and predicate.

Dative. The name regularly given to the indirect object case in such inflected languages as Latin and German, and occasionally used with reference to this construction in English.

Declension. The inflection of nouns, adjectives, and pronouns according to a definite sequence of their case, number, and gender forms. Example: I, my (mine), me; we, our (ours), us. To *decline* a noun, pronoun, or adjective is to give these forms in regular sequence.

Degree. That characteristic of adjectives and adverbs which is indicated by the function of comparison. The three degrees are positive, comparative, superlative. See pages 197, 198.

Demonstrative Adjective. A term sometimes applied to *this, that,* etc., when they are placed before the nouns which they modify: *this* book, *that* horse.

Demonstrative Pronoun. A pronoun which indicates or points out. See page 195.

Dependent Clause. A clause grammatically subordinate or incapable of standing alone. See page 80.

Descriptive Adjective. An adjective which modifies the noun to which it is applied by describing rather than limiting or qualifying its essential meaning: The *red* dress.

Direct Address. The name applied to the construction in which a person is addressed directly: *John,* close the door.

Direct Object. The person or thing directly affected by the action of the verb. See page 190.

Disjunctive. Expressive of disjoining (separation), as the conjunctions *either . . . or, neither . . . nor, but, although.*

Finite Verb. A simple verb, or a member of a verbal construction or verb phrase, which is governed by the subject and agrees with it in number and person. It indicates a specific action or state within definite boundaries of time, and therefore contrasts with the infinitive and the participles. In the sentence *He is going, is* is the finite verb, and *going* is a participle. To be complete, a sentence conventionally requires a finite verb. See pages 74, 75.

Function Word. A word which has little or no independent meaning of its own. It is used chiefly to indicate relations between other words. The roof *of* the house.

Future Tense. See pages 200, 201.

Genitive Case. That form of the noun which is usually written *-'s* for the singular and *-s'* for the plural, used to indicate a number of relationships among which possession is one of the most common. See pages 190–192, Case.

Gerund. A verb form ending in *-ing,* which is used as a noun. See page 211.

Imperative Mood. The form of the verb employed in giving a command.

Indefinite Pronoun. A class of pronouns indicating not one particular thing but any one or more of a class of things: *some, any, everyone.*

Independent Clause. A clause capable of standing alone, or one which makes an independent assertion. See page 80.

Indicative. The mood of the verb which indicates or states an action conceived of as fact. See page 207.

Indirect Object. The person or thing indirectly affected by the action of the verb: I gave *him* the ball. See page 191.

Infinitive. That form of the verb which consists of the *present stem*, frequently preceded by *to*, which indicates the action of the verb conceived of in a *timeless, personless sphere. To come* is an infinitive, as is just *come* in such a verb phrase as *have come*. See page 206.

Inflection. A change in the form of a word by means of which a change of meaning or a relationship to some other word or group of words is indicated. The *-s* in *dogs* and the *-ed* in *played* are inflections.

Intensive Pronoun. A pronoun which serves to intensify or to emphasize its antecedent: I saw him *myself.* See page 196.

Interjection. A part of speech expressing strong feeling or emotion and having no grammatical relationship to the rest of the sentence: *alas, ah, oh.* Other abrupt or ejaculatory words as *pst!* or *tut tut* may be included in this category.

Interrogative Pronoun. A pronoun used in asking a question. See page 195.

Intransitive Verb. A verb which by virtue of its meaning does not permit a direct object. He *goes.* See page 212.

Limiting Adjective. An adjective which modifies the noun to which it is applied by limiting rather than describing or qualifying it: *a* doll, *yonder* tree.

Mood (Mode). The construction or function of the verb that indicates how an act is conceived, whether as a fact, a possibility, a desirability, a command, etc. See pages 205–209.

Nominative. The case name for the subject of a sentence or a predicate noun. See page 192.

Nominative Absolute. See **Absolute.**

Nominative of Address. A noun used in direct address is also sometimes considered to be in the nominative case, although the grammars of some languages use the term *vocative* for this function.

Noun. A part of speech, the name of a person, place, thing, quality, collection, or action.

Number. That property of a substantive or verb which indicates whether the reference is to one or more than one. See page 189.

Object, see **Direct Object, Indirect Object.**

Objective Complement. That portion of the sentence completing the predicate by telling something about the direct object. See page 76.

We think him *a good chairman.*

Obsolete. A word or construction which belongs to an earlier period of the language and is no longer used.

Part of Speech. The grammatical classification of words according to form, function, or meaning. See pages 184–187.

Participle. Forms of the verb ending in *-ing, -ed, -en* (or indicated through internal change, e.g., *sung*), which are used in expanded constructions, as *am going, was driven,* or which may be used as adjectives: *folded* arms.

Participial Phrase. A phrase introduced by a participle. We saw the train *rounding the bend.*

Passive Voice. That construction of the verb which represents the subject as being acted upon rather than acting. See page 210.

> The ball was hit by John.

Past Perfect. That construction of the verb which represents an action as having been completed before another past action took place, in other words a *before-past* tense. See page 204.

Past Tense. That construction of the verb which is usually used to indicate an action as having taken place in the past. See page 200.

Perfect. The name given to those tenses which appear to indicate completed action as opposed to action going on or continuous. See pages 204, 205.

Periphrastic. A construction which accomplishes by means of a phrase or the use of function words what might otherwise be indicated by means of inflections.

> The roof *of the house*. (Periphrastic genitive.)
> The *boy's* hat. (Inflected genitive.)

Person. The property of a verb or pronoun which indicates whether the reference is to the speaker, the person spoken to, or a third person or thing. See pages 193, 194.

Phrase. A group of words which contains less than the minimum subject-verb sequence essential for a clause, and which acts as a grammatical unit.

> The roof *of the house*. (Prepositional phrase used as an adjective.)
> *Rowing the boat* is exercise. (Gerund phrase used as subject.)
> We *have come*. (Verb phrase.)

Plural. That classification of number which refers to more than one.

Positive Degree. See pages 197, 198.

Possessive. See **Genitive.**

Predicate. The active verb of a sentence or clause along with all the words it governs and those which modify it. See pages 73, 74.

Predicate Adjective. An adjective which appears in the predicate but which modifies the subject.

> The grass was *green*.

Predicate Complement. See **Subjective Complement.**

Predicate Noun. A noun which appears in the predicate completing the meaning of a copulative verb.

> He seems a *gentleman*.

Preposition. A preposition is a word showing the relationship of its object and some other word in the sentence. See pages 214, 215.

Prepositional Phrase. A phrase introduced by a preposition.

Present Tense. The construction of the verb which indicates action going on now, habitual, or eternal action. See pages 202–205.

Principal Clause. See **Independent Clause.**

Principal Parts. The forms of a verb from which the various tenses are derived. The principal parts are the present stem, the past tense, and the past participle: *pull, pulled, pulled; sing, sang, sung.*

Progressive. The construction of a verb which represents a specific action going on, in contrast to a habitual, an eternal, or a completed action.

> I am eating. (Present progressive.)
> I was eating. (Past progressive.)

Pronoun. A pronoun is a word used in place of a noun. See pages 193–196.

Proper Noun. The name of a particular person, place, or thing, in contrast to a common noun which merely names one or more of a general class. *Detroit, George Washington,* the *Drake Relays* are proper nouns. See also Common Noun.

Property. A characteristic quality of a part of speech or construction; that which is proper to it. Example:

Gender is one of the properties of English nouns.

Reflexive Pronoun. A pronoun which is the direct object of a verb and has as its antecedent the subject of that verb. See page 196.

He kicked *himself.*

Relative Clause. A clause introduced by a relative pronoun.

Relative Pronoun. A pronoun which is used to relate or connect the various clauses of a sentence to one another. See page 194.

Simple Sentence. A sentence containing a single independent clause.

Singular. That classification of number which refers to only one. See page 189.

Subject. The word or group of words in a sentence naming the topic about which something is said. See page 73.

Subjunctive. That function or construction of the verb which conceives of an action as contrary to fact, hypothetical, or imaginative. See pages 207–209.

Subordinating Conjunction. A conjunction used to connect a dependent or subordinate clause to an independent clause. See page 216.

Substantive. A term applied to any word or group of words used as a noun.

Superlative Degree. See pages 197, 198.

Syntax. That division of the study of grammar which deals with the relationship of the various parts of speech to one another in connected discourse or writing. See pages 216, 217.

Tense. That property of the verb which has to do with the time of action. See pages 200–205.

Transitive. A transitive verb is one which can take a direct object.

Jack *hit* the ball.

Verb. A word that indicates action, state, or being. See pages 199–213.

Vocative. See **Nominative of Address**.

Voice. The characteristic of verbs which indicates whether the subject is acting (active) or being acted upon (passive). See pages 209, 210.

PUNCTUATION AND MECHANICS

1. CONVENTION

*R*ECALL what has been said (particularly in Chapter III) about the relationship of spoken and written English. Punctuation belongs to the written language, and to the written language only. Like the written sentence, punctuation is a system of conventions—that is, of customs tacitly agreed on by the users of the language—whose function is to communicate those elements of speech which cannot conveniently be set down on paper. Pitch, stress, time, and pause are such elements. Before the words *period, colon,* and *comma* came to be applied to the various points of punctuation, they all signified a sentence or segment of a sentence, or a pause. That is to say, they began as names for rhetorical units; they implied a recognition of some of the facts of the spoken language.

Like all conventions, those of punctuation are subject to change, and have changed considerably in the course of time. At any given period, however, methods of punctuation are stable and consistent enough so that, by and large, a reader knows what a writer intends by his punctuation, and the writer can depend on a certain response from his reader. Readers have come to have a certain "visual expectancy": if the page looks very different from what they expect, their understanding of the material will be much hampered.

To illustrate this, one has only to look at the specimens of unconventional punctuation on the opposite page. The first—from the seventeenth century—will reveal at a glance

These things cōcerning the freenesse of people. The like
in effect be considered of these people which are seruile;
namely, whether they be seruiled thorow tyranny & oppres-
sion, or thorow depression & keeping vnder violently; both
sorts being subiects of misery & calamitie. Of the first sort,
we heare of the Tartariãs vnder their *Cam;* for the whole
estate of all they haue standeth at his fancie to dispose of:
the word of whose mouth serueth for a sword to reuenge
him of rebels, and yet they reioyce thereat; neither dare any
man say, This is mine, or anothers: neither can any man
dwell other-where than his Lord assigneth him.

—*An Essay of the Meanes how to Make our Travailes,
into forraine Countries, the more profitable and honourable.*
1606. pt. 2, p. 71.

Now if that is what prose is and that undoubtedly is
what prose is you can see that prose real prose really great
written prose is bound to be made up more of verbs adverbs
prepositions prepositional clauses and conjunctions than
nouns. The vocabulary in prose of course is important if
you like vocabulary is always important, in fact one of the
things that you can find out and that I experimented with
a great deal in How to Write vocabulary in itself and by
itself can be interesting and can make sense. Anybody can
know that by thinking of words. It is extraordinary how it
is impossible that a vocabulary does not make sense. But
that is natural indeed inevitable because a vocabulary is
that by definition, and so because this is so the vocabulary
in respect to prose is less important than the parts of speech,
and the internal balance and movement within a given
space.

—Gertrude Stein, *Lectures in America,* p. 230. Reprinted
by courtesy of Random House, Inc.

that the modern practice of indicating direct quotations by the use of inverted commas was not employed here, and that the colon and semicolon performed functions quite different from those assigned to them today.

The second specimen is the work of a modern author who does not employ the marks of punctuation in a conventional manner. Where the earlier selection uses at least as many punctuation points as would be found in a present-day selection of equal length, the selection from Miss Stein has fewer than the conventional number. The two are alike, however, in being consistent within themselves. More important, though they differ in appearance, they have a similar effect on the reader: as he reads, he must "translate" the punctuation he finds into terms of the punctuation conventions to which he is accustomed. Because ordinary punctuation is not observed, each selection requires a certain amount of re-reading.

That this is necessary is no advantage; in everyday writing it would be a positive disadvantage. Because of convention and the habits which it sets up, therefore, a student who seeks to be understood had better not vary to any serious extent from current practice.

2. MEANING

Although punctuation has been characterized as a convention, do not regard it lightly! It develops from the inability of written language to reproduce certain features of speech. Isolated words in and by themselves are not language; rarely do they communicate meaning. Therefore the part played by punctuation in putting certain words together, and separating these words from other combinations, is vital to communication. Just how vital may be illustrated by the following United Press story:

Slips in phraseology on the part of legislators often result in amusing statutes.

For instance, it is illegal to sleep in a North Dakota hotel. The 1929 legislature approved a law on hotel inspection. A slip in punctuation made it read like this:

"No hotel, restaurant, dining room, or kitchen shall be used as a sleeping or dressing room by an employee or other persons."

Eliminate the comma after the word *hotel* and the section makes some sense. However, judges say it would take a legislative amendment to get rid of that comma.

This is an extreme example, and the unconvinced may argue that the intent of the statute was clear in spite of the superfluous comma. Not so clear was the Michigan law which provided that "every railroad corporation shall provide a uniform, hat or cap and a distinguishing badge" for each conductor, brakeman, and other employees dealing with the public. Two English departments consulted as to the meaning of the sentence interpreted it quite differently. One maintained that the phrase "must be understood grammatically as meaning *either* a uniform *or* hat *or* cap." The other replied that "although the statement is slightly ambiguous it was intended . . . to indicate that the railroad corporation is to provide three things, viz: (1) a uniform, (2) a hat or cap, (3) and a badge." This shows how carefully punctuation must be watched if we do not want the reader to misunderstand us.

The purpose of punctuation, then, is to help make the meaning of a piece of writing clear. *If the structure and grammar are not clear and correct to begin with, punctuation cannot give this help*. But if they are clear and correct, punctuation may emphasize the fact. In other words, punctuation works hand in hand with sentence structure and may best be considered in relation to it. (See Chapter III.)

The parts of a sentence or clause are not of equal value; the basic meaning is carried by the subject-verb-object skeleton, to which are added various details and modifications. Punctuation must help to do two things: *to make the clausal unit clear* and *to make related details clear*. It is therefore treated here so as to illustrate these main functions, and is organized according to types of situation to be met. If you wish to know about punctuation in series, or the pointing of introductory phrases, you may refer directly to these topics. It will not be necessary to go through all the rules for period, colon, semicolon, and so on. The larger and more independent units, the sentence and the co-ordinate clause, are considered first, then the subordinate clauses and phrases, and finally individual words.

Punctuation marks, as used today, may be roughly grouped according to the relative degree of separation which they indicate between groups of words. In speaking, they correspond to pauses of different lengths.

Complete break	. ? !
Considerable break	: ;
Slight break	— ,

Note that the marks used in pairs to "set off" groups of words from their context also show different degrees of separation: in descending order, parentheses, dashes, and commas. They correspond not only to pauses in speech, but often to a drop in the pitch of the voice which lasts through the group of words set off. A sensitive writer uses these marks for contrastive effect, punctuating units of similar value alike and those of unequal value differently.

Note also that for some situations there is only one right punctuation, but in many others there is a choice. No writer will go far wrong if he follows the principle of *clarity without excess*. If one uses more marks than necessary the sentence will be cluttered and broken up, and any lightness or fluency which one may be seeking will be lost. Contrariwise, if one does not make necessary divisions and groupings in the thought, relationships in meaning will not be clear. The student must seek to strike an intelligent balance.

3. SENTENCE OR END PUNCTUATION

(See pages 84, 85, also.)

A. The Complete Sentence. The conventional form for the complete sentence is:

C(apital letter) ———(.) (?) (!)

1. **The ordinary declarative or imperative sentence is punctuated with a period.**

The sun came up bright and early.
Bring me the book that is on the table.

2. **The direct question requires the question mark.**

Is it cold outside?

3. **A sentence declarative in form but interrogative in purpose requires the question mark.**

The baby is awake?

In this case the question mark is really a device for indicating voice pitch. Compare.

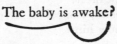

and

The baby is awake.

4. **The indirect question is pointed with a period.**

I asked them why they had come.

For the punctuation of a declarative sentence ending with a directly quoted question, see section P 12, p. 308, in this chapter.

5. In sentences part declarative and part interrogative, the nature of the final clause determines whether a period or a quesion mark is to be used.

At Timothy's it was whispered sadly that poor Roger had always been eccentric about his digestion—had he not, for instance, preferred German mutton to all the other brands? —Galsworthy, *Forsyte Saga*.

And could he relish just a little pot of their very best prune preserve—it was so delicious this year, and had such a wonderful effect. —Galsworthy, *Forsyte Saga*.

6. "Courtesy" questions, of the type which frequently appear in business letters, are usually ended with a period rather than a question mark, although the question mark is sometimes used.

> Will you please send me three boxes of your bond paper.

7. A declarative or imperative sentence expressing particularly strong feeling is punctuated with an exclamation point.

> I will not do it!
> Come here at once!
> Do I know him!

Notice that in the last sentence the exclamation point suggests a wholly different stress and pitch pattern than would be indicated by the question mark.

Do I know him! Do I′ know′ him

Do I know him? Do I′ know him   Do I know′ him

There are sentences which are both exclamatory and interrogative in which the writer may emphasize either aspect.

> What was that odious word!
> What was that odious word?
> Do you think I did that on purpose (?) (!)

8. For a discussion of how much material should be included in a complete sentence, see Chapter III, pages 84–90. **Be careful not to include *more* than one complete sentence within the space between a single capital letter and period** (or other end-punctuation mark).

WRONG: But it was the ride home that counted it began with the usual shouts of leave-taking and confusion of seating arrangements.

RIGHT: But it was the ride home that counted. It began with the usual shouts of leave-taking and confusion of seating arrangements.

B. The Incomplete Sentence.

1. **The conventional symbol for marking a sentence as incomplete is the dash.**

> He has only to understand——

2. **Sometimes suspension periods are used for the same purpose.**

> In southwest Africa we found millions . . .

4. COMPOUNDING PUNCTUATION; CO-ORDINATE CLAUSES

A compound sentence is one which consists of two or more independent clauses. (These may or may not be joined by a co-ordinating conjunction; see Chapter III.)

A. Co-ordinate Clauses with *Grammatical* Connective *(and, but, or, nor, neither)*.

1. The most frequent pattern in this construction is: C(apital letter) _____, gram. conn. _____. The comma shows the end of the first clause and emphasizes the conjunction. Because co-ordinate clauses are on about the same level, and because the conjunction connects them rather closely, this construction normally calls for punctuation no stronger than a comma.

Probably Mr. Thrale never completely recovered from these events, and perhaps it is because he is best known from accounts subsequent to this time that he generally appears so silent and morose a man.
—Krutch, *Samuel Johnson*.

2. This pattern may be varied if the clauses are particularly short, are much punctuated internally, or if the meaning demands it, as follows:

   a. Short clauses connected with *and* are left unpunctuated by many writers and publishers, especially when the omission of the comma does not hinder comprehension.

He had a job now and he might get something better.
—Dreiser, *American Tragedy*.

Her glasses had slipped towards the end of her small nose and her hair had escaped from the tight hat she was wearing over her ears.   —Herrick, *Chimes*.

The omission of the comma suggests a close relationship in idea between the members of the compound sentence. Omit the comma before *and* only when such a close relationship exists. The conjunction *but* is almost always preceded by some mark of punctuation which serves to emphasize the contrast in meaning between the two clauses.

We often read of wonderful manifestations of memory, but they are always instances of the faculty working in some special direction. —Aldrich, *Ponkapog Papers.*

> *b.* **When the clauses of a compound sentence are long and contain much internal punctuation, a semicolon is used by way of contrast to separate the clauses.**

For example, to understand any prophet thoroughly, we ought to know the life, character, and pursuits of that prophet, under what circumstances his book was composed, and in what state and through what hands it has come down to us; and, in general, most of this we cannot now know. —Arnold, *Essays in Criticism.*

> *c.* **When the clauses to be connected are relatively short, a semicolon is sometimes necessary to make the meaning clear or to secure the proper emphasis or sense of separation.**

He heard the rapid murmur of their talk; but what they said, he could not catch.

Here he could find his way blindfold; and freed from the strain of geographical uncertainty, his mind returned to Bosinney's trouble. —Galsworthy, *Forsyte Saga.*

> *d.* **Sometimes, to emphasize a contrast, the dash may be used before** *but:*

> > Wagner changed the face of opera, it is true— but in the Latin lands he never changed its heart.

3. **Do not confuse a compound *sentence* with a compound *predicate*.** A compound predicate does not require connective punctuation, although it is sometimes employed

for clarity when the predicate is long or complicated in structure. Compare example *c* with *a* and *b*.

- *a.* He is one who had no youth or has no memory.
- *b.* We have taken the urbanite away from his fireside and convinced him that winter sports are designed for him.
- *c.* She appeared trim and brisk and yet nervous, and gazed at the street end and looked about like a frightened animal.

B. Co-ordinate Clauses with *Logical* Connective.

By *logical* connectives, as opposed to *grammatical* connectives, are meant such conjunctive adverbs as *so, therefore, hence, however, then, yet, moreover, thus, accordingly, nevertheless, besides, otherwise, still, likewise, also.* Although these connectives do not reduce one clause to a grammatically subordinate position, they do emphasize a meaningful relationship of some kind (causal, temporal, spatial, etc.) between the clauses which they join. See also Chapter VI, p. 216.

1. **The prevalent pattern in this construction is:**

C(apital letter) _____; logical conn. _____.

Because the connective here is relatively less simple than the grammatical connective, the division between clauses needs to be more emphasized; wherfore punctuation stronger than a comma is usually necessary.

He hid; *otherwise* I should have seen him.

I have every belief that the statement was made in utmost sincerity; *still* the question is pertinent.

No man will take counsel, but everybody will take money; *therefore* money is better than counsel.

—Swift.

A hard little thing underneath; *yet* with her moments, when she gazed on beauty, of an almost burning softness.
—Glasgow, *The Romantic Comedians.*

2. **Clauses introduced by the logical connectives** *so, then,* **and** *yet* **are frequently divided from the preceding clause only by a comma.**

She was never out of disgrace, *so* it did not matter to her how she sat.
—Galsworthy, *Forsyte Saga.*

There was no one here, *so* I went away.
—Curme, *Syntax,* p. 168.

It had been snowing, *then* it began to rain.
—*Current English Usage,* p. 18.

The annuity was regularly paid up to 1878, *then* Mr. Harle got into difficulties.
—*Oxford Dictionary* citation, 1895.

The fate of Alsace-Lorraine is properly an international and hence world question, *yet* after all what convinced President Wilson of Teutonic insincerity was less Germany's dubious proposals about the lost provinces than her open and flagrantly predatory and cynical treatment of the Ukraine, Rumania, and the Soviet.
—*Dial,* June 6, 1918, quoted in Summey,
Modern Punctuation.

Use of the comma rather than the semicolon with these three logical connectives is largely the result of newspaper and magazine practice. Of more than a dozen newspaper style books examined, only one recommended the semicolon. Sentence rhythm probably also has its effect, since these connectives, like *and, but,* etc., are monosyllables and make a less definite break than *however, accordingly,* etc.

Clauses beginning with *so, then,* and *yet* should be punctuated according to the closeness of relationship and the length of pause one would normally assign to the break between the two clauses, and the amount of internal punctuation contained within the clauses. Note the difference between the following:

One could understand it and enjoy it; so it became the favorite thing at popular festivals, as well as at the Christmas entertainments in the great hall.

—W. P. Ker, *English Literature.*

There was now no reason why he should not take it with him, so he put it in his pocket.

—S. Butler, *Erewhon Revisited.*

Recall the warning that has been given about the overuse of *so* as a connective. See Chapter IX, Glossary. A sentence which uses *so* preceded by a comma is sometimes weak because *so* is not the best connective for the purpose, or because such a construction does not throw enough emphasis upon the principal clause. Note the difference in emphasis and relationship suggested by:

LOOSE: This problem is insoluble, so let us ignore it.

COMPACT: As this problem is insoluble, we may ignore it.

COMPACT: This problem, being insoluble, may be ignored.

In any case, *so* has a conversational flavor; therefore if you are trying to be formal, use some other word by preference.

C. Co-ordinate Clauses *Without* Connective.

1. When no connective is employed the prevalent pattern is:

C(apital letter) ————; ————.

Nothing could induce him to leave her; nothing could persuade him to go home alone.

He was the first ambassador of any country to be presented to Stalin; he taught a Red army regiment to play polo, taught factory workers to play baseball.
—Janet Flanner, in *New Yorker*, Dec. 17, 1938.

Let us descend into the house; I want to introduce my wife and daughter to you.
—Bellamy, *Looking Backward*.

2. **Sometimes, however, less of a separation than that made by a semicolon seems desirable:** (*a*) **when the coordinate clauses without a connective are very brief,** (*b*) **when they contain little or no internal punctuation,** (*c*) **when they are closely related in idea and seem to form parts of series. In such cases the comma may be used as a mark of separation.**

There are so many of them, they have lots of company, and good company, too, great and small, rich and poor.
—New York *Times*.

Who was she, what was she, did she exist?
—Galsworthy, *Forsyte Saga*.

He touched it with his finger, he wanted to see its eyes. They opened, they were dark—whether blue or brown he could not tell. The eyes winked, stared, they had a sort of sleepy depth in them.
—Galsworthy, *Forsyte Saga*.

The comma splice, as this construction is called, has been discussed at some length in Chapter III, pages 89–91. Be very careful in its use. Some instructors will not permit it under any circumstances—a justifiable attitude, since approximately one-fifth of all errors in punctuation are comma splices that are difficult or impossible to justify. When used with skill, the comma splice can become a convenient and useful device. In narrative writing, for example, where connections need to be less formally logical than in expository writing, this construction can be made to give rapidity and fluency.

3. **When the first clause of a compound sentence serves as an introduction to the second, a colon is frequently used to separate them.**

They got scared of Harris: he carried them too fast.
—Herrick, *Chimes*.

Some things we can, and others we cannot do: we can walk, but we cannot fly.

EXERCISE 1.   1. Observe in the following passage the division into sentences and point out those which might have been combined or compounded and those compound sentences which might have been separated. Give reasons, whenever possible, for the practice which the author did follow.

He wrote operas; and no sooner did he have the synopsis of a story, but he would invite—or rather summon— a crowd of his friends to his house and read it aloud to them. Not for criticism. For applause. When the complete poem was written, the friends had to come again, and hear *that* read aloud. Then he would publish the poem, sometimes years before the music that went with it was written. He played the piano like a composer, in the worst sense of what that implies, and he would sit down at the piano before parties that included some of the finest pianists of his time, and play for them, by the hour, his own music, needless to say. He had a composer's voice. And he would invite eminent vocalists to his house, and sing them his operas, taking all the parts.
—Deems Taylor, *Of Men and Music*.[1]

[1] Reprinted by permission of Simon & Schuster.

2. Punctuate the following passage in the most appropriate and consistent fashion.

perhaps he is right I too have observed like the old policeman that the students are not so frivolous as they used to be but I am not convinced that the new seriousness is meritorious in itself why should it be it is not so important to be serious as it is to be serious about important things the monkey wears an expression of seriousness that would do credit to any college student but the monkey is serious because he itches the war which is credited with having brought on the new seriousness in the colleges merely intensified the conviction of students that it is important to make money the new seriousness is a seriousness about the financial future of the individual reflected in his determination to get some kind of training that will guarantee him what he calls security

3. Although punctuation out of context is frequently meaningless, the following sentences illustrate some errors in student papers. Repunctuate the following sentences according to the conventions and the exceptions given.

1. But look at countries which have submitted to this philosophy in none of them will you find eliminated that hatred which is based on racial prejudice.

2. When I asked him why he did not move to a better location where his efforts would be rewarded. He instantly defended his old farmland.

3. But after all the superstitions are considered; life seems to continue without much regard for them.

4. The boys got on the train and the bus came along just then.

5. Have they not the right to run their own factories without interference.

6. A line was formed and butter tubs were thrown from one to another and the last man placed them on a warehouse floor-truck.

7. We all saw the suffering that went on during the depression, it may not have gone into our own homes but it did come close to most of us.

8. The constitutional rights of the individual are the most vital parts of a government for the majority must rule.

9. It isn't what you learn in college that matters, it's the people you meet and the pleasures you enjoy.

10. Take me for example my train arrived this morning at 8:30 after a thirteen hour trip from New York.

11. The purpose in mind today is basically the same but the outcome is probably somewhat different.

12. It is not possible for one's ideas to be completely correct, thus it is better to listen to all ideas, pick out the aspects of each which are true, and form a new and more accurate opinion.

13. Then the meetings would not be as unproductive as at present and the advisers would become something more than mere rubber stamps for the purpose of approving elections.

14. The belief in God is still prevalent in the hearts of men, it may be buried deep under other ideas but nevertheless it is still there.

15. It may be true that those ideals do not move us easily or do not move us far yet I believe that there is scarcely a person who does not have some reaction when his native land is insulted.

5. INTRODUCTORY MATERIAL

A. Subordinate Clauses (See the Complex Sentence, Chapter III, p. 80).

1. **The normal pattern for subordinate clause preceding its main clause is:**

C(apital letter) sub. cl. ——, main cl.[1] ——.

As the time drew near for their parting, Jessica relaxed somewhat her impersonal discipline.

Almost as soon as he entered office, when the Commerce Department still basked in the glory that Herbert Hoover as Secretary and President had left it with, Mr. Roper made a grand gesture to business by establishing his Business Advisory and Planning Council.

What *Main Street* did for the small town, *Babbitt* did for the metropolis and for its typical hero.

2. **An introductory noun clause followed immediately by its verb need not be set off by a comma.** It is not a good policy to place punctuation points between subject and predicate, since it risks destroying an essential relationship.

What the tourist enjoys most is the unusual scenery.

B. Phrases.

1. **The best plan is to punctuate introductory phrases sparingly; but always punctuate them where you need to make the beginning of the main clause clear, or where ambiguity or misunderstanding would result from lack of punctuation.**

Keep in mind the number of commas and other points which the sentence demands, and also the closeness of

[1] In actual practice, particularly in newspaper writing, *short* introductory clauses are frequently not punctuated.

When they can afford to invest in a few new sheep and goats they come to the open-air trading place at the head of Bethlehem steps.   *—New York Times.*

When I laughed at him he struck me.
     —Chicago *Tribune Rules of Composition.*

connection that you wish to suggest between the phrase and whatever it modifies.

In the first of the examples below, the phrase "the following day" would seem to belong with "promise," rather than with "returned," if there were no comma. (Another way to make the sentence unambiguous would be to place this phrase after "returned" or at the end of the sentence.)

Phrases with Punctuation

True to her promise, the following day Hortense returned to Mr. Rubenstein.

To succeed in business, you must advertise.

In those early days, after it became a custom for each family to prepare its own Christmas potion, the quality of the drink depended upon the wealth of the host.

On the floor, perennially flirtatious and recklessly nimble, he seldom failed to remark several agile septuagenarians, whom he had known as dashing blades when he was a boy.

Phrases without Punctuation

About six miles beyond Belleville the car came to a bend in the hollow where there was a country store.

In the same way an individual noun may turn into a collective.

With better management it will not fail again.

In preparing the wassail of England a great wooden bowl containing cider, beer or wine as a base was placed on the hearth and above it apples were suspended on strings.

Within each one of these forts the strictest organization of industry was insisted on.

Since the first report we have heard nothing.

2. An absolute phrase at the beginning of a sentence is usually followed by a comma:

In the nature of things, the tone of a royal borough is one of leisure, stateliness and a perfect sense of form.

As to publicity, the fat was in the fire.

On the other hand, facts must be faced.

The first package being exhausted, we had to open the second.

3. Certain types of introductory words are frequently followed by a comma:

a. Vocatives.
Sister Falconer, I want to congratulate you on your wonderful meetings.
b. Interjections intended to be only mildly exclamatory.
Oh, he's a pretty bright fellow.
c. Expletives such as *indeed, surely, certainly, moreover, furthermore, why,* and *yes* and *no.*
Indeed, I should be pleased to go.
Well, it's rather complicated.
No, you haven't the answer yet.

In the use of introductory words, develop a feeling for their connection with the rest of the sentence. *Yes* and *no* may be followed by end punctuation if a marked pause is intended.

I don't know. Yes, I guess I do.
Yes. I will.

Words such as *certainly, now,* etc., should not be punctuated at all if they are considered as having adverbial force. Notice how the difference in grammatical function is indicated by the punctuation in the two following sentences:

　　Introductory *now*:　Now, go and sin no more.
　　　Adverbial *now*:　Now go, and sin no more.

C. Formal Introductory Situations.

1. **After introductory clauses and phrases of a somewhat formal or extended nature, the colon is used.**

He had worked out a satisfying parable: The literalist, said he, asserts that a flag is something holy, something to die for, not symbolically but in itself. The infidel, at the other end of the scale, maintains that a flag is a strip of wool or silk or cotton with rather unesthetic marks printed on it, and of considerably less use, therefore of less holiness and less romance, than a shirt or a blanket. But to the unprejudiced thinker, like himself, it was a symbol, sacred only by suggestion but not the less sacred.
　　　　　　　　　　　　—Lewis, *Elmer Gantry*.

Tell me: What really did happen to you?

It's a question of a car: will it be six or eight cylinders?

Note that there is no consistent practice regarding capitalization after the colon. To capitalize is more conservative. See also page 312 in this chapter.

2. *Such as, especially* **and similar introductory words are usually preceded by a comma when they introduce a short series of illustrations, and by a dash or a colon when they introduce a long series, or a series of long illustrations.**

He had the opportunity to hear a number of operas, such as *Rigoletto, Il Trovatore,* and *Siegfried*.

The student is expected to familiarize himself with as many of the aspects of Modern English as possible: such as the sounds of the language and manner of their formation, the sources of the present-day vocabulary, the most active inflectional patterns, and the pertinent facts of English syntax.

3. **The introductory words** *namely, thus, for example,* **and** *that is* **may be preceded by a comma, a dash, a colon, or a period.** When preceded by a comma, no punctuation should follow. When preceded by a dash or colon, a comma may follow. When preceded by a dash or period, a colon may follow.

———————, namely

————————— — namely,

————————— — namely:

———————: namely,

———————. Namely:

4. **The salutation of a letter** *Dear Sir* or *Dear Madam* **is frequently followed by a colon although there is a tendency toward the use of the comma, especially in somewhat informal correspondence.**

6. PARENTHETICAL MATERIAL WITHIN THE SENTENCE

In many sentences it is desirable to insert clauses, phrases or words not essential to the basic structure, and therefore called "parenthetical." Following the general principle already observed, such material may be punctuated in various ways, or left unpunctuated, according to the degree of the break in the thought. The reader's eye is thus aided to recognize an insertion, and he is prepared for its extraneousness to the main thought.

A. Clauses.

1. **Parenthetical clauses within the sentence are set off by commas.**

But bodily health and vigor, it may be said, are not to be classed with wealth and population as mere machinery.
—Arnold, *Culture and Anarchy*.

Germany has already obtained excellent results and is destined, we may depend upon it, however her ineffectiveness may at times make us cry out, to an immense development.

Progress, he said, had come not so much from the enactment of new laws as by the repeal of earlier laws.

2. **A non-restrictive clause should be set off by commas; a restrictive clause should not be set off by commas.** The terms *restrictive* and *non-restrictive* are applied to relative clauses. (The terms *essential* and *non-essential* are also used.) The restrictive clause is one which could not be lifted out of the context without destroying the basic idea of the sentence, whereas a non-restrictive clause could be eliminated and the basic meaning would be the same; hence, it is in a sense parenthetical.

RESTRICTIVE: Our visitor who came yesterday was from the East.

The lack of punctuation here implies that *who came yesterday* is restrictive in its application; that is to say, of a number of visitors we may have had during the past week, we are talking of the one who came yesterday. Or to put it the other way, since the clause and punctuation do show restriction, the implication is that there have been other visitors.

NON-RESTRICTIVE: Our visitor, who came yesterday, had little to say.

With the parenthetical type of punctuation here we now understand that there was only one visitor; the purpose of the clause modifier is not to restrict the meaning of *visitor,* but merely to add a bit of information about him.

NON-RESTRICTIVE: Ann Hathaway's cottage, which we visited, was not at all as I had imagined it.

In one leap, which caused the tiny open boat to quiver like a leaf, he had reached her.

RESTRICTIVE: The belief that atoms are miniature universes is at times questioned.

Mr. Roebuck will have a poor opinion of an adversary who replies to his defiant songs of triumph only by murmuring under his breath.

Men who are intemperate are destructive members of a community.

One of the chief kinds of over-punctuation results from setting off a restrictive modifier, and thus separating an essential element. Students should be careful not to produce such statements as, "All men, who commit murder, should be hanged"—which makes a rather broad charge and calls for a pretty drastic disposal of the adult male population.

Note that these modifiers are not only in the form of *clauses. Phrases* and *words* performing the same function are treated below.

B. Phrases and Words.

1. **Phrases within the sentence are set off by commas when they are absolute or when non-restrictive.**

NON-RESTRICTIVE PHRASES: Letters were folded and sealed, and the postage fees, *collected either from sender or receiver,* were based upon the number of pages.

The trade agreement with Rumania, *being one-sided,* is a case in point.

ABSOLUTE PHRASE: Unquestionably, the advantage which the people of Puerto Rico value most highly, *as a consequence of their being a part of the United States,* is their American citizenship and all that goes with it.

When one looks, *for example,* at the situation in this country, one wonders if, *after all,* we are able to boast.

June, *in the fulness of her heart,* had told Mrs. Small, giving her leave only to tell Aunt Ann.

I did not, *of course,* delude myself that all, *or even many,* of the bad laws I picked out for attention would disappear.

2. Commas are seldom used to set off *also, indeed, nevertheless, likewise, perhaps* **and other parenthetical words; but** *however, moreover,* **and** *furthermore* **are frequently punctuated when they occur as parenthetical expressions within a sentence.**

You will *perhaps* recall that I discussed this matter at some length in my letter of March 14, 1948.

These acts, *however,* were found to be unsatisfactory and ineffectual.

3. A noun used in direct address is set off by commas.

Come, *Mary,* let us go at once.

In conclusion, *Mr. Speaker,* permit me to acknowledge my deep appreciation of your confidence in designating me to serve on this committee.

4. Non-restrictive appositives (that is, those appositives which do not distinguish their principals from other persons or things called by the same name) are usually sepa-

rated by commas. **Restrictive appositives are not set off by commas.**

NON-RESTRICTIVE: Bryant, *the distinguished New England poet,* was a newspaper editor.

RESTRICTIVE: The poet *Bryant* was a newspaper editor.

NON-RESTRICTIVE: In a series of illustrated articles supplied by Ezra Gulick, *the young hustler,* local pride and patriotism were appealed to tactfully.

RESTRICTIVE: The historian *Buckle* emphasized this distinction in his history of civilization.

C. Other Marks of Punctuation to Indicate Parenthetic Material.

Dashes, parentheses, and brackets are also used.

1. **The strongest of these marks are the brackets, which are used chiefly to indicate editorial explanation, especially in quoted matter.**

The time covered is from March to July, 1947. The chief topic of interest is her [Señora Perón's] visit to her husband's political godfather, El Caudillo [General Franco].

2. *a.* **Dashes are generally employed to indicate a more violent interruption of the normal train of thought than would be shown by commas.**

I shall elsewhere, perhaps, be able some day to find an opportunity; but indeed, it is not in my nature—some of my critics would rather say, not in my power—to dispute on behalf of any opinion, even my own, very obstinately.
　　　　　　　　　　　—Arnold, *Culture and Anarchy.*

　　b. **If the parenthetic element already has commas internally, it may be set off with dashes to contrast with the commas.**

Believing that all literature and all education are only useful so far as they tend to confirm this calm, beneficent, and therefore kingly, power—first, over ourselves, and, through ourselves, over all around us—I am now going to ask you to consider with me further, what special portion or kind of this royal authority, arising out of noble education, may rightly be possessed by women.

—Ruskin, *Sesame and Lilies.*

3. **Parentheses are used within the sentence chiefly to enclose brief explanatory items.**

The Speaker then recognized Representative Jones (Illinois).

At the time the book was published (1864) it did not have a ready market.

> *a.* **The question mark enclosed in parentheses is a conventional way of indicating doubt or uncertainty.**

The poem was composed in 1453(?).

> *b.* **The use of the parenthetic question mark as a label for irony or humor is not in good taste and should be avoided.** Use of this question mark implies that your reader will not catch the ironic intent without it. This means that your irony is not clear enough, or not broad enough. In either case, it would be better to rewrite than to punctuate thus.

Avoid: Altogether it was a splendid (?) sight.

7. SUBORDINATE MATERIAL IN FINAL POSITION

There is no essential difference between "after-thought" material and material inserted within the sentence, except that the former is often looser or less formal than the latter. It is merely a parenthetical interpolation tacked on at the end instead of being inserted in the middle.

A. The same practices that determine punctuation of parenthetical material within the sentence apply to punctuation of material at the end.

RESTRICTIVE CLAUSE, NO PUNCTUATION: We all admired the fighting spirit which the opposing team showed.

NON-RESTRICTIVE CLAUSE: The natives labored with a surprising zeal, which effectually aroused our generosity.

PARENTHETIC OR EXPLANATORY CLAUSE: Don't you think you would be more helpless abroad, in case he followed?

PARTICIPIAL PHRASE: But worry he did, walking toward the park.

ADVERBIAL PHRASE: My dear boy, that is a surprise, after all these years.

VOCATIVE: How do you like him, Father?

APPOSITIVE: Quaintly equipped with a black silk umbrella and a pith helmet, he was resting beside a prostrate column when two other travelers approached the lonely temple, a man and a woman.

MORE ABRUPT BREAK—PUNCTUATED WITH A DASH: He smiled at the extraordinarily fine dish which had been set before him—Josephine certainly had a good cook.

EXPLETIVE: She wanted time to think it over, no doubt.

Note that in a sentence where the final expletive is in the form of a clause, there is also the possibility of punctuating with a semicolon, as in clauses without a compounding connective.

> I dislike crowds; don't you?

> I dislike crowds, don't you?

The punctuation here should be chosen to indicate the closeness of the relationship between the two clauses.

Adverbial clauses, particularly those introduced by *though* and *although,* often make stronger sentences if they are *not* put in final position. Compare:

    a. Aluminum alloys are winning wider acceptance today, *although structural steel has been in successful use for over thirty years.*

    b. *Although structural steel has been in successful use for over thirty years,* aluminum alloys are winning wider acceptance today.

    c. *Although aluminum alloys are winning wider acceptance today,* structural steel has been in successful use for over thirty years.

Here, *a* is comparatively weak; *b* and *c* are stronger, each emphasizing a different thing.

B. At times it is necessary to separate a final statement from the rest of the sentence, that an ambiguous reading will not result.

Note the difference between the following:

We found that the average yearly cost of maintaining a car in New York was $250 more than in any other state in the Union.

We found that the average yearly cost of maintaining a car in New York was $250, more than in any other state in the Union.

EXERCISE 2. 1. The following passage has been copied sentence for sentence, but all punctuation within the sentence has been omitted. Punctuate it as you think it should read.

But epochs of concentration cannot well endure forever epochs of expansion in the due course of things follow them. Such an epoch of expansion seems to be opening in this country. In the first place all danger of a hostile forcible pressure of foreign ideas upon our practice has long disappeared like the traveller in the fable therefore we begin to wear our cloak a little more loosely. Then with a long peace the ideas of Europe steal gradually and amicably in and mingle though in infinitesimally small quantities at a time with our own notions. Then too in spite of all that is said about the absorbing and brutalizing influence of our passionate material progress it seems to me indisputable that this progress is likely though not certain to lead in the end to an apparition of intellectual life and that man after he has made himself perfectly comfortable and has now to determine what to do with himself next may begin to remember that he has a mind and that the mind may be made the source of great pleasure.

—Matthew Arnold.

2. Revise, wherever necessary, the punctuation of the following:

1. Because he hasn't any menacing prejudices to hinder his thinking he can create something worth while from many of his ideas.
2. Later, her parents died and she came back to Springfield where she is now going to school.
3. For instance he might have ideas about what a strange world this is.
4. He has a very fine education as is quite apparent but for some unexplainable reason most of his learning has gone for naught.

5. The Dewey of today as compared to the Dewey of ten years ago, is a changed man.

6. All members of the legislative body are party members which means that a large portion of the Russian people are unrepresented.

7. Because of my experience and that of other students I believe that the present system should be radically changed.

8. How different real college life at Michigan or any other institution of higher learning is from movie college life.

9. The real reasons are those that dyed in the wool conservatives cannot or do not attempt to find.

10. This organization which he called the C.I.O., had caused many disputes.

11. The privately owned business enterprises would have to be consolidated thereby eliminating competition.

12. Modern faces peer out through old wigs and costumes giving the effect of a Halloween party instead of a serious drama.

13. In fact I believe that ambition and success go hand in hand.

14. This type of work, where a man is on his own initiative and uses his own ideas to carry out his experiments is what I hope to make my life's occupation.

15. While free schools are open to all the average person rarely has an education equivalent to that of the eighth grade.

16. I obtained the following estimate, that in the same year forty-seven percent of all those gainfully employed, with the exception of farmers or nearly one-half the working population in the cities earned less than $1,000 a year.

17. There are ninety-two of these elements each different from the other.
18. When their market drops the producers immediately slash wages and reduce prices.
19. The cause of, and a direct cure for the common cold is not yet known.
20. However one should not believe everything he hears as most of it may be untrue.

8. ITEMS IN SERIES

The general pattern for items in series is separation by commas:

1   2   3

————————, ————————, ————————

Note that there is no pointing before the first item or after the last.

WORDS IN SERIES: The day was dull, dark, soundless.

PHRASES IN SERIES: Wood on the fire, meal in the barrel, flour in the tubs, money in the purse, credits in the country all come as a result of temperance.

Variations are made in this pattern when the items are longer or more complicated, or when a conjunction is used between the last two items. If heavier punctuation than the comma becomes necessary, the semicolon is usually used.

A. Clauses in Series.

1. Independent clauses in series without a final connecting conjunction are usually separated by semicolons, except for those situations which are discussed on page 279. When there is internal punctuation within the clauses, the semicolon is an absolute necessity.

The number of students will be reduced; the number of teachers will be increased; several new buildings are to be erected.

2. **Independent clauses in series with a conjunction connecting the last two members are punctuated with a comma after each clause except the last.** A comma is almost always necessary before the conjunction when the members of the series are clauses.

The number of students will be reduced, the number of teachers will be increased, and several new buildings are to be erected.

3. **Subordinate clauses in series are separated by commas when they are short, light, and without internal punctuation.** Otherwise they are punctuated with semicolons.

We were informed that the convention had been held in the East last year, that it was to be in the West this year, and that next year it would be held in the South.

I am now trying to demonstrate just exactly in what particulars it was false; that instead of these men being peaceful citizens, honest working men, they were not; that they were men who were acting in violation of the law; that they were defying the law and the officers who were trying to enforce the law.

B. Words and Phrases.

1. **Two or more words modifying the same word should be separated by commas when they are co-ordinate in thought.**

CO-ORDINATE: It was a solemn, impressive ceremony.

They grew gigantic, full, deep, double flowers.

NOT CO-ORDINATE: It has been based upon sound fundamental principles.

Then there is our peculiar American
political party scheme.

Caution: In either case, do not place a comma after the
last member of the series.

a. **The comma is generally used to separate attributive words repeated for emphasis.**

It was a dark, dark sky.

For special emphasis the dash is used.

The times were hard—very hard.

2. **When there are three or more words or phrases in
series with the conjunction *and* between the last two, a
comma need not precede the conjunction unless clarity
demands it.**

NECESSARY FOR CLARITY: We had coffee, fruit, and ham
and eggs.

In situations of this type the comma before the first
and is required to show that *ham and eggs* constitutes a
single item in the series.

NOT NECESSARY FOR CLARITY: The beasts were two lions,
a hart and an ibex.

—*Cambridge History of English Literature.*

In situations like the foregoing there is a wide divergence
of practice. In general, newspapers with their tendency
toward light or open punctuation omit the comma before
and. The style book of the Grand Rapids *Press,* for example, advises its reporters, "Do not use a comma before *and*
in a list: Red, white and blue." Books and magazines show
a stronger tendency toward retention of the comma. What-

ever style of series punctuation you adopt, follow it consistently within the limits of a single paper. Phrases, especially when they are long, are more frequently punctuated
with the comma before the conjunction.

The spectators came on foot, by motor, many by rail,
and some by airplane.

Sea on sea, country on country, millions on millions of
people, all with their own lives, energies, joys, griefs, and
suffering.

9. CONTRASTED ELEMENTS

**The comma often is used to heighten the contrast
of co-ordinate sentence elements, especially when
they are long.**

I speak as a man of experience, not as a theorist.

He too looked like a warrior, unlike the stern-faced
man in bronze above him.

10. BREAKS IN THOUGHT

**A. A dash is used to indicate that the train of
thought is abruptly changed or broken off.**

She would continue to gather minute data, tabulate,
annotate, classify—at present she was occupied with organic compounds.

**B. A dash is used before a repetition or a modi-
fication which has the effect of an afterthought.**

What a faith—in something!

It was cold—bitter cold.

SUMMARY ACCORDING TO USE

I. Period.
   A. End of complete declarative or imperative sentence. P. 271.
   B. End of indirect question. P. 271.
   C. After abbreviations. P. 314.

II. Colon.
   A. In separate clauses of a compound sentence when the first introduces the second. P. 280.
   B. After introductory clauses and phrases followed by an enumeration. P. 286.

III. Semicolon.
   A. In separate long clauses of a compound sentence. P. 275.
   B. Between co-ordinate clauses with logical connective. P. 276.
   C. To separate co-ordinate clauses without connectives. P. 278.
   D. To separate long items in series. P. 297.

IV. Comma.
   A. Between co-ordinate clauses with grammatical connective. P. 274.
   B. Between co-ordinate clauses with certain logical connectives. P. 277.
   C. Occasionally to separate brief co-ordinate clauses without connectives. P. 279.
   D. To set off a subordinate clause at the beginning of a sentence. P. 283.
   E. To separate some introductory phrases from the rest of the sentence. P. 283.
   F. To set off introductory vocatives, interjections, and expletives. P. 285.

EXERCISE 3. 1. Punctuate the following passages in whatever way seems to you to carry out the intention of the author most effectively.

SUMMARY ACCORDING TO USE

[A] His occupying the chair of state was a triumph of the good sense of mankind and of the public conscience. This middle-class country had got a middle-class President at last. Yes in manner and sympathies but not in powers for his powers were superior. This man grew according to the need. His mind mastered the problem of the day and as the problem grew so did his comprehension of it. Rarely was man so fitted to the event. In the midst of fears and jealousies in the Babel of counsels and parties this man wrought incessantly with all his might and all his honesty laboring to find what the people wanted and how to obtain that. It cannot be said there is any exaggeration of his worth. If ever a man was fairly tested he was. There was no lack of resistance nor of slander nor of ridicule. The times have allowed no state secrets the nation has been in such ferment such multitudes had to be trusted that no secret could be kept. Every door was ajar and we know all that befell.

[B] It is well for me that I cannot hear music when I will assuredly I should not have such intense pleasure as comes to me now and then by haphazard. As I walked on forgetting all about the distance and reaching home before I knew I was halfway there I felt gratitude to my unknown benefactor a state of mind I have often experienced in the days long gone by. It happened at times not in my barest days but in those of decent poverty—that someone in the house where I lodged played the piano and how it rejoiced me when this came to pass! I say played the piano a phrase that covers much. For my own part I was very tolerant anything that could by the largest interpretation be called music I welcomed and was thankful for even five-finger exercises I found at moments better than nothing. For it was when I was laboring at my desk that the notes of the instrument were grateful and helpful to me. Some men I believe would have been driven frantic under the circumstances to me anything like a musical sound always came as a godsend it tuned my thoughts it made the words flow. Even the street organs put me in a happy mood; I owe many a page to them written when I should else have been sunk in bilious gloom.

[C] But oh what a difference in the morning! He awakes in the dark startled perhaps from some pleasant dream by the wild alarm-m-m-m of a clock under his pillow and outside the snug island of warmth on which he lies the Universe stretches away in every direction above below and on every side of him cold dreary and unfit for human habitation to and beyond the remotest star. In that cold Universe how small he is how warm and how weak! Instantly he thinks of the furnace and the remotest star seems near by comparison. The thought of getting up and going down cellar seems as unreal as the thought of getting up and going to meet the sun at that pale streak which through his easterly window heralds the reluctant coming of another day. Yet he knows that he *must* and that eventually he *will* get up. In vain he tells himself how splendid how invigorating will be the plunge *from his warm bed* right into the fresh brisk hygienic morning air.

SOME MECHANICAL APPLICATIONS OF PUNCTUATION

There are other conventions of punctuation which are more or less mechanically applied. A discussion of these follows.

11. THE APOSTROPHE

The word *apostrophe* comes from a Greek root meaning "turning away" or "elision" and the punctuation mark bearing that name has come to be used where certain vowel sounds are omitted, or where vowels which existed at an earlier period of the language are no longer pronounced. It is chiefly a mark of omission or contraction.

A. Possessives.

1. The apostrophe followed by *s* is used to indicate the genitive (possessive) singular of all nouns, and the genitive (possessive) plurals of those nouns whose common plural form does not end in *s*.

girl's toy	John's book
men's clothing	children's party

2. The apostrophe alone is added to plural nouns ending in *s* to form the genitive (possessive) plural.

dogs' kennel	wolves' cry	Joneses' house
girls' club		foxes' lair

3. The apostrophe and *s* is used to indicate the genitive singular of the indefinite pronouns.

one's   other's   either's

Caution: The plural personal and relative pronouns do not add the apostrophe to indicate the genitive case.

hers	not	*her's*
whose	not	*who's*
yours	*ours*	*theirs* *its*

4. Practice varies in respect to the formation of the genitive singular of proper nouns ending in *s*.

Charles's   or   Charles'
Jones's   or   Jones'

When the addition of the *'s* would result in a series of three sibilant sounds, the apostrophe is almost always omitted, even in common nouns.

Kansas' son
Moses' commandment
conscience' sake

5. The apostrophe is frequently omitted in the names of organizations when the possessive case is implied, and in certain geographic designations.

Citizens League   Teachers College
Merchants Association   Actors Equity Association
Pikes Peak (recommended by the U. S. Geographic Board)

B. The apostrophe is used in place of the omitted letters or numbers in writing contracted forms.

aren't   it's (it is)   who's (who is)
can't   ne'er   you're (you are)
don't   o'clock   '39

Caution: Do not confuse *its* (possessive pronoun) with *it's* (*it is*) or *whose* (possessive pronoun) with *who's* (*who is*). This is a frequent error.

C. The apostrophe followed by s is used to form the plurals of letters and symbols.

a's and *b*'s
size 7's

12. QUOTATION MARKS

In general quotation marks are used to enclose all matter that is *directly* quoted, whether from a written or spoken source. Indirect quotations are not punctuated with quotation marks.

Direct Quotation: "I was looking for you," he said.
Indirect Quotation: He told her that he had been looking for her.

A. The punctuation *after* the introductory statement preceding a quotation varies with the close-

ness of the structure, the formality of the statement, and the length of the quotation.

1. A short emphatic quotation requires no punctuation.

He shouted "Thief!" and took up the chase.

2. A short quotation, informally introduced, is punctuated with a comma after the introductory word.

The elder girl said casually, "It is so quaint living down here in the Square."

3. A long quotation, formally introduced, is punctuated with a colon after the introductory word.

After quiet was restored the speaker proceeded: "During the past month I have consulted with a large number of individuals on the increasingly difficult problem of railroad transportation."

B. When the explanatory statement, such as *he said*, follows the quotation, the quotation is concluded with a comma, question mark, or an exclamation point; the explanatory phrase begins with a small letter, and stands outside the quotation marks.

"It is my mother," he said in a low voice.

"Can't you see it?" she asked.

"Take it away at once!" he commanded.

C. When the explanatory phrase comes between parts of the quotation, the quotation itself is followed by a comma, but the explanatory statement is followed by whatever mark of punctuation would normally follow the first portion of the quotation.

EXPLANATORY STATEMENT AT THE BEGINNING: Stephen replied, "Oh, I know the old proceedings were bad enough, but I am trying to improve them."

EXPLANATORY STATEMENT IN THE MIDDLE: "Oh, I know the old proceedings were bad enough," replied Stephen, "but I am trying to improve them."

EXPLANATORY STATEMENT AT THE BEGINNING: He said, "Then I'll see you tomorrow. Can you be ready at nine?"

EXPLANATORY STATEMENT IN THE MIDDLE: "Then I'll see you tomorrow," he said. "Can you be ready at nine?"

EXPLANATORY STATEMENT AT THE BEGINNING: James said, "We'll just go down to Hampstead; the horses want exercise, and I should like to see what has been going on down there."

EXPLANATORY STATEMENT IN THE MIDDLE: "We'll just go down to Hampstead," said James; "the horses want exercise, and I should like to see what has been going on down there."

D. Relative Position of Quotation Marks and Other Marks of Punctuation.

1. The dash, question mark, and exclamation point are placed within the quotation marks when they apply to the quotation only, and outside the quotation marks when they apply to the whole statement.

He said, "Are you coming?"

Did he say, "I am going now"?

"Summer courses—out here on the lake—history and art and cooking and swimming—" Beatrice chimed in enthusiastically.

"You think you are sufficient in yourself"—then he stopped suddenly and began again, "Some day you will see that you have been mistaken."

2. **The comma and the period normally precede the quotation mark.**

"I don't feel natural when I express them your way," she admitted, "in words."

At times placing the period within the quotation marks seems illogical (*i.e.,* According to Johnson's opinion, "the first Whig was the Devil.") but the practice is general.

3. **The colon and semicolon always follow the quotation marks.**

A judge, like a marshal or a postmaster, is just so much "recognition"; another piece of patronage.

E. A quotation within a quotation is indicated by single quotation marks.

"But he did say," Charles pointed out, " 'I won't come if I don't finish my work,' so apparently he hasn't finished it!"

F. When the quoted material consists of several paragraphs, quotation marks are placed at the beginning of each paragraph and at the end of the quotation.

G. When someone's exact phraseology is included within an indirect quotation, quotation marks are frequently placed around the directly quoted material.

A distinguished Conservative statesman tells us from the town hall of Tamworth that "in becoming wiser a man will become better"; meaning by wiser more conversant with the facts and theories of physical science.

H. In formal writing it is customary to enclose slang in quotation marks.

Gentlemen, if I may say so, this plan appears to be completely "cockeyed."

Do not employ this in informal writing. Moreover, do not enclose colloquialisms in quotation marks in any kind of writing. Students frequently overuse quotation marks in this way. Unfamiliar technical terms may be enclosed in quotation marks, but present practice favors italics for these, or underlining in hand-written and typewritten manuscripts. Underlining is the printer's sign for italics.

I. Titles of literary, musical, and artistic works may be enclosed in quotations marks, but present practice favors italics.

J. For the paragraphing of quoted material, see Chapter II, pages 61-64.

13. ITALICS

The use of italic type is a mechanical device to secure distinctness on the printed page, and it has come to be employed where emphasis or distinctness is desired. Italics have taken over many of the conventional functions performed in earlier times by quotation marks, different sizes of type, or capitals. In hand-written or typewritten manuscripts, italics are indicated by underlining.

A. Book titles, titles of publications, musical selections, and works of art are italicized.

I suppose you have read *The Hucksters.*

1. **The names of ships are generally italicized.**
The ship was called *Wanderlust.*

B. Words from other languages are italicized.

It is a *de facto,* not a *de jure* government.

C. Words or letters spoken of as words or letters are italicized.

What can you tell us about the derivation of *telephone?*

The plural inflection generally ends in *-s.*

D. Italics are occasionally used for emphasis.

Employ this device with caution.

He avows also that the fortunate individual whom he is describing, by "being accustomed to such contemplations, will feel the *moral dignity of his nature exalted."*

14. CAPITAL LETTERS

Capital letters serve two uses: to mark the beginning of a structural unit, and to distinguish *proper* nouns and adjectives.

A. To Indicate Beginnings.

1. A capital letter begins the first word of a sentence.

2. A capital letter is used for the beginning of each line of poetry when it is printed in the traditional way.

3. A capital letter is used to begin the first word of a quoted sentence.

4. **A capital letter is generally used for the first word after a colon when the statement following the colon is a rather long complete sentence.** Observe:

We have followed one plan throughout our history with two small exceptions: One was when President Wilson entered upon his second term, and the other was when Mr. Roosevelt was just about to enter his second term.

The reason for his failure was plain: he had not prepared himself.

See also p. 286.

B. To Indicate Proper Names.

1. **The personal pronoun *I* is always capitalized.**

2. **All nouns referring to the Deity are capitalized, as are all attributive names of the Deity and of Christ.**

God, the Lord, the Son of God, the Virgin Mary, the Trinity, the Supreme Ruler, the Redeemer, the Omnipotent

3. **The days of the week, the names of months, holy days, and names of festivals are capitalized.**

Monday, January, Good Friday, Labor Day, Passover, Yom Kippur

3*a*. **The names of seasons are not capitalized unless personified.**

spring, autumn

4. **Official titles before the name of the bearer are capitalized.**

Mayor Keneally, Governor Green, King Christian. [*Note, however:* Mr. Keneally is mayor of Chicago.]

5. In titles of books, musical selections, magazine articles, etc., the important words are capitalized. Articles, conjunctions, and prepositions are usually not capitalized except when they occur first in the title.

War and Peace
And So—Victoria

6. Words denoting family relationship are capitalized when they are prefixed to the name of a person. When they are used as a substitute for a person's name, practice varies.

I called Mother Brown on the telephone.
I called (Mother) (mother) on the telephone.
She called her mother on the telephone.

7. *North, south, east,* and *west* and their compound forms are not capitalized unless a particular and well-defined section of the country is referred to.

First he came to the Middle West, and subsequently he traveled farther west.

8. Nouns and adjectives of races and languages are usually capitalized: Indian, Caucasian, Mongolian, English. *White* is never capitalized when referring to a race; the practice with *negro* and *gypsy* varies.

9. School subjects are not capitalized unless a particular course is referred to. The names of the various classes are not capitalized.

I took history as a sophomore.
I took History IV in the twelfth grade.

10. The greatest variation in the capitalization of other proper names occurs in the last word of the title when that

word indicates the general class, i.e., *Harvard College, Mississippi River, Blithedale Country Club* or *Harvard college, Mississippi river, Blithedale country club.* In general, newspapers print the class word with a small letter, while books and magazines capitalize. When the general term comes first, however, it is always capitalized:

Bank of Italy, Church of the Disciples.

15. THE HYPHEN

The hyphen has two uses, to indicate compound words, particularly those coined for the occasion or those which are still in the process of becoming one word, and to indicate syllabic division at the end of a line.

Consult your dictionary whenever you suspect a word should be hyphenated. If the dictionary gives more than one form, choose one and use it consistently.

The same advice will hold for the use of the hyphen in word division. Monosyllabic words cannot be separated, and words may be divided only between syllables.

See also Chapter XIII, p. 434.

16. THE PERIOD

The period is used after an abbreviation, as *Dr., A.B., i.e., p., U. S. A.* If in doubt about the proper form of the abbreviation, or how many periods are demanded, consult your dictionary. (See pages 435, 436, also.)

17. THE COMMA

Commas are used to separate items in dates and addresses. See page 301, also.

23 Burbank Avenue, Altadena, California.
Monday, January 12, 1948.

EXERCISES

EXERCISE 4. Punctuate the following passages:

[A] Leaving this part of the temple we made up to an iron gate through which my companion told me we were to pass in order to see the monuments of the king accordingly I marched up without further ceremony and was going to enter when a person who held the gate in his hand told me I must pay first I was surprised at such a demand and asked the man whether the people of England kept a *show* whether the paltry sum he demanded was not a national reproach whether it was not more to the honor of the country to let their magnificence or their antiquities be openly seen than thus meanly to tax a curiosity which tended to their own honor as for your questions replied the gate-keeper to be sure they may be very right because I don't understand them but as for that there threepence I farm it from one who rents it from another who hires it from a third who leases it from the guardians of the temple and we all must live I expected upon paying here to see something extraordinary since what I had seen for nothing filled me with so much surprise but in this I was disappointed there was little more within than black coffins rusty armor tattered standards and some few slovenly figures in wax I was sorry I had paid but I comforted myself by considering it would be my last payment a person attended us who without once blushing told a hundred lies he talked of a lady who died by pricking her finger of a king with a golden head and twenty such pieces of absurdity Look ye there gentleman says he pointing to an old oak chair there's a curiosity for ye in that chair the kings of England were crowned you see also a stone underneath and that stone is Jacob's pillow I could see no curiosity either in the oak chair or the stone could I indeed behold one of the old kings of England seated in this or Jacob's head laid upon the other there might be something curious in the sight but in the present case there was no more reason for my surprise than if I should pick a stone from their streets and call it a curiosity merely because one of the kings happened to tread upon it as he passed in the procession

[B] Thus it happens that your true dull minds are generally preferred for public employ and especially promoted to city honors your keen intellects like razors being considered too sharp for common service I know that it is common to rail at the unequal distribution of riches as the great source of jealousies broils and heartbreakings whereas for my part I verily believe it is the sad inequality of intellect that prevails that embroils communities more than anything else and I have remarked that your knowing people who are so much wiser than anybody else are eternally keeping society in a ferment happily for New Amsterdam nothing of the kind was known within its walls the very words of learning education taste and talents were unheard of a bright genius was an animal unknown and a bluestocking lady would have been regarded with as much wonder as a horned frog or a fiery dragon no man in fact seemed to know more than his neighbor, nor any man to know more than an honest man ought to know who has nobody's business to mind but his own the parson and the council clerk were the only men that could read in the community and the sage Van Twiller always signed his name with a cross

[C] I get the feeling that your aunt is a very remarkable woman he said in his slow precise English with its faint trace of accent she should have been what is it you say a career woman yes that is what I see in her a career woman without a career she should have painted all the time lived alone in a big room with a skylight made herself one meal a day out of tin cans walked alone in the fields and wept over sunsets he had risen and stood looking as he spoke at Aunt Palms scene of early spring no he said now reflectively perhaps she should even have lived in a city bought her plants from pushcarts seen sunsets only two weeks out of a year had no children of her own so that she could have really longed for them and maybe then painted them yearningly like Mary Cassatt Fredericka asked as he hesitated yes if that is one of whom I am thinking

—From Nancy Wilson Ross,
The Left Hand is the Dreamer.[1]

[D] number one says the voice now two and from high up somewhere two cans of fog let out spurts of vapor which billow slowly into layers in the air now down and to your left Mac the voice says and the man on the jib boom finally moves and sends a stream of fog from his can directly down to the water and across the camera field save it says the voice and the fog stops coming and the billows and layers of what has been sent out merge slowly in the air which is now being set softly in motion by two giant noiseless fans turning slowly one at the water's edge one trained down from the dock above Jimmie looks through his finder and says something to the lighting director and the voice picks up again Al can you bring that junior

[1] Reprinted by permission of William Sloane Associates.

SPELLING

*W*E AMERICANS have come to place a high value
upon the ability to spell correctly, and conversely we associate poor spelling with illiteracy. Newspapers and the
radio have developed the spelling bee on a national, even
an international, scale, and the skill which enables one to
keep the confusing consonant combinations straight in the
word *phthisis* is interpreted as an indication of superior
intelligence. Accept this or not, many readers will judge
you and your work by your spelling. Therefore, you must
correct deficiencies in spelling that you may have.

1. OUR INCONSISTENT SPELLING

Its system of spelling is one of the blackest marks against
the English language. The chances for the adoption of
English as an international language would be heightened
if the spelling could be made at least as consistent as that
of German, Spanish, or Italian. Frequent efforts from the
sixteenth century on to reform English spelling have made
little headway.

The contradictions and difficulties of English spelling
are not the result of mere chance, however. They are
caused partly by the variety of elements of which our language is composed. Several classes of words retain more or
less exactly a type of spelling distinctive of the language
from which they have been borrowed; while they are consistent with each other, they are at variance with those
words similar in sound but derived from a different source.
Notice such pairs of words as *vane* and *vein* (to say noth-

ing of *vain*), *thyme* and *time, phase* and *faze* (sometimes spelled *feeze* or *feaze*).

A second reason for the inconsistencies of English spelling may be found in the large number of changes in pronunciation occurring in the language since 1500, when printing developed and spelling became generally fixed. Even the names which we give to the letters of the English alphabet (*ay, bee, see, dee, ee*) are different from those given to the letters of the Roman alphabet in any other language (*ah, bay, say, day, ay*); this indicates the extent to which our sounds have changed. Although many of our sounds have changed, the spelling of these sounds did not. Therefore we have "silent" letters such as *b* in dum*b* and *gh* in thou*gh*t, fossilized remains of sound which are no longer pronounced. We have also various ways of spelling the same vowel sound, as in *knead* and *need* where the spelling once served to indicate a distinction in pronunciation no longer present.

We must finally remember that it is less than two hundred years since writer, printer, and reader began to set much value on spelling the same word in the same way. Until that time a man's spelling was his own concern, his own property, and no one bothered to see if Monday's spelling matched Wednesday's. People seem to have got along well enough under this free and easy system, but it happens not to be ours.

We have glanced briefly at the history of our spelling, not to excuse or justify bad spelling—the conventions of the twentieth century do not permit this—but rather to show why our rules for spelling have such frequent exceptions.

2. WHY WE MISSPELL

The extent of the eye span and the speed of reading have much to do with misspelling. Some of us have a visual memory. We recall or think of words as we see them on a printed page, whereas others hear them. Naturally, the visually minded person will have less difficulty with spelling.

A knowledge of other languages also plays an important part. A student conscious of Latin *evitare,* "to avoid," even if he has not met the Latin adjective *evitabilis,* is less likely to spell English *inevitable* as *ineviatible,* and certainly Latin *usura* or French *usure* would prevent him from making such a blunder as *usery.*

3. PRONUNCIATION AND SPELLING

Do not attempt to correct spelling errors through a conscious distortion of pronunciation.

This is contrary to advice frequently offered. One is often told to create such artificial distinctions in pronunciation as begg*a*r, doct*o*r, advis*e*r, though Webster's dictionary uses the same symbol to indicate the phonetic value of all three vowels. We must remember that spelling began as an attempt—and not a very good one—to reproduce pronunciation. To fashion our pronunciation according to what is in origin a rather bad attempt at reproducing it, is putting the cart before the horse.[1]

4. WORD DERIVATION AND SPELLING

Develop an awareness of the component parts of derivative words. Learn how a word is composed and associate it with as many similar or related words as you can. Notice that *infantile* is composed of *infant* and *-ile;* if you associ-

---

[1] "I was surprised to notice how few cases of uncertainty as to the spelling were based on mispronunciations. Uncertainty as to the meaning of a word leads to far more uncertainties of spelling than does the uncertainty as to the correct pronunciation." "Linguistic Cowardice and Verbal Timidities," *English Journal* (College Edition) XXV (September, 1936), p. 577. Professor J. M. Steadman.

ate this word with such related words as *infancy, infantry, infanta, infanticide,* then the group as a whole, and particularly the shifted accent on the *a* vowel in the last two words, will keep you from such a spelling as *infintile.*

5. PREFIXES

Some spelling errors arise from the confusion of prefixes which look alike but are so different in meaning that they cannot be affixed to the same roots. Outstanding examples are:

ante, "before": *antecede*   *anti,* "against": *antidote*
de, "from, down, away": *debate*   *di,* "twice": *diploma*
dis, "separation": *dismiss*   *dys,* "hard, ill": *dyspepsia*
per, "through": *perforate*   *pre,* "before": *prescribe*

6. WORDS WITH SIMILAR SPELLING BUT OF DIFFERENT MEANING

Many pairs of words, different in origin, meaning, and spelling, have come to be pronounced alike or somewhat alike. Test yourself on the following pairs, and if uncertain about the meaning or use of any one member of the pair, look up both of them in your dictionary.

accept	angel	breath
except	angle	breathe
advice	bare	canvas
advise	bear	canvass
aisle	baring	capital
isle	barring	capitol
alley	bearing	
ally		cite
altar	born	site
alter	borne	sight

clothes
cloths

coarse
course

complement
compliment

consul
council
counsel

costume
custom

dairy
diary

decent
descent
dissent

desert
dessert

dual
duel

formally
formerly

forth
fourth

gamble
gambol

holly
holy
wholly

hoping
hopping

instance
instants

its
it's

loath
loathe

morn
mourn

passed
past

peace
piece

personal
personnel

plain
plane

planed
planned

precedence
precedents

presence
presents

principal
principle

quiet
quite

rain
reign
rein

right
rite
write

serf
surf

shone
shown

sole
soul

staid
stayed

stake
steak

stationary
stationery

steal
steel

than
then

there
their
they're

to
too
two

villain
villein

wander
wonder

weak
week

weather
whether

who's
whose

7. "EI" AND "IE" SPELLINGS

These spellings are easily confused. Memorizing this jingle will help:

> Write *i* before *e*
> Except after *c*
> Or if sounded like *a*
> As in *neighbor* or *weigh*.

Words with *ie* not after *c* are: *chief, fief, besiege, field, fiend,* etc.

Words with *ei* after *c*: *ceiling, deceive, receive, conceive*.

Words with *ei* pronounced as *a* in *care: heir, their*.

Words with *ei* pronounced as *ay* in *way: weigh, neighbor, veil, reign, freight*.

Exceptions to this rule are: *either, neither, height, leisure, seize, foreign, sovereign, forfeit*.

8. THE DICTIONARY

The dictionary is your best help. Learn to use and apply the spelling rules contained in the preface of every good dictionary. The following exercises are designed to give practice in discovering and applying rules for correct spelling.

1. Under what circumstances are the final consonants of words doubled when adding suffixes, and when do they remain single? Add the suffixes *-ed* and *-ing* to the following words: *fan, lag, plot, label, surfeit, confer, develop, admit, shop, sham, mimic*.

Information necessary to answer this and the three following questions may be found on page xx of Webster's *Collegiate Dictionary* (Fifth Edition).

2. Before what kinds of suffixes do words ending in silent *e* retain the *e*, and before what kinds of suffixes do

they drop it? Write the present participle of each of the following words: *shave, argue, mate, decree, prove, awe, tinge, inquire, deserve, hoe.* Add one appropriate suffix, either *-ful, -ly,* or *-ment,* to each of the following words: *ease, judge, bare, grace, true, whole, move, use.*

3. Give rules concerning the behavior of words ending in *-y* when a suffix is added. Form the plural of each of the following nouns: *toy, baby, key, contemporary, husky, valley, country, army, bay.*

4. Give the plural form of each of the following: *halo, echo, memento, piano, tomato, motto, folio, cargo, punctilio, hero.*

5. By an examination of the derivation, etymology, and meaning of the separate elements of the following words, explain:

    a. Why there should be two *m*'s in *committee.*

    b. Why there are two *m*'s in *immigrate* but only one *m* in *emigrate.*

    c. What in the etymology accounts for the two *t*'s in *battle* and *battalion.*

    d. Why *excellent* has two *l*'s and why the last vowel is *e,* not *a.*

    e. Why *accord* has two *c*'s.

    f. Why *appear* has two *p*'s.

    g. Why *readable* takes the *-able* suffix and not *-ible.*

    h. Why *tractable* takes the *-able* suffix and not *-ible.*

    i. Why *legible* takes the *-ible* suffix.

    j. The difference in spelling of *intercede* and *supersede.*

9. PREFERRED SPELLINGS

Remember that some words have at least two "acceptable" spellings. In some instances there is a difference between British and American practice; in others, both forms are current in America.

Form the habit of always spelling the same word in the same way. It is better if you spell consistently all of the words in the same class; that is, if you spell *humor* and not *humour,* then spell *odor* rather than *odour.*

Consult your dictionary for preferred spelling of the following pairs:

adviser—advisor	naturalise—naturalize
center—centre	gray—grey
endorse—indorse	mediaeval—medieval
enquire—inquire	reflection—reflexion
analog—analogue	enrolment—enrollment
fledgeling—fledgling	smolder—smoulder
program—programme	caliber—calibre
gipsy—gypsy	shew—show
odor—odour	orthopaedic—orthopedic
pretence—pretense	encase—incase
manoeuvre—maneuver	

10. SIMPLIFIED SPELLING

The question of simplified or reformed spelling has already been discussed. (See Chapter V, p. 180.) Remember that the status of certain reformed spellings varies. Some are acceptable in formal writing; others are appropriate only when the writer is being informal or humorous. If, in a composition, you decide upon the spelling *thru,* spell it that way throughout. Your spelling must not be of the hit-and-miss variety.

11. IMPROVING YOUR SPELLING

Begin by analyzing your own particular difficulties. After every theme is returned, make a list of the words you have misspelled. Break up this list into the various types of error represented. If most of the words in it represent a confusion of *ei* and *ie,* put most of your effort on this particular problem. Examine the misspelled words in the light of the rule that has been given. Find out if you have been missing the words that fit the rule or the exceptions. In your reading, make a special effort to notice *ei* and *ie* spellings.

If your chief difficulty is in doubling consonants that should be single, or vice versa, approach this problem in the same way. Have you been confusing the consonants at the ends of root syllables before a suffix, or those doubled when a prefix is added? Look up the troublesome words in the dictionary and see if the etymology and the derivation of the words will not help you to spell them correctly.

Your instructor can do little more than to mark the words which you misspell and to insist that you improve. Devising some means of improvement and carrying it out is your responsibility.

12. WORDS FREQUENTLY MISSPELLED

acceptable	argument	capitalism
accessible	arising	catastrophe
accommodation	armament	category
accustom	arousing	ceiling
acquaintance	bankruptcy	censor
adequate	bargain	cite
adherents	basis	comedy
adjournment	beginning	committed
adopt	belief	comparatively
aggressive	beneficial	competition
aisle	brilliance	condemns
allege	brutality	conscience
analyze	budget	conscious
apparent	bulletin	considerable
appreciate	camouflage	considered

WORDS FREQUENTLY MISSPELLED (*continued*)

consistent	endeared	hypocrisy
controllable	endurance	icicle
controversies	enormous	idea
co-ordinate	entirely	imagine
counsel	entrance	implied
corollary	environment	impossible
counterfeit	equipped	impromptu
curricular	exaggerate	impure
completely	expense	incentive
conceive	existence	incessantly
concentrate	faculties	incidentally
deceive	fallacies	incompetent
decision	fascinate	independent
defense	fascism	indispensable
definite	federal	inefficient
department	flourish	inherent
dependents	foreign	initiative
descendant	foremost	inseparable
descriptive	formerly	inveigle
desert	fraternities	involve
desirable	friend	Japanese
desperate	fundamental	kidnapping
develop	furtherance	knowledge
development	group	laboratories
different	guarantee	laborer
disappear	haphazard	later
disappointed	happen	latter
disastrous	happiness	laziness
discriminate	hardening	lead
dissatisfaction	hereditary	led
disturbance	hindrance	legitimate
ecstasy	homely	leisure
efficient	hospital	letting
embarrassed	hungry	license
emphasize	hurriedly	maintenance

WORDS FREQUENTLY MISSPELLED (*continued*)

machinery	privilege	significant
material	probably	similar
medieval	prominent	similarly
Mediterranean	propaganda	stagnant
menace	prove	stimuli
merely	quiet	stratagem
miniature	readily	strenuous
mortgage	realistically	studying
necessarily	receive	subscribe
necessities	recommend	subsistence
neither	refer	substantial
occurrence	referred	subtle
opinion	reluctant	sufficiently
optimist	remedy	suffrage
paid	ridiculous	surprising
peasant	sacrifice	sympathize
performed	satisfied	systematically
perhaps	scarcity	tentative
permanent	schedule	terribly
personally	scheme	tragedy
piece	scholarly	unanimous
politicians	scholarship	unscrupulousness
possess	seize	variety
practice	senses	various
precede	separate	villain
preceding	shriek	warring
prejudice	siege	whims
prerequisite	sight	woolen

CHAPTER IX

USAGE

*T*HERE ARE many questions of usage which cannot be decided according to rules of grammar or by the application of general principles of propriety in diction. Such disputed points are individual matters, and a judgment on them can be reached only after a painstaking examination of the most competent authorities and, more important still, of the language itself.

It is the purpose of this section to deal with such troublesome questions and to give the student a practical decision in respect to each of them. Because we firmly believe that the English language itself is the final arbiter in these matters, many of our conclusions are supported by actual citations or illustrations from present-day and sometimes earlier English—some from literature, some from newspapers and other forms of contemporary writing.

More often the judgments here expressed have been based upon the most reliable and authentic collections of the facts of the English language. Of these, the *Oxford Dictionary* is unquestionably the most important, but in all instances Webster's *New International Dictionary* (Second Edition) and Wyld's *Universal Dictionary of the English Language* have been consulted as well. The following works are also essential whenever an investigation of usage is to be made: J. Lesslie Hall, *English Usage;* R. C. Pooley, *Grammar and Usage in Textbooks on English,* and *Teaching English Usage;* O. Jespersen, *A Modern English Grammar;* C. C. Fries, *American English Grammar,* and G. O. Curme, *Syntax. Current English Usage* by S. A. Leonard is valuable also as a survey of *opinion about* usage.

Whenever you consult the glossary, read carefully and

completely everything that is said about the expression under discussion. Be certain hereafter you will use that expression only on those levels of usage, formal or informal, where recommended. Remember that, although the term *colloquial* is not a condemnation of any word in the gloss, a colloquialism is not appropriate in very formal writing.

Preceding the glossary is a list [1] of the "worst errors of usage," found frequently in the language of the least educated, but not acceptable in current standard speech or writing.

It should be noted that many of these usages were altogether acceptable at other stages in the history of the English language, and that some are, in fact, more logical than the corresponding forms which are "correct" today. Usage does not always follow logic. From the point of view of the student, however, the important thing is to know what is acceptable current usage.

Many points of usage are disputed or variable, but there is no question about those included in this list. Read the list carefully. If you find that you make any of these errors, rid yourself of them as quickly as possible.

1. WORST ERRORS OF USAGE

A. Matters of Number.

1. **Failure to pluralize nouns of measure:**

WRONG: three *year* ago; five *mile* away; ten *pound* of salt.
RIGHT: three *years* ago; five *miles* away; ten *pounds* of salt.

2. **Pluralizing wrongly:**

WRONG: *farm's; dog's; hat's.*
RIGHT: *farms; dogs; hats.*

(The apostrophe shows genitive case or contraction. Obviously, this error is limited to writing.)

[1] Based on Fries' *American English Grammar.*

3. Using *was* with plural subjects:

WRONG: we *was;* you *was;* the men *was.*
RIGHT: we *were;* you *were;* the men *were.*

B. Matters of Grammatical Form.

1. Incorrect form of demonstratives:

WRONG: *them* people; one of *them* kind.
RIGHT: *those* people; one of *that* kind.

2. Case form in reflexive pronouns:

WRONG: He did it *hisself.* They thought of *their* own *selves.*
RIGHT: He did it *himself.* They thought of *themselves.*

3. Using adjectives for adverbs:

WRONG: He washed it *good;* She treated him *kind.*
RIGHT: He washed it *well;* She treated him *kindly.*
(See further, Chapter VI, Grammar, p. 214.)

4. *Don't* with third person singular subject:

WRONG: He *don't* care; It *don't* matter.
RIGHT: He *doesn't* care; It *doesn't* matter.

5. Confusing principal parts of verbs:

a. **Leaving -*ed* (pronounced -*t*) off the past tense and past participle.**

WRONG: He *talk* to me. We've often *work* after dark.
RIGHT: He *talked* to me. We've often *worked* after dark.

b. **Adding -*ed* where it does not belong:**

WRONG: He was *drowneded.* They *knowed* better.
RIGHT: He was *drowned.* They *knew* better.

(The second occurs in the attempt to regularize an irregular preterite.)

c. **Using the present form for the past tense:**

WRONG: I *give* it to him yesterday. I *see* he was ready.
RIGHT: I *gave* it to him yesterday. I *saw* he was ready.

d. **Using the past participle for the past tense.**

WRONG: The water *run* down. She *done* him wrong. They *seen* us.
RIGHT: The water *ran* down. She *did* him wrong. They *saw* us.

e. **Using the past tense for the past participle:**

WRONG: I've *did* it many a time. The children have *went* home.
RIGHT: I've *done* it many a time. The children have *gone* home.

f. *Ought* **used as a participle:**

WRONG: He hadn't *ought* to tell.
RIGHT: He *ought* not to tell, or He *should* not tell.

See also pages 345, 346.

C. Redundancies.

1. Multiple negatives:

WRONG: He's *not* going there *no* more. There *ain't never* been *nobody* like her. He *can't hardly* talk.
RIGHT: He's *not* going there any more. There has *never* been anybody like her. He can *hardly* talk.

2. Double comparatives (and superlatives):

WRONG: *more kinder* people; *most unpleasantest* work.
RIGHT: *kinder* people; *most unpleasant* work.

D. Miscellaneous Faults (see the individual articles in the Glossary).

1. Use of *ain't.*
2. Confusion of *lay* and *lie.*

3. **Confusion of** *as regards* **and** *in regard to.*
4. **Use of** *that there* **and** *this here.*

2. *GLOSSARY OF USAGE*

The following abbreviations are regularly used throughout the Glossary:

Oxford Dictionary: OD
Webster's *New International Dictionary: WD*
Wyld, *Universal Dictionary of the English Language:*
Wyld
Horwill, *Dictionary of Modern American Usage: DAU*

Above. The argument that *above* is either a preposition or an adverb and therefore may not be used as an adjective, i.e. *the above paragraph,* is no longer valid. The *OD, WD,* Wyld, and Funk and Wagnalls all recognize this use. Often this adjectival use of *above* may be objectionable on grounds of style. It is most properly classified as legal and commercial jargon. See pages 151–153.

Ad. A clipped or shortened form of *advertisement. WD* and *OD* classify it as colloquial.

Aggravate. Colloquial in the sense of "exasperate, vex, annoy." The *OD* has citations for this use of *aggravate* from the seventeenth century to the present time, including the novelists Richardson and Thackeray.

Ain't. Not acceptable, except possibly in one situation, the first person singular interrogative, *ain't I,* where it may be considered only as a possible colloquial form. Here the speaker must choose from among one of three possible forms: *aren't I, am I not,* and *ain't I. Aren't I* is objectionable because it uses the plural or second person singular verb *are* with the first person singular subject *I. Am I not* is felt by many to be awkward or formal because all the other short, frequently used auxiliary verbs place the contracted *n't* between verb and subject in the interrogative, e.g. *don't I, can't I, haven't I.* The form *ain't* is historically regular, having developed from an earlier *an't.* Remember that any other use of *ain't* is wholly without justification, and that *ain't* should never be used in any formal situation either in speech or writing.

Alibi. American colloquial for "an excuse." *WD* and *OD.* In formal writing use *alibi* only in its technical legal sense.

All of. According to *WD, all* is often followed by *of* and a pronoun, and in recent usage by *of* and a noun. *All of the books* is thus quite as acceptable as *all the books.*

All the farther. *All the farther, all the faster, all the higher,* etc., are not acceptable usage when intended to mean *as far as, as fast as, as high as;* use the latter. This idiom seems to have been formed on the pattern of *all the more;* but *all the more* is adjectival, whereas *all the farther,* etc., are adverbial.

All the farther, etc., when used to mean *farther yet* or *even farther, even faster, even higher,* etc., are quite acceptable usages.

Alright. Although this spelling is used unconsciously by some who are ignorant of the conventional spelling, and consciously by certain writers who wish to defy the conventions, it cannot be said to have found general acceptance. The conservative spelling is still *all right.*

Among. See *Between.*

And etc. The *and* is superfluous, since *etc.* is already an abbreviation for *et cetera,* "and so forth." Do not use *etc.* as a substitute for specific ideas.

Angle. Although the use of *angle* for "point of view, aspect, phase," is recognized by *WD* as wholly legitimate, students frequently overuse the word. Vary it with some of the words suggested.

Anybody's else. See *Else.*

Anyone. The dictionaries show both one- and two-word spellings for *anyone* (*any one*), *everyone,* and *someone.* The dual spelling is useful because it makes possible the distinction between any person indiscriminately and any particular or single person, for example: Did anyone go? Did any one of them go? For the agreement of *anyone* with a pronoun, see Chapter VI, p. 222.

Anyplace. Recognized as a colloquialism by *WD* and spelled there as a single word.

Anyways. An appropriate form when the word means "in any way or manner, anywise," as for example: "Nor was such interference . . . anyways injurious."—De Quincey. The form with *-s* is a provincialism when the word means "in any case, at all events." Use *anyway* in place of it. "Anyway, I am glad you came."

Anywheres. This form is a remnant of the genitive or possessive case, which at one time had an adverbial as well as a possessive use. It is not standard English. Use *anywhere* in place of it.

Apt. In British English *apt* is used to indicate something which may happen because of habit or inherent tendency; *likely* indicates merely the probability of something taking place. *WD:* "An impulsive person is *apt* to blunder. An angry dog is *likely* to bite." In American English *apt* is often used interchangeably with *likely* to indicate probability. "Sentences averaging more than 20 to 25 words are *apt* to become involved and confusing."—*Style Book* of the Jackson (Mich.) *Citizen Patriot.*

Around. The use of *around* to mean "about, nearly" is labeled *U. S. colloquial* by *WD,* but *DAU* and the supplement to the *OD* indicate that it has gained some recognition as literary usage. "The convention adjourned *around* four o'clock." W. G. McAdoo.

As. (1) *As* for *because* or *since* in introducing a clause has been overworked: *As* you are not ready, we must go without you. The objection to it is on grounds of style rather than of grammar. *WD* suggests that *as* assigns a less immediate and explicit cause than *since* or *because*.

(2) *As* for *that,* introducing a noun clause after the verbs *know, say, think* (I don't know *as* I can go) is an old usage which has dropped out of the standard language and is now provincial. Do not use it.

As . . . as . . . Many authorities used to hold that *as . . . as* should be used in positive comparisons (I am *as* old *as* he) but that *so . . . as* was required in negative comparisons (I am not *so* old *as* John). An examination of the actual usage of many recognized writers shows that the *as . . . as* construction has been used with negative comparisons as well as positive for the last two hundred years. *He did not do as well as we expected* was classified as established in *Current English Usage*.

As to. Often overused as in the following: "The question *as to* whether they should remain at work or go on strike was still unsettled." This sentence would be just as clear without the *as to*. It is better omitted. Faulty: He said nothing *as to* the score. Better: He said nothing *about* the score. The chief function of *as to* is introductory. It may be used to place at the beginning of a sentence some element that without it would have to be placed in a less prominent position: *As to* the accuracy of the information, we are not in a position to specify.

Asset. Although the use of *asset* in a non-commercial sense for "resource, support, source of strength, valuable object, favorable circumstance," is recognized by *WD* and by Wyld as wholly legitimate, it is frequently overused. Vary it with the expressions suggested.

GLOSSARY OF USAGE

Auto. A clipped form of *automobile*. *WD* labels it colloquial; the *OD* does not indicate such a limitation of use. *DAU* cites instances from serious writing. Note that it, rather than the full form, *automobile*, has been used in forming such compounds as *autoist, auto-bus*.

Awful, Awfully. About a century ago these two words were overused and as a result their meaning, in such phrases as *awful time, awfully bad weather*, has weakened to that of a mere intensive, depending upon the context for meaning. Most of the dictionaries still label them slang. Probably colloquial.

Back of. Used in both spoken and written American English where British English would employ *behind* or *at the back of*. "Various motives were back of this reversal of policy."—Professor H. Robinson.

Bad. *Bad* instead of *badly* as an adverb is not used in writing. "He writes *badly*," not "He writes *bad*."

Badly. Colloquial as an intensive after the verbs *need, want*. Informal: I need it *badly*. Formal: I need it *very much*. *Badly* with such verbs as *feel* and *look* is not in general use; here *bad* is used and is construed as a predicate adjective: *it looks bad; I feel bad*.

Balance. Originally, commercial jargon for "remainder, rest." Now recognized as colloquial by *WD* and Wyld. *DAU* cites examples to show that this use of the word is coming into literary English. "He spent the balance of his life in travel."—*Dictionary of American Biography*. You may still encounter some objections to this use. Avoid them by employing other words.

Because. See Chapter III, pages 107, 108.

Beside. Generally a preposition, meaning "by the side of." I rode *beside* him.

Besides. "Over and above, moreover." Generally used as an adverb: I don't want to go out; *besides*, it is already too late. As a preposition: Have you anything to tell us *besides* what we already know?

Between. (1) Be careful neither to say nor to write: Between you and *I*. Right: Between you and *me*. *Between you and I* arises from the intensive drill on *you and I* in a nominative case construction, but here the pronouns are objects of the preposition *between*.

(2) The rule that *between* implies two, whereas *among* implies more than two is not accurate. *Between* has been used to apply to more than two for the last thousand years. Concerning the use of *between* and *among,* the *OD* says, "It is still the only word available to express the relation of a thing to many surrounding things severally and individually, *among* expressing a relation to them collectively and vaguely: we should not say 'the space lying among the three points,' or 'a treaty among three powers,' or 'the choice lies among the three candidates in the select list,' or 'to insert a needle among the closed petals of a flower.' "

Blame on. The expression "He blamed it on me" is a colloquialism arising from the use of *blame* as a noun: "He placed the blame upon me." If the verb is used in formal writing, the preposition *for* should be used with it: "He blamed me for it."

Burst. The forms *bursted* and *busted* for the past tense and past participle are several hundred years old, but have now been replaced by *burst* for both functions. *Bust* is perhaps provincial or humorously colloquial in the United States.

But what. In such a sentence as "I have no doubt but what he will come," *but what* is a colloquialism. Literary English demands *that:* I have no doubt that he will come.

Calculate. An American provincialism, in the sense of

"to intend, plan, expect." Use one of the words suggested in place of it.

Can. According to the conventional rules, *can* means "to be able to" while *may* means "to have permission." Citations from the *OD* indicate that throughout the last half century *can* has been moving in the direction of *may*. It has gone so far in England that dictionaries reflecting British usage give "to have permission" as one of the meanings of *can,* without qualification.

Cannot help but. This is a mixed construction arising from a confusion of "I can but do it" and "I cannot help doing it." It has some literary authority. "He could not help but see them."—Walpole, *Jeremy.* "Professor Raleigh, from whose work on style I quoted above, often writes forcibly and suggestively, but we cannot help but feel . . . that it is more the work of a stylist than a thinker."—John Burroughs, *Literary Values.*

Can't hardly. A double negative which is no longer in acceptable use.

Can't seem. See *Seem.*

Claim. "In America the verb *claim* has lost its distinctive meaning of *demand as one's due,* having become a mere synonym for assert, state."—*DAU.* Both Horwill and the supplement to the *OD* furnish ample citations from reputable American writings. "A citizen of a foreign country claiming to be imprisoned for some act committed with the sanction of his government." —C. A. and M. Beard, *The American Leviathan.*

Complected. According to the *OD* and *DAU,* American colloquial for *complexioned.* Do not use in writing.

Considerable. American colloquial when used absolutely as a noun: They lost *considerable* in the fire. Appears occasionally in serious writing in combination with *of.* "Considerable of the moisture for which farmers have been eagerly watching has fallen this past week over the wheat belt."—New York *Evening Post*.

Contact (verb). "To come or to bring into contact with." Although this verb appears without a restricting label both in *WD* and *OD,* there is still much prejudice against it as commercial jargon. Avoid it.

Could of (for **could have**). Do not write this. In normal unemphatic speech the unstressed forms of the verb *have* and of the preposition *of* are pronounced alike, that is, with a neutral vowel followed by [v]. Hence the spelling *could of* is one way of representing what is actually pronounced, but it indicates that the writer is ignorant of the grammatical construction involved.

Cunning. In the sense "quaintly interesting, pretty, attractive," it is confined primarily to American colloquial English.

Cute. This is really the word *acute* with the initial vowel cut off. Two hundred years ago the word meant "sharp, keen-witted," but now it has a meaning similar to *cunning*. It has always been colloquial and often overused.

Data. The plural of Latin *datum,* and formerly always used with a plural verb or pronoun. At present, according to *WD,* it is "not infrequently used as a singular," because of the collective conception of *data* as a unified mass of information. *DAU* contends however, that the singular use of *data* is confined to America. "No provision was made for the publication of this data."—Professor F. J. Haskin.

Definitely. Frequently overused for the purpose of giving emphasis or intensity. If you have acquired this habit, guard against it. Use synonyms, such as *certainly, surely,* etc.

Different than, Differently than. This appears to have arisen from a confusion of *differ from* and *other than*.

It is frequent in literature from the seventeenth century on and is recognized as an alternate form in Webster, but with the warning "considered incorrect by many." Pooley has made the sound observation that *than* tends particularly to appear when it is a substitute for *from that which,* as in the following sentence: "Provision is made for happiness of a quite *different* nature *than* can be said to be made for misery."

Don't. A colloquial contraction for *do not* which, according to *WD* is "Sometimes loosely used for *does not.*" The supplement to the *OD* cites a number of examples, all from American English. There is a widespread feeling against *he, she, it don't.* Avoid it, both in speech and writing.

Due to. In origin *due* is an adjective; therefore the argument is sometimes advanced that it may modify only a substantive, and that it is incorrect when used prepositionally to introduce an adverbial phrase, *e.g.,* Due to the blizzard, we were obliged to remain in Madison.

J. S. Kenyon asserts that "some highly respectable writers admit" this construction. The supplement to the *OD* considers this use of *due to* more frequent in America than in England, although it seems to have developed as early as the seventeenth century. Notice that this development of *due to* exactly parallels the development of *owing to,* which is always accepted without question as an introductory prepositional phrase.

To avoid the prejudice against this use of *due to,* you may substitute *owing to* or *because of.*

Each other. The textbook rule that *each other* must be used in referring to two persons and objects, and that *one another* is to be used in reference to more than two, has rarely been observed in the language itself. The earliest citation for *each other* in the *OD* is from the *Battle of Maldon,* written before 1,000, and here the reference is to more than two. Other quotations show that it has been in constant use since. Both *WD* and the *OD* indicate that *each other* and *one another* are used interchangeably.

Either, Neither. Originally used to designate one of two persons or things. Since the seventeenth century, the terms have occasionally been used to designate one of a larger number. To avoid criticism, use *any* or *any one* and *none* or *no one* when your reference is to more than two. Questionable: Either of the three books will do. Right: Any of the three books will do.

It is possible that *either* and *neither* are chiefly used to refer to more than two in situations where the context would demand *any of these* or *none of these,* as in the following sentence: "Heat, light, electricity, magnetism . . . are all correlatives . . . neither, taken abstractly, can be said to be the cause of the others." But since the expression is not clear, it is better to limit *either* and *neither* to groups of two.

Else. The possessives *anybody's else, everybody's else, somebody's else* are old forms which have been generally abandoned. Use *anybody else's,* etc.

Enthuse. "To become enthusiastic." *WD:* "generally colloquial."

Everyplace. See *Anyplace.*

Expect. Colloquial or provincial when used to mean "suspect."

Extra. In the sense of "unusually" has occasionally been condemned, *e.g.,* "An extra fine day." This use may be questioned on grounds of taste, since the more recent quotations from the *OD* suggest that it is commercial jargon.

Factor. Sometimes overused for *element, circumstance, influence.*

342

Falls. Authorities are agreed that this word is usually plural and requires a plural verb. "The falls are one mile from here."

Farther, Further. In theory *farther* is supposed to indicate distance, and *further* to indicate degree, time, or quantity: "The house is three miles *farther* down the road." *"Further* than this I cannot say." In actual practice *further* and *farther* are interchanged in all uses except that of "in addition" or "more," where only *further* is permissible. Unidiomatic: *farther* details. Right: *further* details.

Feature (verb). The use of *feature* as a verb in the sense "to exhibit, make a special attraction of" began as an American colloquialism, but it has been adopted in England also, as the supplement to the *OD* shows. There is still much objection to this use.

Fellow. Colloquial when used to mean "a person."

Fine. This word has been used as a general term of approval for the last five hundred years, nor does it seem to have been confined to colloquial English. Unfortunately it frequently happens that this is one of the few terms of general approval in a student's vocabulary, and he tends to use it on all occasions. If you have the *fine* habit, try first to be somewhat more specific in your expressions of admiration, and if this is beyond you, find some synonyms for *fine.*

    Fine used as an adverb meaning "well" is colloquial.

Fix (noun). Colloquial for "predicament, plight."

Fix (verb). American colloquial for "repair, arrange, prepare."

Folks. Colloquial for "relatives," "family," sometimes "parents." For formal use the more specific words are better.

Funny. Colloquial in the sense of "strange, queer, odd."

Get. The *OD* lists thirty-four meanings for this verb used independently and thirty-eight more in combination with prepositions. Many of these are colloquial, and certain others are provincial. Thus the word is very easy to overuse or to use vaguely. We could hardly do without it in conversation or daily speech, but we had better use it with caution in writing, especially in those senses which are farthest removed from the early meaning of the verb, "to acquire." Consult the dictionary whenever in doubt. See also *Got, Gotten.*

Good. No longer correct as an adverb. Archaic: He reads good. Right: He reads well.

Good and. Colloquially used as an intensive: *good and* cold.

Got. *Have got* is common for *have* in the sense "possess" and has been criticized as repetitious. The construction very possibly arose because of a desire for emphasis. After *have* came to be used more and more as an auxiliary verb, speakers undoubtedly felt that it was weak and unsatisfactory when used as an independent verb, consequently the *got* was added to intensify the meaning. *Have got* for *have* began as a colloquialism in the sixteenth century, and according to Jespersen, *A Modern English Grammar,* the nineteenth-century examples show its extension to higher forms of literature. J. Lesslie Hall, *English Usage,* mentions among others Carlyle, Thackeray, Dickens, Lamb, Ruskin, Holmes, as using it.

Have got in the sense "to be obliged to" parallels the development of the verb *ought.* Both of them at one time meant "to possess" and in both verbs there was a shift of meaning from possession to obligation and a displacement of the present tense by a past tense form. The dictionaries usually label this use of *have got* colloquial, but an examination of the occurrences of this expression in such writers as Disraeli, Ruskin, Wilde,

Shaw, Trollope, and Wells, suggests that the expression is quite firmly established in written English. There is undoubtedly less prejudice against these uses of *have got* in British than in American English.

Gotten. An older form of the past participle of *get*. It is the more frequent form in American English where it is used in the senses "become, acquire, receive," but not "possess, have." "So, I think the State of Wyoming could not be charged . . . with *having gotten* itself into a position . . ." Senator McAdoo, February 23, 1938.

Guess. American colloquial for "think, suppose, believe."

Had better. In "I had better go," *had better* is somewhat more common than *would better* although both do occur.

Do not use *better* in writing without an auxiliary verb. Not appropriate for formal use: You better come. Revised: You had (would) better come.

Had have, Had of, Hadn't of.. . .*Had of, had have,* etc. are wholly inappropriate for written English. In spoken English the idea may be more satisfactorily indicated by the use of *had* alone.

INAPPROPRIATE: Had he have come.
REVISED: *Had he come* or *if he had come.*

Had ought, Hadn't ought. The verb *ought,* like many other auxiliaries, is defective; that is, it does not have all of the principal parts which a normal verb ordinarily possesses. At one time in its history, when *ought* and *owe* were still considered as forms of the same verb, and when the verb meant "to possess" as well as "to be under obligation," the form *ought* was used as the past participle as well as the past tense. It is this old use which still prevails in the forms *had ought* and *hadn't ought,* both of which are inappropriate to written English.

The status of these expressions in spoken English is more difficult to define. *Had ought,* the affirmative, is probably a provincialism, but because of the American hesitation to use *oughtn't,* it is quite possible that the negative *hadn't ought* is common colloquially. Avoid criticism by saying or writing, *Shouldn't you have* . . . *Ought you not to have* . . .

Had rather. *Had rather* and *would rather* are equally acceptable.

Hardly. See *Can't hardly.*

Have got. See *Got.*

Healthy. *WD:* "conducive to health." *OD* indicates it has been used synonymously with *healthful* since 1552.

Help but. See *Cannot help but.*

Himself. See *Self.*

Honorable. A courtesy title used very widely in this country. *DAU* says that it is applied "to (1) the President and members of his Cabinet, (2) members of either house of Congress, (3) state governors and holders of the more important State offices, (4) members of State Legislatures, and (5) almost any other politician or government official, major or minor, to whom one desires to pay a compliment." Conventionally, the word *honorable* should always be preceded by *the* and followed by the initials or first name of the person so addressed or by the title Mr., e.g. *The Honorable Charles J. Williams, The Honorable Mr. Graham.* In actual practice the *the* is sometimes omitted when the title and name do not appear in connected context, as on programs and announcements. Some newspapers are hesitant to apply the title to an American at all, viz., "There is no such title as *Hon.* in the United States."—*Style Book,* Washington *Evening Star.*

Human(s). Sometimes vaguely used as a noun for *human beings, persons, people,* etc. It is properly used as a noun

346

only in a collective sense to indicate the species or human race.

If. There has been some objection to the use of *if* in introducing a noun clause indicating doubt or uncertainty, as, "I do not know *if* I can go," and *whether* has been recommended in its place. The facts of recorded usage do not justify such an objection to *if,* as the construction has been in constant use in both colloquial and literary English for the last thousand years.

In. Generally used to indicate a situation already existing within limits of space, time, or circumstance; *into* is used for direction toward: He walked *into* the room. He walked *in* the room. In a sentence such as "He went *in to* dinner," notice that *in* is an adverb and *to* is a preposition; hence they must be separated in spelling.

In back of. Not appropriate for formal or written English. This is an American colloquialism formed after the pattern of *in front of.* In writing, substitute *behind, at the back of, back of.*

In regards to. A confusion of *in regard to,* where *regard* is a noun, and *as regards,* where *regards* is a verb. Substitute either of the two preceding expressions.

Inside of. A colloquialism for "within," *e.g.,* "Inside of the house." When used in reference to time, "Inside of three hours," it is an American and British colonial colloquialism. *Of* is wholly permissible in all circumstances when *inside* is a noun and not a preposition: The inside of the box was also carved.

Kind. In formal English, preceded by the demonstrative and followed by *of* and a noun, should be in the singular throughout: *This kind* of man has his use.

"The feeling that *kind of* was equivalent to an adjective modifying the following substantive, led to the use of *all, many, other, these, those,* and the like, with a plural verb and pronoun, when the substantive was plural, as in *These kind of men have their use*. This is still common colloquially . . ."—*OD*.

Kind of. Colloquial when used adverbially, "somewhat, in a way, to some extent."

Kind of a. In formal writing, use *kind of* followed directly by the noun: That is a *kind of* settlement customary with the ancient Greeks. *Kind of a . . .* is common colloquially.

Lady. *Woman* is properly used as the feminine form in all situations where *man* would be the normal masculine form. *Lady* is properly the feminine equivalent of *gentleman*.

>   INAPPROPRIATE: Three *ladies* came out of the theatre just as I passed.
>
>   REVISED: Three *women* came out of the theatre just as I passed.
>
>   RIGHT: Her manners and speech were those of a *lady*.

Lay. Used only as a transitive verb, one which takes an object. The verb *lie* is the corresponding intransitive verb. Now I *lay* the book on the table. He *lies* on the bed. The verb *lie* is a strong or irregular verb, and has as its principal parts the forms *lie, lay, lain*. *Lay* is a weak or regular verb, and has as its principal parts *lay, laid, laid*. Much of the confusion between the two verbs arises from the fact that the past tense of *lie* and the present tense of *lay* are identical. Note the following illustrations of the past tense forms: I *laid* the book on the table. He *lay* on the bed.

Leave. Means "to cause or allow to remain; to depart"; generally not used in the sense of permit.

>   FAULTY: They would not *leave* me go.
>
>   REVISED: They would not *let* me go.

"Leave me alone" and "Let me alone" are both ac-

348

ceptable, although they may be interpreted somewhat differently.

Liable. Originally used only to indicate the possibility of something undesirable happening, *e.g.,* He is *liable* to break a leg. Since about 1900, there has been a tendency in America to use the word where an Englishman would use *likely;* that is, to indicate something that is probable without reference to its desirability. "Norman Hunter's new record . . . is liable to stand unmolested for many years."—N. Y. *Evening Post.*

Like. Originally *like* was a preposition and therefore could govern a noun, but could not introduce a clause; *as* was a conjunction whose function was to introduce clauses. Examples: The sun looked *like* a ball of fire. The sun looked *as if* it were a ball of fire. Do it *as* I do.

Concerning the substitution of *like* for *as* (not *as if,* however) the *OD* comments, "Now generally condemned as vulgar or slovenly, though *examples may be found in many recent writers of standing.*" So far as written English is concerned, then, the safest course is to use *like* and *as* as illustrated in the preceding paragraph.

In colloquial English, it is doubtful if anything can stem the tide of the substitution of *like* for *as.* Some who, through hyper-correctness, substitute *as* for all uses of *like* fall into the opposite and quite ridiculous extreme.
Like for *as if* is heard much less frequently.

Likely. See *Apt, Liable.*

Loan (verb). "Loan is in modern (British) English usage a noun only, though it was once a verb also. In America it is still a verb."—Horwill, *DAU. WD* records this verb without any comment. "Carlyle *loaned* me Maurice's novel."—Conway, *Autobiography.*

Locate. According to the *OD,* the transitive use of *locate,* "to settle, establish" (He *located* the factory near the river) is in acceptable usage both in England and America. The intransitive use (He *located* at Terre Haute) is found chiefly in American colloquial English. To avoid criticism, use *settle* in place of the intransitive use of *locate* in formal writing.

Lose out. The word *out* has been used to intensify the verbs *lose* and *win* in American English for the last fifty years. *DAU* shows that *lose out* and *win out* appear in formal literary English.

Lots of. Colloquial for "a great deal, much."

Mad. American colloquial and British English dialect when used to mean "angry." This is an old meaning of the word, recorded as early as 1300.

May. See *Can.*

May of. See *Could of.*

Mean. American colloquial when used to indicate "ill-tempered, characterized by petty selfishness or malice."

Might of. See *Could of.*

Most. In formal written English *almost* is an adverb meaning "nearly"; *most* is an adverb meaning "in the greatest degree." We are *almost* there. I am *most* grateful. In American colloquial and British English dialect *most* is sometimes substituted for *almost.*

Muchly. No one at all familiar with the language would use this word seriously.

Must of. See *Could of.*

Mutual. Sometimes confused with *common. WD* comments, "That is *common* in which two or more things share equally or alike; *mutual* properly implies reciprocal action." This intention is *common* to all of us. The transaction was of *mutual* benefit to buyer and seller. Concerning *mutual friend* and *mutual acquaintance,*

OD comments, "Still often used on account of the ambiguity of *common*."

Myself. See *Self*.

Neither. For reference to more than two objects, see *Either*.

Since the seventeenth century, *neither* has been used occasionally with a plural verb, usually when a prepositional phrase containing the antecedents of *neither* stands between it and the verb. "Neither of them *declare* themselves eyewitnesses of Christ's resurrection."—Cardinal Newman.

"After *neither-nor* we still often find the plural verb after singular subjects since there has long been a tendency to give formal expression to the plural idea which always lies in the negative form of statement."—Curme, *Syntax*. "Neither Leopardi nor Wordsworth *are* of the same order with the great poets. . . ."—Matthew Arnold.

Prejudice against this construction appears to be increasing in the United States, however.

Nice. Often condemned as a term of general approval. *OD* writes, "In common use from the latter part of the eighteenth century as a general epithet of approval or condemnation, the precise signification varying to some extent with the nature of the substantive qualified by it." No modern dictionary disapproves of the word. Avoid overusing it.

No place. See *Anyplace*.

Nobody else. See *Else*.

None. *WD* comments, "As subject, *none* with a plural verb is the commoner construction." The argument that *none* is properly singular because historically it is equivalent to *no one* is false. When we wish to emphasize the singular, we usually say *no one* or *not one*.

Not. Although common and acceptable in earlier English, the double negative is not acceptable today.

> WRONG: I could not hear nothing. I didn't have no apples.
> RIGHT: I could hear nothing. I couldn't hear anything. I had no apples.

Nowhere near. Frequently condemned as colloquial, and even at times called vulgar. There seems to be no dictionary justification for this. It is mentioned without a restrictive label in *OD* and in Wyld. In writing it may be advisable to use *not so old as* or *not nearly so old as* for *nowhere near as old.*

Nowheres. A provincialism. See *Anywheres.*

Of. See *Could of, Inside of, Had of.*

Off of. This expression, formerly in standard use, is now dialect.

> DIALECT: He jumped off of the barn.
> STANDARD: He jumped off the barn.

One . . . one. It was once insisted that *one* be consistently used throughout a sentence: *One* rarely enjoys *one's* luncheon when *one* is tired." Writers today do not hesitate to insert forms of the pronoun *he: One* rarely enjoys *his* luncheon when *he* is tired.

Only. See Chapter III, pp. 103, 104.

Onto. Frequently condemned either as a colloquialism or as a misspelling. There are instances where it is necessary to avoid the ambiguity of *on* or *upon* after certain verbs. Notice that "He jumped *on* the deck" and "He jumped *onto* the deck" are not the same in meaning, nor would "He jumped *on to* the deck" agree exactly with either. *WD* records *onto* without a restrictive label. Notice, however, that the more economical *on* or *to* alone will often satisfy the requirements of the situation.

Ought to of. See *Could of*.

Out. See *Lose out*.

Out loud. Frequently condemned as a colloquialism, but is recorded in the *Oxford Dictionary* with citations from literary sources. *Aloud* may be used in its place without fear of pedantic criticism.

Outside of. Accepted usage when the phrase means "beyond the bounds of." "The sepulchre lay outside of the ancient city." American colloquial when it means "except, besides."

COLLOQUIAL: I see no one outside of my servants.
LITERARY: I see no one except my servants.

Over with. A colloquialism for *over, concluded, ended*.

Per. The argument that *per* is a Latin word and accordingly must be used only before other Latin words is not in accord with the facts. It has been used with English words ever since 1588. It may be used in phrases relating to conveyance, *per express;* in phrases relating to manner of statement, *per invoice;* or in expressions denoting rate or proportion, *per foot, per pound. Per usual* is humorous slang; a phrase such as *fifteen per,* omitting the object, is jargon and should be avoided.

Per cent, percent. Although *per cent* is in origin an abbreviation for *per centum,* "by the hundred," it is not usually followed by a period according to American practice. There is objection on the part of some authorities to the use of *per cent* (or *percent*) in situations other than after a numeral: A high percent was demanded. Here it is preferable to use percentage: A high *percentage* was demanded.

Except in commercial writing, write out *per cent;* do not use the sign %. *Per cent* may, according to Webster, be spelled as one or two words. *Percentage* is now always written as one word.

Phenomenon. This word, borrowed from Greek, has kept for its plural inflection the *-a* inflection of the Greek neuter nouns; however, both *WD* and the *OD* recognize the native plural *phenomenons* as well. Neither dictionary gives any justification for the use of *phenomena* as a singular. "The phenomena *were* (not *was*) of interest to us."

Plan (on). "In America the word *plan* may mean not only 'devise," but 'intend, hope.' "—*DAU.* This use is not colloquial, as is sometimes suggested. In this sense *plan* is followed either by the infinitive with *to,* or by the gerund preceded by *on:* I plan to go tomorrow. I plan on going tomorrow.

Plenty. Colloquial when used as an adverb. The house was *plenty* large. In American English *plenty* does appear as an adjective, but only when used predicatively. "In the early days when land had been *plenty.*"—James Truslow Adams.

Pretty. *Pretty* as an adverb, meaning "fairly, moderately, tolerably," has been in constant use since the middle of the sixteenth century. Hall, *English Usage,* records two hundred instances from sixty of "the best essayists, scholars, novelists, and historians of the last two hundred and fifty years." It tends to be overused. Vary it with some of the synonyms just suggested.

Proposition. Colloquial or commercial jargon for "proposal, scheme, project, undertaking." Avoid overuse.

Proven. This older form of the past participle, archaic in England, is in current use in America. The *OD* shows a range of citations from 1536 to 1899 and comments, "Properly in passive." *DAU* has a number of examples from current American writing. Hall points out that *proven* is Tennyson's regular form. There need be no hesitation about the use of either *proved* or *proven;* both are acceptable.

Providing. Some authorities insist on *provided* in a sentence such as "I will come *provided* everyone else does." *Providing,* in this sense, appears as early as the seventeenth century and has been used by George Eliot, Ruskin, and other accepted writers.

Quite. Frequently labeled a colloquialism in the sense "to some extent, rather," but the *OD* records instances of this use from the middle of the eighteenth century up to the present time, including Richardson, Fielding, and Ruskin.

Raise. *DAU* comments, "In England one *grows* farm or garden products, *breeds* animals, and *rears* children. In America one raises them all." The citations show that the verb *raise,* "to bring up, foster children," occurs frequently in established writers in this country.

Raise as an intransitive verb (Both leaves of the drawbridge *raise*) is obsolete in England but still appears occasionally in American writing. There is so much prejudice against it that it is preferable to use *rise* in its place.

Real. As an intensive adverb, chiefly an American colloquialism. Its meaning has developed in the same path as that of *very,* which was originally an adjective only.

COLLOQUIAL: real good.
FORMAL: very good.

Reason is because. See Chapter III, pages 107, 108.

Refer back. This expression appears repetitious but there are situations which seem to demand its use. If a matter, which has at some previous time been referred to a committee, is brought up for discussion and is again referred to the committee which considered it originally, the simple verb *refer* will not suffice, for the matter has already been *referred* once. *Sent back* might be preferable, but since *refer* is already so firmly fixed in parliamentary lan-

355

guage, *refer back* seems to be here to stay, but only in similar instances. The alternative *re-refer* is clumsy.

Reverend. According to the conventional rules, the word *reverend* should always be preceded by *the* and followed by Mr. or by the initials or first name of the person so addressed. In this country the practice of omitting *the* is widespread, according to E. C. Ehrensperger, who, some years ago, made a careful study of American practice in this matter. He mentions the *Harvard Alumni Bulletin,* the Boston *Transcript,* and many church periodicals, in which *the* is regularly omitted. The omission of the name, initials, or *Mr.* after *Reverend* is provincial.

Right. With intensive force, *right* soon (*right* good, Southern U. S.) equals "very"; archaic in England and provincial in America. *Right* meaning "straight" with temporal connection (He went *right* home) is American rather than British usage.

Right along. "Continuously," colloquial.

Right away. "Immediately," colloquial.

Seem. The logic of "I can't seem to solve this problem" is often questioned. The difficulty lies in the lack of an infinitive for *can.* To state the idea fully, one would have to say "I seem not to be able to solve this problem," "I seem unable to," or "I do not seem able . . . ," all of them cumbersome. Since inability is expressed by means of verbs far more frequently than it is through adjectives, the *can't seem* construction developed. It is recognized as acceptable by *WD.*

Seldom ever. No longer acceptable.

Self. The use of the intensive forms *myself, himself, yourself* in place of the personal pronouns *I, me, you, he, him* is frequently given blanket condemnation. The problem is too complex to be made the subject of a single rule. Excerpts from Pooley's analysis follow:

"As a matter of fact there are five uses of *myself* as the substitute for a personal pronoun, disregarding the reflexive uses. They are:

1. Sole subject of a verb. '*Myself* when young did eagerly frequent doctor and saint . . .' (Fitzgerald). Archaic, poetic, not acceptable in current prose usage.

2. Second member of a compound subject. 'John and *myself* brought the Yule log home.' Frequently heard, but not fully enough established to gain recognition.

3. After comparisons with *than* or *as*. 'Enough to make a better man than *myself* . . . run into madness' (Richardson); 'No one knew this as well as *myself*.' Acceptable informal usage, not at all rare in literature.

4. Sole object of a verb or preposition. 'To *myself* mountains are the beginning and end of all natural scenery' (Ruskin). Not quite as acceptable in current usage as No. 5.

5. The second or later member of a compound object of a verb or preposition. 'He invited . . . John Wilson and *myself* to visit him for a day or two' (Lockhart, *Life of Sir Walter Scott*). This use is fully established in literature and current English."

The same conclusions apply to the other persons of the intensive pronoun, *yourself, himself, herself,* etc.

Set. A transitive verb, frequently confused with *sit,* intransitive.

> WRONG: The dowel sets firmly in the hole.
> RIGHT: The dowel sits firmly in the hole.
> RIGHT: The dowel is set firmly in the hole.

Sit is an irregular or strong verb, and its principal parts are *sit, sat, sat*. *Set* is a regular or weak **verb.** Its principal parts are *set, set, set*.

Setting hen is wholly acceptable.

Shall. See Chapter VI, pages 200, 201.

Should, Would. The following generalizations will help:

1. *Would* express a conditional willingness.

   I *would* try out for the play if I had time.
   You *would*
   He, she, it *would*
   We, you, they *would*

2. *Would* expresses customary action in past time.

   I *would* light the fire every evening.
   You *would*
   He, she, it *would*
   We, you, they *would*

3. *Should* expresses obligation.

   I *should* go.
   You *should*
   He, she, it *should*
   We, you, they *should*

4. *Should* and *would* express a kind of future dependent upon a condition.

   I, we *would* or *should* be glad to help (if I, we could).
   You *would*
   He, she, it, they *would*

Should of. See *Could of.*

Show up. Colloquial for "appear, arrive, be present." Slang for "expose."

Sit. See *Set.*

Size. Present-day usage sanctions *size* used elliptically with a noun following: a large *size* plate. The *OD* shows it in use from the eighteenth century down to the present.

Size up. Colloquial for "estimate, judge."

Slow. Has been used adverbially since 1500. Considerations of euphony generally decide between *slow* and *slowly.*

So. 1. Student themes frequently lead one to believe that *so* is one of the few co-ordinating conjunctions in the student's vocabulary. For this reason, many teachers have been led to condemn *so* in a sentence like: "They had no guest room; *so* we went to a hotel." *So* has been used in this fashion for the last seven hundred years, but for the sake of variety it would be well for the student to become aware of *accordingly, therefore, on that account,* and to avoid an overuse of *so.*

2. The use of *so* for *so that* in the sense "in order that" is not in the best modern usage.

> FAULTY: I waited a few minutes *so* I would not be too early.
> REVISED: I waited a few minutes *so that* I would not be too early.

3. *So* as an intensive adverb, *so* sad, *so* fresh, has been in continuous literary use for as long as we have any record, and is wholly justifiable, but use it with discretion.

Some. American colloquial or provincial when used as an adverb for "somewhat, a little."

> I worked *some* today.
> He is *some* better.

Slang when used as an intensive: He is *some* ballplayer.

Someplace. See *Anyplace.*

Somewheres. Dialect. Use *somewhere.*

Sort of. See *Kind of.*

Sort of a. See *Kind of a.*

Such. When *such* is completed by a relative clause, the relative clause should be introduced by *as:* "Such words as occur in the first three sentences . . ." When *that* is used in this situation, the *such* changes in meaning and acquires intensive force: Such words that occur in the first three sentences!

Such is used adverbially to intensify an adverb both in informal and literary English; guard against overuse. "All comes of his gaining an archer's place at *such* early years." (Scott)

Such used colloquially with a noun gives intensive force: *Such* a place!

Sure. American colloquial when used as a substitute for *yes, certainly.* "Sure, it is true; they all have merit." American colloquial and English dialect when used as an adverb; formal English today demands *surely.* "That surely is a difficult poem."

In your writing use *sure* only as an adjective. "He walked with a *sure* and steady pace."

Suspicion (verb). Formerly used as a verb in literary English but now a dialect form only in America. Use *suspect.*

Take and. Dialect in such an expression as, "I'll take and saw this board."

Take sick. Dialect for *become sick.*

Taxi (verb). In accepted usage (1) to travel in a taxicab, (2) to run an airplane or seaplane along the ground or on the water under its own power.

Tend. When *tend* is used to mean "attend, care for" the *to* is omitted. "He tends the sick."

That there. No longer current in Standard English.

WRONG: That there dog is a good hunter.
RIGHT: That dog is a good hunter.

These kind. See *kind.*

This here. No longer current in Standard English.

WRONG: This here book is torn.
RIGHT: This book is torn.

Through. Colloquial when used adverbially for "finished" in the pre-adjective position: I am through writing. Satisfactory for all occasions when used predicatively after the verb *to be:* He did not arrive until the speech was half through.

Thusly. Do not use.

Toward, Towards. *Towards* is prevalent in British usage; *toward* is more common in American usage except where emphasis is desired. His back was *toward(s)* me.

Transpire. *WD:* "To come to pass; happen; occur;—a sense disapproved by most authorities but found in writings of authors of good standing." "I am fearful of supporting the conference report after what has transpired." It may be objected to on stylistic grounds as jargon.

Try and. The use of *and* instead of *to* with the infinitive after *try* goes back to the seventeenth century. It may be found in Milton, Coleridge, Lamb, Thackeray, Arnold, George Eliot, and Charles Kingsley. However there is considerable prejudice against this construction in American usage.

Ugly. *OD,* definition 6: "Offensive to refined taste or good feelings, disagreeable, unpleasant, not nice." Citations range from 1621 to the present time.
OD, definition 8: "Cross, angry, ill-tempered."
Obviously any objection to these extended meanings of *ugly* is not supported by literary use. When you do employ the word in either of these senses, make certain that the context indicates clearly which of the meanings you intend. Do not use it ambiguously.

Unique. Logically, *unique* means the only one of its kind, and therefore it does not admit of comparison, i.e. a thing cannot be *more* or *most* unique, or even *very* unique. *OD* comments, "From the middle of the nineteenth century it has been in very common use, with a tendency to take the wider meaning of 'uncommon, unusual, remarkable.'"

Up. The adverb *up* furnishes great sport to those critics who expect language to be consistent in its logic and who totally neglect the psychological factor. They point out that *up* in combinations such as *fill up a glass, open up a box,* is wholly superfluous because it adds nothing to the meaning of the verb. In the consciousness of the speaker, however, *up* does add emphasis and a sense of finality or completion. Just when *up* is superfluous is at times very difficult to decide. Is *folding* a paper exactly the same as *folding* it *up?* Is *cleaning* a room exactly the same as *cleaning* it *up?* It takes the *OD* three full columns to settle some of these questions of meaning, and nowhere does it condemn *up* as superfluous. The tendency to complete or emphasize verbs with *up* seems to be about seven centuries old.

Used to could. Not Standard English. The construction arises from the same situation that is responsible for *can't seem,* namely the lack of an infinitive form of *could.* Say *used to be able, formerly was able.*

Very. According to some authorities *very* must be followed by *much* or *well* or some other adverb when it modifies a participle. (I was *very much* interested.) The *OD* definition of *very,* B 2c, reads, "Qualifying past participles used predicatively or attributively=Very much." This clearly indicates that *very* does occur in Standard English as the modifier of a past participle.

A common sense rule would be that *very* may be used alone with any participle that can be used attributively as an adjective. Since we can say *a swollen foot,* it is permissible to say *the foot was very swollen.*

Viewpoint. Although there has been some objection to the use of this word, it has been in existence for almost a century and is in good usage. "I think, however, if I have the right viewpoint . . ." Senator Norris, *Congressional Record,* Feb. 11, 1938.

Wait on. No longer used in Standard English in the sense "to wait for." It is dialectal in America.

Want (for). *Want,* "desire, wish for," is normally followed by the direct object, which may in turn serve as the subject of an infinitive but not of an active verb. "I want you to go," not "I want you should go." *Want* followed by *for* preceding the infinitive ("I want for you to come") is a provincialism.

Want in (out, up, etc.). Scotch, Irish, and U. S. colloquial, according to the *OD*. Dialectal would probably be a more accurate classification.

Way. On the use of the noun *way,* "manner in which something is done," without a preposition, the *OD* comments, "Now somewhat rare, the form with *in* being commonly preferred." "Be happy *in* your own way."

Ways. "In America the use of *ways* as a singular in such expressions as *a long ways* is not a solecism as it would be in England."—Horwill, *DAU.* "We are a good ways apart." Generally colloquial.

Where. *Where* in a sentence such as, "I read in the paper *where* a plane was lost," is no longer used in written English. Use *that* in its place. "I read . . . that a plane was lost." Some modifications of this construction are acceptable colloquially. Avoid it in writing.

Where . . . at. Examples of *at* after *where* (Not knowing *where* she was *at*) are cited by the Supplement to the *OD* from American writings, but the quotations seem to be primarily colloquial. Avoid in writing.

Where . . . to. Colloquial with *from* or *to* at the end of a sentence or clause. "Where did it go to?"

Which. See Chapter VI, pages 195, 227, 228.

While. Frequently overused as a conjunction, meaning

"whereas, besides, in addition, on the contrary." Generally, *and* or nothing at all will serve the purpose.

> Faulty: To the right of us was the river, while the mountains were on our left.

> Revised: To the right of us was the river; the mountains were on our left.

Who.   See Chapter VI, pages 194, 195, 226, 227.

Whose.   See Chapter VI, pages 227, 228.

Will.   See Chapter VI, pages 200, 201.

Win out.   See *Lose out.*

Woods.   *WD:* "More often in the plural and often, chiefly in colloquial use, construed as a singular."

Would better.   See *Had better.*

Would of.   See *Could of.*

PART III

The Long Paper

*I*N PART I we considered the shorter kind of composition which forms the staple of most beginners' work. In addition the student needs to have practice in handling larger units, which present a more difficult problem of organization. Most composition courses therefore include the writing of a long paper, due at the end of the term, which requires the student to collect information or opinion from printed sources, to evaluate and digest it, and to adapt it to the purposes of his own writing.

In the following pages the process of preparing such a "term paper" is taken up: the initial planning, methods of note-taking, the use of the library in gathering source materials, outlining, and finally the standard forms for footnotes and bibliography. Thus the paper may be prepared step by step with the study of the chapters following.

PART III

The Long Paper

CHAPTER X

PLANNING AND NOTE-TAKING

1. FIRST STEPS

A. The Subject.

If a specific subject for your paper has not been assigned, follow the suggestions already made in Chapter I, with necessary adaptations. The short paper usually covers a single idea or narrow range; the subject for a long paper must be capable of fuller development. Yet it is still necessary to avoid too broad a subject. If *Communism and Literature* is enough for a two-hundred page book, it is too extensive for a two- or five-thousand word paper. You had better select some certain aspect of the question: academic freedom, the organization of the curriculum, or the dissolution of student organizations. It is just as desirable to write a long paper on some topic of which you already know a little as it is to base a short theme upon personal knowledge and experience.

B. The Plan.

There is no one best way to write a long paper. Obviously, if you could have a ready-made outline and then search out the specific information necessary to develop the paper from it, that would be a great simplification. But how can you make the outline before you have studied the subject and discovered its possibilities? You will need to do more reading and note-taking, in other words, than will appear in the final paper, just because you cannot tell exactly, as you read, what the final limitations of the paper will profitably be. Your reading must be done, in part, to give you a perspective of the subject; after this you can make a final outline from which the paper will actually be written. At the same time, your collection of materials should not be haphazard. As you read and take notes the latent pattern of the subject will gradually emerge. You will become aware of what points are the important ones and why. *Keep a record of these;* it will save much labor when you come to making the outline.

C. Finding Materials.

In the next chapter are bibliographies or lists of books sufficient to give you a start in your search for information upon almost any topic you choose. Remember that any bibliography which pretends to cover a dozen or more fields of knowledge and interest in as many pages must be very sketchy indeed. It will serve only as a beginning. In the bibliographical section devoted to the special fields (pages 399–407), there is at least one reference to a bibliography or an encyclopedia for every field. An encyclopedia of music will be useful not only for the information which it may give about any one topic—let us say the development of folk music—but it will mention special articles and studies entirely devoted to such a topic. Follow up these references, and do not neglect the newspaper and magazine bibliographies (pages 395–397). Do not stop collecting information until you find yourself going round in a circle—until the material you come upon merely repeats the information which you already have.

2. *NOTE-TAKING*

It is not usually possible to keep on one's desk all the books and other sources that may be needed in writing a long paper. Nor is this necessarily the most desirable procedure. It is usually more practical and efficient to take what you are likely to need once and for all from each source and to keep your notes in some handy and consistent form.

Furthermore, the exact words in which your sources are written are usually less important than what they say. To quote them at length word for word would be wasteful, and may indicate that you have not digested them adequately. Quote only those things which are said in a particularly effective way; condense the rest as you read. The most useful devices for restating and condensing are the paraphrase, the synopsis, and the précis.

3. THE PARAPHRASE

Frequently you will find material which is expressed in difficult or technical language. The sentences are involved; the words are abstruse. One of the best ways to understand such passages is to rewrite them in your own words, that is, to *restate* or *paraphrase* them. Examine carefully the two portions of essays which follow and the paraphrases which accompany them:

[A] *Original:*

Studies serve for delight, for ornament, and for ability. Their chief use for delight is in privateness and retiring; for ornament, is in discourse; and for ability, is in the judgment and disposition of business. For expert men can execute, and perhaps judge of particulars, one by one; but the general counsels, and the plots and marshalling of affairs, come best from those that are learned. To spend too much time in studies is sloth; to use them too much for ornament is affectation; to make judgment wholly by their rules is the humor of a scholar. They perfect nature, and are perfected by experience; for natural abilities are like natural plants, that need pruning by study; and studies themselves do give forth directions too much at large, except they be bounded in by experience.

—Bacon, *Of Studies*.

Paraphrase:

Studies have three uses. They please us when we are alone; they improve our conversation; and they show us how to conduct our affairs. A man with experience of the world but without learning will be able to dispose of particular details, but a learned man is the more able to make plans and to carry them out. To spend too much time on studies results in inaction. To show off your learning is affectation. Never to add the fruits of practical experience to the learning found in books is the tendency of the impractical scholar. Studies bring our natural abilities closer to perfection, and they in turn are aided by experience. That is, our natural abilities have to be cut back and trimmed just as a shrub has to be pruned. And since abstract ideas tend to run away with us, studies need to be restrained and bounded in by experience.

[B] *Original:*

The historical and psychological researches of the past century have rendered the theory which lies behind the practice of modern democracy entirely untenable. Reason is not the same in all men; human beings belong to a variety of psychological types separated one from another by irreducible differences. Men are not the exclusive products of their environments. A century of growing democracy has shown that the reform of institutions and the spread of education are by no means necessarily followed by improvements in individual virtue and intelligence. At the same time biologists have accumulated an enormous mass of evidence tending to show that physical peculiarities are inherited in a perfectly regular and necessary fashion. Body being indissolubly connected with mind, this evidence would almost be enough in itself to prove that mental peculiarities are similarly heritable. Direct observation on the history of families reinforces this evidence, and makes it certain that mental idiosyncrasies are inherited in exactly the same way as physical idiosyncrasies. Indeed, mind being in some sort a function of brain, a mental idiosyncrasy is also a physical one, just as much as red hair or blue eyes. Faculties are heritable: we are born more or less intelligent, more or less musical, mathematical, and so on. From this it follows that men are not essentially equal, and that human beings are at least as much the product of their heredity as their education.

—Aldous Huxley, "The Idea of Equality" from *Proper Studies*.[1]

Paraphrase:

The investigations of historians and psychologists during the past century have made it impossible to accept the theory behind the practice of modern democracy. Men are not equally intelligent; they belong to a variety of types which differ from one another by very small yet actual degrees. Nor are men wholly the product of their surroundings. From the democracies which have grown up during the past century, one may observe that the reform of institutions and the spread of education have not made particular men better or wiser. Also, biologists have collected much evidence which seems to show that physical peculiarities are inherited according to certain definite and inescapable laws. Since body and mind are so very closely connected, one might conclude that peculiarities of the mind are passed on in the same fashion. This conclusion is strengthened by observing the history of certain families. Moreover, since mind is the working of the brain, which is a physical organ, a mental peculiarity is just as physical as the color of the hair or eyes. Abilities are inherited—we

[1] Reprinted by courtesy of Harper and Brothers.

are born musical, mathematical, and so on. Then it must follow that men are not essentially equal, and that they are at least as much the product of their heredity as of their education or environment.

4. SUGGESTIONS FOR PARAPHRASING

A. **Read the passage over a number of times before beginning to write your paraphrase.** Find out the meaning of all words which you do not understand or which are not unmistakably clear from the context.

B. **For every unfamiliar or difficult word, substitute a common word.** What, in the second paraphrase (B), was used in place of each of the following words in the original: *untenable, irreducible, idiosyncrasy, faculties?* In any of these instances was more than a single word used as a substitute?

C. **Watch out for unusual or older uses of familiar words.** What, in the first paraphrase (A), was used in place of *expert, plot, humor?*

D. **Break up sentences which have a complicated or unusual construction.** Compare the following sentence with its three-sentence paraphrase:

Original:

But let us suppose a new law to be perfectly equitable and necessary, yet, if the procurers of it have betrayed a conduct that confesses by-ends and private motives, the disgust to the circumstances disposes us, unreasonably indeed, to an irreverence of the law itself; but we are indulgently blind to the most visible imperfections of an old custom.

Paraphrase:

A new law may be wholly just and necessary. If those who are responsible for it, however, have clearly acted in the light of their selfish interests, we are so disgusted that we quite illogically do not respect the law. On the other hand, even though an old custom may be unreasonable, it pleases us to observe it anyway.

E. **Make certain that your paraphrase reflects the essential plan of the original.** Read the last sentence of the selection from Bacon. Compare it with the paraphrase. What words in the paraphrase indicate its author's conception of the relationship of the various elements in Bacon's last sentence?

F. Caution: **a paraphrase should leave out no idea that is in the original, nor should it add any idea which is not there. All it changes are the words in which the ideas are expressed.**

EXERCISE I. 1. Look up the derivation of *paraphrase* in your dictionary. What does the prefix *para-* mean? What would be the difference between a paraphrase and a translation?

2. Write paraphrases of the following selections, following the suggestions given above:

[A] The general story of mankind will evince, that lawful and settled authority is very seldom resisted when it is well employed. Gross corruption, or evident imbecility, is necessary to the suppression of that reverence with which the majority of mankind look upon their governors, and on those whom they see surrounded by splendor, and fortified by power. For though men are drawn by their passions into forgetfulness of invisible rewards and punishments, yet they are easily kept obedient to those who have temporal dominion in their hands, till their veneration is dissipated by such wickedness and folly as can neither be defended nor concealed.

It may, therefore, very reasonably be suspected that the

old draw upon themselves the greatest part of those insults which they so much lament, and that age is rarely despised but when it is contemptible. If men imagine that excess of debauchery can be made reverend by time, that knowledge is the consequence of long life, however idly or thoughtlessly employed, that priority of birth will supply the want of steadiness or honesty, can it raise much wonder that their hopes are disappointed, and that they see their posterity rather willing to trust their own eyes in their progress into life, than enlist themselves under guides who have lost their way?

There are indeed, many truths which time necessarily and certainly teaches, and which might, by those who have learned them from experience, be communicated to their successors at a cheaper rate; but dictates, though liberally enough bestowed, are generally without effect, the teacher gains few proselytes by instruction which his own behavior contradicts; and young men miss the benefit of counsel, because they are not very ready to believe that those who fall below them in practice, can much excel them in theory. Thus the progress of knowledge is retarded, the world is kept long in the same state, and every new race is to gain the prudence of their predecessors by committing and redressing the same miscarriages.

—Samuel Johnson, *The Rambler.*

[B] When Mrs. Allen seeks the explanation of the impoverishment of a nation in the existence of foreign investments she is reversing the causal relationship. An impoverished nation under our present economic system must perforce resort to foreign capital or proceed by tedious and uncertain methods to economic development. She evidently forgets that it is only three decades since we were a debtor nation. The part that European capital has played in our development can hardly be overstated. Had we at any time during our development stage driven out foreign capital by adopting a confiscatory policy such as Mexico has adopted, it would be impossible to estimate the deterring effect.

If it were not for the evident belief held by Mrs. Allen in the principles here set forth one would feel that she was advocating the overthrow of the entire capitalistic system and as a part of this the making of a handsome gift to the present political powers that be in Mexico at the expense of her own American fellow-citizens. If she really held this view I should not presume to dissuade her from the broad economic view inimical to capital, but I would ask her to consider carefully the respective merits of the American citizen whom she would divest of these rights and properties and the particular class in Mexico to whom she would hand them over gratis.   —From a letter to the N. Y. *Times.*

[C] Yet hence arises a grave mischief. The sacredness which attaches to the act of creation, the act of thought, is transferred to the record. The poet chanting was felt to be a divine man: henceforth the chant is divine also. The writer was a just and wise spirit: henceforward it is settled the book is perfect; as love of the hero corrupts into worship of his statue. Instantly the book becomes noxious: the guide is a tyrant. The sluggish and perverted mind of the multitude, slow to open to the incursions of reason, having once so opened, having once received this book, stands upon it, and makes an outcry if it is disparaged. Colleges are built on it. Books are written on it by thinkers, not by Man Thinking; by men of talent, that is, who start wrong, who set out from accepted dogmas, not from their own sight of principles. Meek young men grow up in libraries, believing it their duty to accept the views which Cicero, which Locke, which Bacon, have given; forgetful that Cicero, Locke, and Bacon were only young men in libraries when they wrote these books.

Hence, instead of Man Thinking, we have the bookworm. Hence the book-learned class, who value books, as such; not as related to nature and the human constitution, but as making a sort of Third Estate with the world and the soul. Hence the restorers of readings, the emendators, the bibliomaniacs of all degrees.

—Ralph Waldo Emerson, *The American Scholar.*

[D]   THE MEANS TO ATTAIN HAPPY LIFE

Martial, the things that do attain
The happy life be these, I find:
The riches left, not got with pain;
The fruitful ground; the quiet mind;
The equal friend; no grudge, no strife;
No charge of rule, no governance;
Without disease, the healthful life;
The household of continuance;
The mean diet, no delicate fare;
True wisdom joined with simpleness;
The night dischargèd of all care,
Where wine the wit may not oppress;
The faithful wife, without debate;
Such sleeps as may beguile the night:
Contented with thine own estate,
Ne wish for death, ne fear his might.

—Henry Howard, Earl of Surrey.

TYPES OF CONDENSATION

The paraphrase results in no reduction in the size of the original. If you have read a long article and want to incorporate the essence of it in a theme, if you have read a chapter of a textbook, you will need some written record in reduced form. Since the answer to an examination question may require a summary of some reading or of a portion of a lecture, you must learn how to make such abridgments competently.

5. *SYNOPSIS*

The most familiar and least difficult form of condensation is the *synopsis,* a brief or condensed statement. In present use the term is most often applied to a summary of material that is narrative rather than reflective, story rather than essay. We speak of the *synopsis* of a motion picture. A theatre program has a *synopsis,* in acts and scenes, of the whole play. Here is the synopsis of the first act of Shakespeare's *Merchant of Venice:*

Antonio, a merchant of Venice, has many dear friends who are beholden to him for his good qualities; but most of all he loves Bassanio, for whom he would make any sacrifice. Bassanio is in love with Portia, a wise and wealthy lady, but since he lacks worldly means wherewith to press his suit, he is constrained to borrow of his friend Antonio three thousand ducats ere he can visit her. Antonio's wealth is entirely represented just then by various ships at sea. However, he bethinks himself of a Jewish money-lender named Shylock, who lends him the money under agreement that Antonio shall forfeit a pound of his flesh in default of payment on the day his bond falls due. The merchant signs the bond, thinking it a mere form of no significance.

—J. W. McSpadden, *Shakesperian Synopses.*[2]

In writing a synopsis:

A. **Leave out everything that does not directly advance the plot of the story.** McSpadden did not give the names of those suitors who are paying court to Portia as the play opens: The Neapolitan prince, the Count of the Palatinate, M. LeBon, and the others mentioned by Nerissa in the second scene. Since these suitors are not heard of again, there would be no point in mentioning them.

[2] Reprinted by courtesy of the Thomas Y. Crowell Company.

B. **Do not omit any detail that is necessary to understand or account for later happenings in the story.** McSpadden took care to characterize Portia as a "wise and wealthy lady." If her wisdom had not been mentioned at the very outset of the synopsis, as it is indicated early in the play itself, we should have been at a loss to account for her successful defense of Antonio and her prosecution of Shylock in court later on in the play.

C. **Jot down on a piece of paper those incidents which you think are important enough to be included in your condensation.** Read the selection through a second time, making a second list of important incidents. Then compare these lists and decide on a final list of incidents. Using the revised list as an outline, write your synopsis.

EXERCISE 2. 1. Write a synopsis of a short story or of a chapter in a novel which you have recently read.

2. Write a synopsis of a motion picture or of a play which you have recently attended.

3. Write a synopsis of the account of some recent athletic contest which has been described at some length in your college paper. In such a case it will be helpful, of course, for you to have seen the contest; but base your synopsis on the account that has been written of the game, and not on what you saw.

4. Write a synopsis of the following narrative:

THE GREAT FIRE OF LONDON

2 SEPTEMBER, 1666 (Lord's day). Some of our maids sitting up late last night to get things ready against our feast to-day, Jane called us up about three in the morning, to tell us of a great fire they saw in the City. So I rose and slipped on my night-gown, and went to her window, and thought it to be on the back-side of Mark Lane at the farthest; but, being unused to such fires as followed,

I thought it far enough off; and so went to bed again and to sleep. About seven rose again to dress myself, and there looked out at the window, and saw the fire not so much as it was and further off. So to my closet to set things to rights after yesterday's cleaning. By and by Jane comes and tells me that she hears that above 300 houses have been burned down to-night by the fire we saw, and that it is now burning down all Fish Street, by London Bridge. So I made myself ready presently, and walked to the Tower, and there got up upon one of the high places, Sir J. Robinson's little son going up with me; and there I did see the houses at that end of the bridge all on fire, and an infinite great fire on this and the other side the end of the bridge; which, among other people, did trouble me for poor little Michell and our Sarah on the bridge. So down, with my heart full of trouble, to the Lieutenant of the Tower, who tells me that it begun this morning in the King's baker's house in Pudding Lane, and that it hath burned St. Magnus's Church and most part of Fish Street already. So I down to the water-side, and there got a boat and through bridge, and there saw a lamentable fire. Poor Michell's house, as far as the Old Swan, already burned that way, and the fire running further, that in a very little time it got as far as the Steelyard, while I was there. Everybody endeavoring to remove their goods, and flinging into the river or bringing them into lighters that lay off; poor people staying in their houses as long as till the very fire touched them, and then running into boats, or clambering from one pair of stairs by the water-side to another. And among other things, the poor pigeons, I perceive, were loath to leave their houses, but hovered about the windows and balconies till they some of them burned their wings, and fell down. Having stayed, and in an hour's time seen the fire rage every way, and nobody, to my sight, endeavoring to quench it, but to remove their goods, and leave all to the fire, and having seen it get as far the Steelyard, and the wind mighty high and driving it into the City; and everything, after so long a drought, proving combustible, even the very stones of churches, and among other things the poor steeple by which pretty Mrs. ———— lives, and whereof my old schoolfellow Elborough is parson, taken fire in the very top, and there burned till it fell down: I to Whitehall (with a gentleman with me who desired to go off from the Tower, to see the fire, in my boat); to Whitehall, and there up to the King's closet in the Chapel, where people come about me, and I did give them an account dismayed them all, and word was carried in to the King. So I was called for, and did tell the King and Duke of York what I saw, and that unless His Majesty did command houses to be pulled down nothing could stop the fire.   —Samuel Pepys, *Diary*.

6. PRÉCIS WRITING

By definition a *précis* is a concise or abridged statement of any kind of material. In business, legal, and diplomatic circles, the subject matter of which précis are required falls into three broad classes: reports, correspondence, and minutes of evidence. To illustrate: The report of a commission investigating a Federal project might consume several thousand pages. A member of the President's cabinet is to make a speech, utilizing the essential facts of this report. Having neither the time nor the opportunity to study the several thousand pages of the document, he directs one of his secretaries to prepare a précis for him. This précis must contain, greatly condensed, all the essential facts and conclusions of the original report. Précis of evidence are equally useful to lawyers and judges, while précis of correspondence are regularly prepared for members of the diplomatic service.

The précis writer must be careful to say in about thirty

words what the original says in one hundred; in addition, in those thirty words he must give the very meanings and attitudes expressed in the full version. The précis must be just what its name implies: *precise*.

Lately a particular kind of précis writing has become very popular in the magazine world. The success of the *Reader's Digest* led to a number of similar journals: *Fact Digest, Digest and Review, Science Digest,* and *Everybody's Digest*.

Your notes on a chapter of assigned textbook reading are also a kind of précis. Notes made solely for use in preparing a long paper should be in the form of a précis. Class lecture notes are again a type of condensation which must include the essentials of the lecture. How often have you looked at notes that were "cold" and have been unable to make anything out of them? That was, of course, because you had failed to catch the essentials but had instead put down unrelated facts or comments in a helter-skelter fashion. Your condensation had not been *precise*.

Examine carefully the following three selections and the précis which have been made from them.

[A] *Original:*

Having sacrificed blood and treasure to win the war, having failed to establish quickly and at the first stroke a good and lasting peace, it was too hard, it was too much trouble, to keep on trying. We gave up. We took the easy way, the way that required us to do nothing, and we passed resolutions and made pious declarations saying that there was not going to be any more war, that war was henceforth outlawed.

Thus we entered the twenties, refusing to organize the peace of the world because that was too much trouble, believing, because that was no trouble at all, that peace would last by declaring that it ought to last. So enchanted were we with our own noble but inexpensive sentiments that, though the world was disorganized and in anarchy, we decided to disarm ourselves and the other democracies. That was also the easy way. It saved money. It saved effort.

(256 words)   —Walter Lippmann,
Our Squandered Inheritance of Freedom.[3]

Précis:

After sacrificing to win the war, and failing in the first attempt to establish lasting peace, we gave up trying and took the easy way. Thus during the twenties we made pious declarations about peace while doing nothing effective to achieve it. We disarmed the democracies before world stability had been won, because that saved us money and effort.

(59 words)

[B] *Original:*

"Nec ulla deformior species est civitatis quam illa in qua opulentissimi optimi putantur." The reflection of Cicero upon the dissolution of the commonwealth he served is matched by the insistence of Horace that when money is rated above all things, an unearned love is unattainable by men. Why should our fate be different from that of Rome? We can read in the pages of our own moralists that the lesson of the Industrial Revolution made the same impact upon themselves. Wordsworth, Southey, Carlyle, Mill, Matthew Arnold, Morris, all in their period warned us that an unequal society contains within itself the seeds of its own dissolution. We inherit the results of a century's refusal to give serious heed to their warning.

(121 words)   —Harold J. Laski, *Democracy in Crisis.*[4]

[3] Reprinted from a newspaper column published June 22, 1940.
[4] Reprinted from *Democracy in Crisis* by permission of The University of North Carolina Press. Copyright, 1933, by The University of North Carolina Press.

PRÉCIS WRITING

Précis:

"No state is worse than that in which the wealthiest are considered the best." So Cicero reflected, thinking of the fallen commonwealth of Rome; and Horace similarly condemned materialistic values. Wordsworth, Southey, Carlyle, Mill, Arnold, Morris, reflecting on the influence of the Industrial Revolution, have all warned us that our unequal society must have the same fate. Today we suffer because their warning went unheeded.
(65 words)

[C] *Original:*

Wire-tapping got its start in New York in 1895 when a former telephone worker who had joined the city police suggested that it might be a good idea to listen in on wires used by criminals. William L. Strong, who was mayor at the time, gave the project his blessing and for years after that wire-tapping flourished secretly. It was something the public of that period wouldn't worry about, anyhow, because in the nineties the telephone was not generally regarded as a household fixture. In those days police wire-tappers just walked into the telephone company's offices, asked for the location of the wires they were interested in, and got the information without fuss. Lines were usually tapped right in the cellar of the house or at an outside wall box.

There was an uproar when people got wind of the prevalence of wire-tapping. An investigation of public utilities in 1916 called attention to it. Those, of course, were war days, and eavesdropping of all kinds was widely encouraged. The government was tapping thousands of lines. A complete central-office switchboard had been set up in the New York Customs House, with taps running into it from all parts of the city. Every time a suspected alien lifted his receiver a light showed on this board and a stenographer, with headset clamped on, took a record of the conversation.

Inevitably it was claimed that wire-tapping violated a citizen's rights, and a large section of the press cried out against the practice, but nothing ever came of it. The furor, however, made the wire-tapper's job more difficult, because the Telephone Company, finding itself in an uncomfortable position, refused from then on to coöperate with the police in helping them locate suspect wires.

(289 words)   —Morris Berger, "Tapping the Wires,"
The New Yorker.[5]

Précis:

Wire-tapping got its start in New York in 1895 when a former telephone worker suggested that the police listen in on criminals. In those days police wire-tappers just walked into the telephone company's offices and learned the location of the wires they were interested in without fuss. Lines were usually tapped right in the cellar of the house or at an outside wall box.

Later, during World War days, when eavesdropping was widely encouraged, the government tapped thousands of lines. A complete central-office switchboard had been set up in the New York Customs House, with taps running into it from all parts of the city. Every time a suspected alien lifted his receiver a light flashed and a stenographer, with headset clamped on, recorded the conversation.

When people got wind of the prevalence of wire-tapping, the press denounced it, but nothing happened. The furor, however, made the wire-tapper's job more difficult, because the telephone company refused from then on to coöperate with the police.

(164 words)   —*Reader's Digest*.[6]

[5] Reprinted by courtesy of *The New Yorker*. Copyright, 1947, *The New Yorker Magazine, Inc.*

[6] Reprinted by courtesy of *Reader's Digest*.

PRÉCIS WRITING

Notice in these selections that the proportion between original and précis is somewhat different in each case. Prècis A is the most condensed; it has less than one-fourth as many words as its original. Précis B is somewhat less reduced, having about one-half as many words as the original, while Précis C has more than one-half as many words as the article it represents.

Some authorities fix upon one-third of the number of words in the original as the most desirable proportion for a précis, but the length of the original material and the kind of subject matter have much to do with the amount of reduction possible. Observe that of the three précis chosen for illustration, the one which succeeds in attaining the greatest compactness follows least closely the wording of the original passage, while Précis C, the least compact, lifts many sentences bodily from its source.

7. SUGGESTIONS FOR PRÉCIS WRITING

A. **Read over the article carefully. Be sure that you understand everything that is said.** Try to formulate a statement of the intent or purpose of the passage.

B. **After you have read the passage through and have a conception of its intent, make notes of the important points.** Here, for example, are the notes upon which Précis A, page 382, was based:

> Sacrifices to win the war.
> Failure to establish lasting peace.
> We stopped trying, took the easy way.
> Passed resolutions during '20's outlawing war, but did nothing to organize peace.
> We disarmed the democracies, though the world was in anarchy.
> Saved money and effort.

C. **Expand the notes into your précis, striving for as much economy of phrasing as possible.** It is preferable to write the first draft of the précis from your notes without looking at the original. This will help you to put the précis into your own words. After you have written your first draft, then compare this with the original and make whatever alterations seem necessary to give the exact shades of meaning demanded.

D. 1. **Use a single word in place of a phrase whenever possible.** Note that in Précis B *unheeded* replaces *refusal to give serious heed.*

2. **Try to use adjectives in place of phrases and clauses:** *materialistic values* replaces *when money is rated above all things.*

3. **Use phrases in place of clauses or sentences.** What in B is the equivalent of *the same fate* in the précis?

EXERCISE 3. Write précis of the following selections, putting to use the suggestions just given:

[A] About this time, our club meeting, not at a tavern, but in a little room of Mr. Grace's, set apart for that purpose, a proposition was made by me that, since our books were often referred to in our disquisitions upon the queries, it might be convenient to us to have them all together where we met, that upon occasion they might be consulted; and by thus clubbing our books to a common library, we should, while we liked to keep them together, have each of us the advantage of using the books of all the other members, which would be nearly as beneficial as if each owned the whole. It was liked and agreed to, and we filled one end of the room with such books as we could best spare. The number was not so great as we expected; and, though they had been of great use, yet, some inconveniences occurring for want of due care of them, the collection, after about a year, was separated, and each took his books home again.

And now I set on foot my first project of a public nature, that for a subscription library. I drew up the proposals, got them put into form by our great scrivener, Brockden, and, by the help of my friends in the Junto, procured fifty subscribers of forty shillings each to begin with, and ten shillings a year for fifty years, the term our company was to continue. We afterwards obtained a charter, the company being increased to one hundred: this was the mother of all the North American subscription libraries, now so numerous. It is become a great thing itself, and continually increasing. These libraries have improved the general conversation of the Americans, made the common tradesmen and farmers as intelligent as most gentlemen from other countries, and perhaps have contributed in some degree to the stand so generally made throughout the colonies in defense of their privileges.

—Franklin, *Autobiography.*

[B] On any scheme of cosmogony, life must be limited to an exceedingly small corner of the universe. To our baby's wonderings whether other cradles and other babies exist, the answer appears to be that there can at best be very few cradles, and there is no conceivable means of knowing whether they are tenanted by babies or not. We look out and see a universe consisting primarily of matter which is transforming itself into radiation, and producing so much heat, light, and highly penetrating radiation as to make life impossible. In rare instances, special accidents may produce bodies such as our earth, formed of a special cool ash which no longer produces radiation, and here life may be possible. But it does not at present look as though Nature had designed the universe primarily for life; the normal star and the normal nebula have nothing to do with life except making it impossible. Life is the end of a chain of by-products; it seems to be the accident, and torrential deluges of life-destroying radiation the essential.

—Sir James Jeans, "Man in the Universe." [7]

[7] Reprinted from *Eos, or The Wider Aspects of Cosmology,* reprinted by permission of Routledge and Kegan Paul, Ltd.

[**C**] Idealism must always prevail on the frontier, for the frontier, whether geographical or intellectual, offers little hope to those who see things as they are. To venture into the wilderness, one must see it, not as it is, but as it will be. The frontier, being the possession of those only who see its future, is the promised land which cannot be entered save by those who have faith. America, having been such a promised land, is therefore inhabited by men of faith: idealism is ingrained in the character of its people. But as the frontier in America has hitherto been geographical and material, American idealism has necessarily a material basis, and Americans have often been mistakenly called materialists. True, they seem mainly interested in material things. Too often they represent values in terms of money: a man is "worth" so much money; a university is a great university, having the largest endowment of any; a fine building is a building that cost a million dollars—better still, ten millions. Value is extensive rather than intensive or intrinsic. America is the best country because it is the biggest, the wealthiest, the most powerful; its people are the best because they are the freest, the most energetic, the *most* educated. But to see a materialistic temper in all this is to mistake the form for the spirit. The American cares for material things because they represent the substance of things hoped for. He cares less for money than for making money; a fortune is valued not because it represents ease, but because it represents struggle, achievement, progress. The first skyscraper in any town is nothing in itself, but much as an evidence of growth; it is a white stone on the road to the ultimate goal.

—Carl Becker, *Kansas.*[8]

[**D**] And to urge another argument of a parallel nature: if Christianity were once abolished, how would the freethinkers, the strong reasoners, and the men of profound

[8] Reprinted by permission of Henry Holt and Company, Inc.

learning be able to find another subject so calculated in all points whereon to display their abilities? What wonderful productions of wit should we be deprived of, from those whose genius by continual practice hath been wholly turned upon raillery and invectives against religion, and would therefore never be able to shine or distinguish themselves upon any other subject! We are daily complaining of the great decline of wit among us, and would we take away the greatest, perhaps the only topic we have left? Who would ever have suspected Asgil for a wit, or Toland for a philosopher, if the inexhaustible stock of Christianity had not been at hand to provide them with materials? What other subject, through all art or nature, could have produced Tindal for a profound author, or furnished him with readers? It is the wise choice of the subject that alone adorns and distinguishes the writer. For, had a hundred such pens as these been employed on the side of religion, they would have immediately sunk into silence and oblivion.

—Jonathan Swift,
The Abolishing of Christianity in England.

[E] Late one Saturday afternoon last month, a youthful London couple named Eddie and Brenda Smithson stepped on board a Skymaster at Northolt Airport, half an hour's drive from Victoria Station, and headed west toward a new life in a strange land. In doing so, Mr. and Mrs. Smithson were following the drift of more and more young English men and women, both married and single, who feel oppressed by the difficulties of a drab existence in England today and want to try their luck in the Dominions. The emigration figures make gloomy reading for officials of the British government, who would prefer to keep these exports at home. In the first six months of 1939, for instance, the number of English who felt that for them the answer to a frightening world outlook lay in Canada was under two thousand; in the first six months of this year, close to ten thousand people went there. During the same period of 1939, South Africa lured just under three thousand recruits from the old country; during the first six months of this year, eleven thousand Britons who had experienced the rigors of a crisis winter succumbed to the appeal of posters advertising the sunny South African climate and set out to sample it. All British shipping companies have waiting lists of would-be emigrants, many of whom, because of the jam, cannot hope to get on a boat before sometime next year.

—Mollie Panter-Downes, "A Reporter in England,"
The New Yorker.[9]

[F] Once, from eastern ocean to western ocean, the land stretched away without names. Nameless headlands split the surf; nameless lakes reflected nameless mountains; and nameless rivers flowed through nameless valleys into nameless bays.

Men came at last, tribe following tribe, speaking different languages and thinking different thoughts. According to their ways of speech and thought they gave names, and in their generations laid their bones by the streams and hills they had named. But even when tribes and languages had vanished, some of those old names, reshaped, still lived in the speech of those who followed.

After many centuries a people calling themselves Americans held the land. They followed the ways of the English more than of any others, especially in their speech. Yet they gathered together in their blood and in their manner of life something of all those who had lived in the land before them. Thus they took as a heritage many names of the past. Adding more names, they gave to their children with every generation the heritage richer than before.

A few hundred were great names, known to all Ameri-

[9] Reprinted by permission of The New Yorker. Copyright, 1947, The New Yorker Magazine, Inc.

cans, of states and cities, mountains and rivers. But most of them were little names, known only to those who lived near by, of ponds and swamps and creeks and hills, of townships and villages, of streets and ranches and plantations, of coves and gulches and meadows. These little names arose by so many thousands that at last they were numbered by millions.

—George Stewart, *Names on the Land.*[10]

[10] Reprinted by permission of Random House, Inc.

CHAPTER XI

THE LIBRARY

*Y*OU SHOULD now be ready to learn about your library
and to discover what its facilities are. Does it have a reference room where encyclopedias, dictionaries, yearbooks, and
works of general reference are kept? Are there special
reading rooms devoted entirely to books in particular fields
of study or divisions of knowledge, such as mathematics,
literature, philosophy, history, and economics? Has your
library made any special collections of books on any one
topic, such as English gardens or colonial furniture, and
are such collections housed in a special building or special
room? Are there rooms devoted to magazines and newspapers? And perhaps the most important question: Where
is the card catalogue?

1. CARD CATALOGUE

A card catalogue is a collection of the titles of all the
books in the library, each title being entered on a 3″ by 5″
card, along with the name of the author, the publisher, and
other significant information. These cards are filed alpha-
betically according to author, and sometimes according to
subject and title as well.

Catalogues vary in their completeness, but you may always be certain that there will be a card for every book
in the library filed under the name of its author. Here is
a reproduction of a typical "author card" from a library
catalogue:

P2
305   Eastman, Max, 1883–
.E13e
1935   **Enjoyment of poetry,** by Max Eastman . . .
             [Rev. ed.] New York, Chicago [etc.]
             C. Scribner's sons [1935]

             xiii, 254 p. 19½ cm.

The various items of information contained on the card are as follows:

1. The series of letters and numbers in the upper left corner is the library "call number"; it tells the librarian where and on what shelf he will be able to find that particular volume, and if your library is at all large, this is the number which you must give the attendant to get the book.

2. The top line of the card contains the author's name, the last name first, followed by his given name or names in their regular order.

3. The date of the author's birth, and of his death if he is no longer living, follows his name.

4. On the second line, usually in bold-faced type, the title of the book is given; and the sub-title, if there is any, follows in lighter type.

5. Many catalogue cards will then give the author's name a second time, but this time just as it appears on the title page of the book in question (which may not always correspond to the entry at the top of the card).

6. If the particular book which is catalogued is not the first edition, the card must specify what edition it is. The reason for this is clear enough. Later editions may represent revisions, and a reference to a certain page or to a quotation from the first edition of the book may not apply to later editions.

7. The place of publication, the name of the publisher, and the date of publication follow next in order.

8. Near the bottom of the card there is a statement about the number of pages contained in the book, the number of full-page illustrations and maps, if there are any, and the height of the book measured in centimeters. This information is rarely of concern to anyone except a highly trained scholar or bibliographer. It is called the *collation*.

2. SUBJECT HEADINGS

To assist the student who knows only the general topic he wants to pursue in preparation for a long theme or term paper, many libraries include in their catalogues cards which have subject as well as author headings. These may be in a separate section of the catalogue or filed along with the author cards.

If you were interested in finding out something about the history of the names of various places, you would look in the catalogue under the general topic *Names*. This topic might have under it several subdivisions, such as *Names, Family; Names, Geographical; Names, Personal,* and so on. It is the second of these which refers to the subject we have in mind, and here is a typical card which might be found in this division of the catalogue:

800.3
T 24
1883   Taylor, Isaac   (1829–1901)

Words and places: or Etymological
Illustrations of history, ethnology, and
geography. By Isaac Taylor . . .

With maps. London, Macmillan and co., 1893

xii, 375 p. illus., 2 fold. maps. 17½ cm.

NAMES, GEOGRAPHICAL

This card is sufficiently like the previous one illustrated
so that no detailed explanation of it is necessary. Notice
that no particular edition is specified, hence this must be
a card for the first edition of the work. Note also that the
last line tells you that the book has a twelve-page preface
in addition to the three hundred and seventy-five pages in
the body of the work, that the work is illustrated, and that
it contains two folded maps.

3. TITLE CARDS

To aid the reader or student who remembers the title
of a book but either does not know or has forgotten the
author, some card catalogues contain title cards as well.
These are usually confined to a limited number of works,
those sought after most frequently, and the arrangement on
the card follows that of the author cards except that the
title of the book is placed at the top of the card and the
name of the author comes below it.

4. MAGAZINES AND NEWSPAPERS

The card catalogue has in it at least one card for every
book in the library. It would be impossible, however, for

any library to include in its catalogue the author and title of every magazine article it possesses. Yet frequently the information to be found in magazines is concise and recent, exactly what a student needs to help him write a theme. Magazine articles are indexed yearly in the following publications:

Poole's Index to Periodical Literature. This covers the period from 1802 to 1907.

Reader's Guide to Periodical Literature. This covers the period from 1900 to the present time.

International Index to Periodicals. The sub-title of this tri-annual publication indicates that it deals chiefly with those magazines which are concerned with the humanities and sciences. The first volume begins with 1913.

(Annual) Magazine Subject Index.

There are also a number of indexes devoted to articles in special fields of study and interest:

Art Index.
The Education Index.
The Agricultural Index.
The Industrial Arts Index.

In using these indexes you must familiarize yourself with the standardized system of volume and page reference employed by nearly all magazines. All the issues of a magazine for one year (in some cases, six months) constitute a *volume* of that magazine, and at the close of the year those numbers are bound together. All the issues of the first year of any magazine will constitute *Volume 1,* those for the second year, *Volume 2,* and so on. Most magazines begin their page numbers with the first issue of the volume and number continuously until the end of that volume has been reached. Accordingly, references to magazines in some of these indexes and in many other bibliographical sources will be to the volume and page; the year and month may not be mentioned at all. References to weekly magazines will more often give the particular date of issue, since many of them do not number their pages continuously from the beginning of the volume.

It is often difficult to find newspaper material on many topics. Fortunately, yearly indexes are issued by two of the finest newspapers in the English language. The (London) *Times* publishes as *Official Index to the Times,* and the *New York Times Index* serves the newspaper of that name.

5. GENERAL REFERENCE WORKS

In beginning your investigation of some topic you will find it convenient to consult an encyclopedia or general reference work. From such general works you will extract the titles of books and articles which deal with your subject at greater length.

ENCYCLOPEDIAS

Encyclopedia Americana, revised edition, 1945, 30 vols. The publishers also issue an annual supplement called *Americana Annual.*

Encyclopædia Britannica, 14th edition, 1929, 24 vols. (latest printing 1943). This now has an annual supplement, *Britannica Book of the Year.* Many authorities consider the eleventh edition of this encyclopedia (29 vols., 1910) superior to anything that has appeared since.

New International Encyclopædia, 2d edition 1914–16, revised 1922–30, 23 vols. and 4 supplementary. The annual supplement to this encyclopedia is *New International Yearbook.*

SPECIAL DICTIONARIES

Allen, F. S. *Allen's Synonyms and Antonyms,* 1921; revised ed. by T. H. V. Motter, 1938.

Bartlett, John. *Familiar Quotations,* 10th edition, 1922; 11th edition, 1937.

Benham, W. G. *Book of Quotations, Proverbs and Household Words,* rev. ed., 1929.

———— *Dictionary of Classified Quotations,* 1921.

Brewer, E. C. *Dictionary of Phrase and Fable,* 1923.

———— *Reader's Handbook* of famous names in fiction, allusions, references, proverbs, plots, stories, and poems. New ed., 1923.

Craigie, Sir William and Hulbert, James R. *Dictionary of American English,* 1938–44.

Century Cyclopedia of Names, 1911. (Vol. 11 of the *Century Dictionary and Cyclopedia.*)

Crabb, George. *Crabb's English Synonyms,* 1917.

Fernald, J. C. *English Synonyms and Antonyms,* 1931.

Fowler, H. W. *A Dictionary of Modern English Usage,* 1926, reprinted 1930, 1940.

Harbottle, T. B. *Dictionary of Quotations* (classical). 1905.

Henderson, I. F. and Henderson, M. A. *A Dictionary of Scientific Terms,* 3d ed. rev. by J. H. Kenneth, 1939.

Horwill, H. W. *A Dictionary of Modern American Usage,* 1935.

Hoyt, J. K. *New Cyclopedia of Practical Quotations,* 1922.

Mawson, C. O. Sylvester, *International Book of Names,* 1942.

Roget, P. M. *Thesaurus of English Words and Phrases,* 1946.

Skeat, W. W. *An Etymological Dictionary of the English Language,* 4th ed., 1910.

Smith, W. G. *Oxford Dictionary of English Proverbs,* 1935.

Weekley, E. *An Etymological Dictionary of Modern English,* 1921.

YEARBOOKS

These give statistical facts chiefly about trade, population, governmental affairs, and biographical information about important men and women.

American Year Book, 1911–1920, 1925–
Chicago Daily News Almanac and Yearbook, 1900–
Europa, 1930–
Information Please Almanac, 1947–
New International Year Book, 1907–
Public Affairs Information Service, 1911–
Statesman's Year-Book, 1864–
Who's Who in America, 1899–   A biographical account of living Americans.
Who's Who, 1849–   Biographical accounts of living British subjects. There are also similar publications for various other countries and for the various professions. *Europa,* mentioned previously in this list, is the most comprehensive collection of European biographies.
World Almanac, 1885–

6. REFERENCE GUIDES TO
SPECIAL SUBJECTS

In almost every field of interest there are encyclopedias of special subjects, yearly guides to magazine articles, dictionaries of the basic terminology, and yearbooks which summarize the significant developments in that field. A list of the more important reference sources for a number of fields of interest follows:

AGRICULTURE

Agricultural Index, 1916–
Bailey, L. H. *Cyclopedia of American Agriculture,* 1908, repr. 1917, 4 vols.

——— *Standard Cyclopedia of Horticulture,* 1914–17, repr. 1925, 3 vols.

Bush-Brown, L. and J. *America's Garden Book,* 1939.

Taylor, Norman. *The Garden Dictionary,* 1936.

U. S. Department of Agriculture. *Experiment Station Record.*

U. S. Department of Agriculture. *Yearbook of Agriculture.*

ART AND ARCHITECTURE

A.L.A. Portrait Index, Library of Congress, 1906. This is an index to portraits contained in printed books and periodicals.

American Art Annual, 1899–

Ars Una, 1909–28. A series of one-volume histories of art, each volume being devoted to the art of a single country.

Art Index, 1930–

Champlin, J. D. Jr., and Perkins, C. C. *Cyclopedia of Painters and Painting,* 1892, 4 vols.

Fielding, M. *Dictionary of American Painters, Sculptors and Engravers,* 1927, 1945.

Harper's Encyclopedia of Art, 1937, 2 vols.

Index of Twentieth Century Artists, 1933–37.

Sturgis, R. *Dictionary of Architecture and Building,* 1901–2, 3 vols.

Who's Who in American Art. Published biennially.

Who's Who in Art. Third ed. 1934.

BIOGRAPHY

Appleton's Cyclopædia of American Biography, 1887–1924, 6 vols. and 4 supplementary.

Century Cyclopedia of Names, 1914. (Vol. XI of *Century Dictionary and Cyclopedia.*)

Dictionary of American Biography, 1928–36, 20 vols. and index. A supplement, to Dec. 31, 1935, pub. 1944.

Dictionary of National Biography, 1885–1901, 63 vols., supplements: 1901, 3 vols.; 1912, 3 vols.; 1927, 1937. Biographical data about Englishmen who are no longer living. There is also a one-volume *Concise Dictionary of National Biography*, which is an epitome of the larger work.

Encyclopedia of American Biography, New Series, 1934–, 19 vols.

National Cyclopedia of American Biography, 1893–1937, 30 vols.; 6 supplementary volumes are devoted to the biographies of living persons.

Similar biographical dictionaries and encyclopedias exist for countries other than England and America.

CLASSICAL LITERATURE AND ANTIQUITIES

Peck, H. T., editor. *Harper's Dictionary of Classical Literature and Antiquities*, 1897.

Smith, W., Wayte, W., Marindin, G. E. *A Dictionary of Greek and Roman Antiquities*, 3d ed., 1890–91, 3 vols.

Walters, H. B. *A Classical Dictionary of Greek and Roman Antiquities*, 1916.

COMMERCE, ECONOMICS, BUSINESS, FINANCE

American Business Encyclopædia, 1913, 5 vols.
Census of Business, U. S. Bureau of the Census.
Commerce Year Book, U. S. Department of Commerce.
Encyclopædia of the Social Sciences, 1930–35, 15 vols.
Mulhall, M. G. *Dictionary of Statistics*, 4th ed. repr., 1909.

Munn, G. G., *Encyclopedia of Banking and Finance,* 1927, 1937.

Newark, N. J. Free Public Library. *Business Information and its Sources,* compiled by M. C. Manley, 1931; supplement, 1939.

────── *Business Books:· 1920–1926,* 1927.

Survey of Current Business (U. S. Department of Commerce).

Statistical Abstract (U. S. Department of Commerce).

EDUCATION

American Business Education Yearbook, 1944–

Biennial Survey of Education (U. S. Office of Education).

Education Index, 1930–

Marsh, C. S., *American Colleges and Universities,* 4th ed., 1940.

Monroe, P. ed. *Cyclopedia of Education,* 1911–13, 5 vols.

Monroe, W. S. *Encyclopedia of Educational Research,* 1941.

National Survey of Secondary Education (U. S. Office of Education).

Survey of Land-Grant Colleges and Universities (U. S. Office of Education), 1930, 2 vols.

Watson, F., ed. *Encyclopædia and Dictionary of Education,* 1921–22, 4 vols.

ENGINEERING AND INDUSTRIAL ARTS

Engineering Index, 1884–

Industrial Arts Index, 1913–

Tweney, C. F., and Shirshov, I. P. *Hutchinson's Technical and Scientific Encyclopædia,* 1935, 4 vols.

HISTORY

Adams, J. T. *Atlas of American History,* 1943.

Beers, H. P. *Bibliographies in American History,* 1938; 2d ed. 1942.

Channing, E., Hart, A. B., and Turner, F. J. *Guide to Study and Reading of American History,* 1912.

Dictionary of American History, 1940, 5 vols. and index.

Dutcher, G. M., and others. *Guide to Historical Literature,* 1931.

Jameson, J. F. *Dictionary of United States History,* 1931.

Keller, Helen R. *Dictionary of Dates,* 1934.

Larned, J. N., ed. *Literature of American History,* 1902.

Writings on American History, 1902–

LAW

Black's Law Dictionary, 3d ed., 1933.

Bouvier's Law Dictionary and Concise Encyclopedia, 9th ed., 1934.

Corpus Juris, 1914–   Annotations from decisions in important cases.

Index to Legal Periodicals, 1908–

LITERATURE AND THE STAGE

Baker, E. A., and Packman, J. *Guide to the Best Fiction,* 3d ed., 1932. Although this is primarily an index of English and American fiction, translations from foreign languages are included.

Baker, E. A. *Guide to Historical Fiction,* 1914.

Book Review Digest, 1905–

Clark, B. H. *Study of the Modern Drama,* 1934.

Cambridge History of American Literature, 1917–21, 4 vols.

Cambridge History of English Literature, 1907–27, re-issued 1932, 15 vols.

Dramatic Index, 1910–

Firkins, I. *Index of Plays, 1800–1926,* 1927. Supplement: *1927–34,* 1935.

———— *Index to Short Stories,* 1923. Supplement, 1929.

Hefling, H., and Richards, E. *Index to Contemporary Biography and Criticism,* 2d ed., 1934.

Logasa, H., and Ver Nooy, W. *Index to One-Act Plays,* 1924–40, 3 vols.

Magnus, Laurie. *Dictionary of European Literature,* 1926.

Mantle, Burns, *Best Plays of 1909–1919,* and annual volumes after that date.

Harvey, Sir Paul. *Oxford Companion to English Literature,* 1934.

Sharp, R. F. *Short Biographical Dictionary of Foreign Literature,* 1933.

Stage Year-Book, 1908–28. A yearly review of the English stage, no longer current.

Who's Who Among Living Authors of Older Nations, 1931–

Who's Who Among North American Authors, 1921–

Who's Who in Literature, 1924–

MUSIC

Allen, H., and others. *Dictionary of Modern Music and Musicians,* 1924.

Cobbett's Cyclopedic Survey of Chamber Music, 1929–30, 2 vols.

Grove's Dictionary of Music and Musicians, 3d ed., 1935, 6 vols.; supplementary vol., 1940.

Kobbé, G. *The Complete Opera Book,* rev. ed., 1935.

Oxford History of Music, 1929–34, 7 vols.

Pierre Key's Music Year Book, 1925–38. A yearly survey of musical organizations, artists, and festivals in this country.

Pratt, W. S. *New Encyclopedia of Music and Musicians,* 2d ed., 1929.

Sears, M. E. *Song Index,* 1926; supplement, 1934.

Scholes, P. A. *Oxford Companion to Music,* 1938.

Thompson, O. *International Cyclopedia of Music and Musicians,* 1939.

Wier, A. E. *Macmillan Encyclopedia of Music and Musicians,* 1938.

MYTHOLOGY AND FOLKLORE

Chambers, Robert. *Book of Days,* 1914, 2 vols.

Edwardes, M., and Spence, L. *Dictionary of Non-Classical Mythology,* 1923.

Hazeltine, Mary E. *Anniversaries and Holidays,* 1928; 2d ed., 1944.

Hazlitt, William C. *Faiths and Folk Lore,* 1905, 2 vols.

Mythology of All Races, 1916–32, 12 vols. and index.

Spence, L. *Introduction to Mythology,* 1931.

PHILOSOPHY AND PSYCHOLOGY

Baldwin, James M. *Dictionary of Philosophy and Psychology,* 1901–05; 2d ed., 1910, 3 vols.; corrected ed., 1928. The third volume also appears under the title: Rand, B. *Bibliography of Philosophy, Psychology and Cognate Subjects.*

Bibliography of Philosophy, 1934–   A yearly bibliography of scholarly philosophical literature.

Psychological Abstracts, 1927–

Psychological Index, 1894–   A yearly bibliography.

Warren, Howard C. *Dictionary of Psychology,* 1934.

POLITICAL SCIENCE

Cyclopedia of American Government, 1914, 3 vols.

Encyclopedia of the Social Sciences, 1930–35, 15 vols.

Langer, W. L. *Foreign Affairs Bibliography, 1919–42,* 1933–45.

Palgrave, R. *Palgrave's Dictionary of Political Economy,* 1923–26, 3 vols.

Political Handbook of the World, 1927–

Student's Guide to Materials in Political Science, prepared by L. Burchfield, 1935.

United Nations Review, published by the United Nations Information Office, 1941–

United Nations Weekly Bulletin, U.N. Department of Public Information, 1946–

RELIGION

Addis, W., and Arnold, T. *Catholic Dictionary,* 9th ed., 1917.

Case, S. J., McNeill, J. T., and others. *A Bibliographical Guide to the History of Christianity,* 1931.

Catholic Encyclopedia, 1907–22, 15 vols. and 2 supplementary.

Encyclopedia of Religion and Ethics, 1911–27, 12 vols. and index.

Jewish Encyclopedia, 1901–06, 12 vols.

Mathews, S., and Smith, G. B. *Dictionary of Religion and Ethics,* 1921.

New Catholic Dictionary, 1929.

Schaff, P. *New Schaff-Herzog Encyclopedia of Religious Knowledge,* 1908–14, 12 vols. and index.

Universal Jewish Encyclopedia, 1939–43, 10 vols.; index, 1944.

Yearbook of American Churches, 1916–

SCIENCE

Atomic Information, published monthly by National Committee on Atomic Information, 1946–

Bibliography of North American Geology, 1931–34, 2 vols.

Botanical Abstracts, 1918–26. After 1926 this monthly publication was united with *Abstracts of Bacteriology.*

Bulletin of the Atomic Scientists, published by the Atomic Scientists of Chicago, fortnightly, 1945–

Crane, E. J., and Patterson, A. M. *Guide to the Literature of Chemistry,* 1927.

Glazebrook, Richard. *Dictionary of Applied Physics,* 1922–23, 5 vols.

Henderson, I. F., and Henderson, W. D. *Dictionary of Scientific Terms in Biology, Botany, Zoology, Anatomy, Cytology, Embryology, Physiology,* 2d ed., 1929.

Schoengold, M. D., ed. *Encyclopedia of Substitutes and Synthetics,* 1943.

Soule, B. A. *Library Guide for the Chemist,* 1938.

Standardized Plant Names, published by American Joint Committee on Horticultural Nomenclature, 1923.

Thorpe, E. *Dictionary of Applied Chemistry,* 1922–27, 7 vols. Supplement, 1934–35, 2 vols.

Willis, J. C. *Dictionary of the Flowering Plants and Ferns,* 6th ed., 1931.

SOCIOLOGY

Dictionary of Sociology, ed. H. P. Fairchild, 1934.

Encyclopedia of the Social Sciences, 1930–35, 15 vols.

Public Affairs Information Service, 1915–

Social Science Abstracts, 1929–

If the field in which you are interested is not represented

in the list of books which has been given, here are two detailed works on the use of the library:

Hutchins, M., Johnson, A., and Williams, M. *Guide to the Use of Libraries,* 1936.

Mudge, I. G. *Guide to Reference Books,* 6th ed., 1936. With supplements to 1940.

7. COLLECTING SOURCE MATERIAL

Once you know your way about the library and have chosen the topic for your paper, you are ready to collect source materials. Where you go first will depend on your subject. Is it on something recent or contemporary? Then newspapers and magazines may have to satisfy you—there may be no book on it. Is it historical? Then you may have to rely on books alone.

In either case, the first thing to do is to make a list of sources in which you are likely to find something of the kind you want. Look up your subject in the card index and the periodical indexes, and keep a careful record of everything you find. The best way—in fact, the only good way —to do this is to get cards or slips of paper similar to the library cards, and to put each separate title on one slip. *Do not merely make a list in a notebook.* The use of cards or slips may appear slow when you begin, but it will pay for itself in the end. For you will have to sort things out and alphabetize them, which is very easy with cards but intolerably clumsy with a notebook list. Bookstores supply cards in various sizes.

Get your cards or slips, then, and make one for each of the sources you may find useful. From these you will make your *bibliography.* Be sure to be accurate and inclusive; take down *all* the information which you will ultimately need. (It might be wise to look up the requirements of footnotes and bibliography as given below, pages 425–431, that you may omit nothing essential.) Do not collect sources indiscriminately. The library cards, read wisely, will often guide you. The date will tell how recent a book is; the number of pages and subject references will suggest its scope; and in other ways you can decide without seeing them that some books are not worth listing or looking at for your present need.

In addition to your bibliography cards, keep another set of cards or slips on which to take *notes* as you read. Be sure to make your notes legible and accurate, and do not forget page references. A quotation without a page reference is almost impossible to find again. Punctuate to show quotation, omissions, your own words, etc.

EXAMPLE

Turn back for a moment to page 393, on which is shown a library card for Max Eastman's *Enjoyment of Poetry*. Suppose you wanted to use this book for your paper. You would first make a bibliography card very much like the library card, keeping most of the information it gives, except perhaps the last line.

Now for each of the notes you take from this book you would make a card like this:

Eastman   Language of Poetry

"He [the poet] not only gives to our mind the indication, or the general information that he wishes, but he gives to our bodies an acute impression less easy to forget. To read in practical language is to be told, but to read in poetry is to learn by experience."

p. 193

Note that "Eastman" at the top, left, is all you need to connect this with the bibliography card, which has the information about the book itself. At the top, right, you indicate with a phrase the subject of your note. If this phrase corresponds to one division of your outline, the sorting of your collected notes will be greatly facilitated. The material on this card is quoted exactly, with two explanatory words added by you in brackets. The page reference follows.

As you collect your materials, remember that *it is easier to discard extra notes than to go back to the source and find a statement which you could now use, but of which you made no record.* Do not depend on memory; write your notes.

8. USE OF SOURCE MATERIALS

Remember that your task is not finished when you have amassed a great body of material from books, magazines, and newspapers. You are assigned a long paper to make you do some thinking on your own account. Since you cannot think in a vacuum, the information that you have gathered is the material for your thoughts. This information should appear in your paper, but the paper must be concerned primarily with your ideas and conclusions *about* this information.

In short, your paper must have a purpose: the discussion and presentation of your own conclusions about a particular problem which you have succeeded in isolating in the course of your reading. You must have a point to prove, an attitude to maintain, a conclusion to present. This point of view must be supported in terms of actual fact. A possible opposite point of view or a possible set of conclusions differing from yours will have to be refuted in terms of actual fact. In other words, your next task is the sifting, digesting, and putting in order of your material.

CHAPTER XII

ORGANIZING THE PAPER

*I*F YOUR PAPER is to be successful it must be planned. You may seem to write short papers altogether without plan, and you may even do some without an outline, because their limited scope permits you to plan them in your head—almost without knowing it. Besides, some simple subjects virtually plan themselves: if you are explaining how something is manufactured, you will naturally follow the raw material through a series of processes until the product is finished. But the longer the paper you write, the more deliberate and considered must be your plan. You can hardly do without an outline.

1. OUTLINING

It is instructive to see how another writer has used the outline. Let us take a recent essay on education, isolate the topic statements (see above, page 45) from each paragraph, and discover the underlying pattern, if such there be.

WHY NOT TEACH SOME OF THESE THINGS? [13]

1. "What shall I teach?" A great many of us who teach have wondered about this very matter.

2. I do not think that there is in general any clearly defined understanding in America as to the real end of education.

3. Firsthand experience in public-school teaching furnishes one with many illustrations of the fundamental absurdity of the assumption that we educate for culture.

[13] Claire Williams, "Why Not Teach Some of These Things?" Reprinted by courtesy of *The Forum*.

4. Others seem to assume that the end of education is to train youth to earn its living. That seems to me also a mistaken assumption.

5. I think that the end of education is to improve slowly, steadily, decade by decade, the quality of the populace.

6. Before we set out to educate, we should decide exactly what things schools can teach which will tend to grade up the population.

7. The gap in mental development between the civilized man and the savage is most easily estimated by observing the difference in language.

8. In normal cases the power to express thought measures the power to think.

9. For the welfare of the state, then, its people should be able to think. To do this they must be in command of language, which is the instrument of thought.

10. It would be much more efficient to train children to speak well at the start than to have them waste time and strength trying to unlearn habits ineradicably established.

11. I emphasize the value of this early training in language, not only for the sake of correct speech, but for another reason: in infancy, knowledge of things advances at the same pace as our knowledge of language.

12. The more children know by seven, the better their chances are to learn a reasonable amount by the time they are seventeen.

13. Next, I should teach formal manners.

14. If a state is to have a civilized population, its children must be taught to behave like civilized beings.

15. About the most important thing the child has to learn is that the world is full of other people, whose rights he must observe, and with whom he must be scrupulous in the fulfillment of his obligations.

16. Next I should include in my school a great deal of physical training.

17. It does lie within our power to do a great deal toward perfecting our pupils' physique.

18. A child should study drawing to learn how to use his hands with precision and neatness and to help him retain the faculty of observation.

19. I should require some sort of handwork to give pupils practice in the use of tools.

Having assembled the topic statements, we read over this summary and decide what the purpose of the essay is. It appears clear that the author is considering what subjects should be taught in the schools; the idea is readily confirmed by a glance at the first topic statement: "What shall I teach?"

In analyzing the essay, then, let us first ask ourselves, "What subjects does this author want the schools to teach?" Paragraphs 7–11 all deal with the teaching of language and paragraph 12 continues the argument begun in the preceding paragraph, so we can tentatively set down as one division of the essay a note which would read something like this:

¶s 7–12 Language

Next notice that paragraph 13 and the two following deal with manners and forms of behavior. A second division of the essay could be set down then as follows:

¶s 13–15 Manners

We may next note that paragraphs 16 and 17 select physical training as one of the subjects to be taught, that paragraph 18 is devoted to drawing, and finally that paragraph 19 deals with manual training. Following the example of the preceding paragraphs, we might add to our notes:

¶s 16, 17 Physical training
¶ 18 Drawing
¶ 19 Manual training

Since all these subjects have to do with the development of skill rather than of the intellect, it would be possible to consider them under one head and to organize them as follows:

> Development of skill:
> > Physical exercise
> > Drawing
> > Manual training

All of the things which our author believes should be taught in the schools have now been covered, but the first six paragraphs of the essay still remain to be organized. The first paragraph is an introductory statement of the topic of the essay. Paragraph 2 states that there are a number of opinions about the aims of education. The following three paragraphs illustrate this point by showing how varied such opinions actually are. Therefore, we might make a temporary note something as follows:

> No agreement as to aims of education.
> > Culture not the chief end
> > Training for earning a living not the chief end
> > Education should improve the quality of the populace

This is not the only possible organization for these statements; we might put statement 2 with the opening paragraph and call them both introductory:

I. No agreement in America as to certain phases of education.

> A. What shall be taught?
> B. What is the end of education?

Notice that we might then place as subsections under B paragraphs 3, 4, and 5.

B. What is the end of education?

1. We do not educate for culture.
2. We do not educate to train students to earn a living.

It is precisely this rearranging of statements that gives outline making its value. In the course of it, the path of the author's argument is impressed upon you ever more clearly; you come to see just how one statement follows or depends upon another. Moreover, if one statement does not logically depend upon something which has gone before, or, if there is a serious break in the writer's train of thought—which may weaken the validity of his conclusion —the processes involved in making the outline will certainly bring the weak points to light. The procedure is reversed, of course, when you make an outline for a paper that *you* are going to write; but the effect of clarifying the pattern is the same.

Now that we have assembled topic statements in various ways and have tried a number of possible groupings, the final step is to join the main headings into a connected outline. We may make two distinct types of outlines from this essay.

2. SENTENCE OUTLINE

I. In the American educational world there is little or no agreement on certain of the most vital problems.

A. Many teachers are not certain about what should be taught.
B. There is not a clearly defined understanding as to the real end of education.

1. Culture is not the primary aim.
2. Training youth to earn its living is not the chief end.

II. The end of education is to improve the quality of the populace.

III. We must teach those subjects which will accomplish this end.

    A. Training in language works toward this end.
        1. The power to express thought measures the power to think.
        2. Knowledge of things advances at the same pace as the knowledge of language.

    B. Training in formal manners improves the quality of the populace.
        1. It teaches children to behave like civilized beings.
        2. It gives children a sense of the rights of other people.

    C. The development of skills is also necessary.
        1. Physical training will perfect the children's physiques.
        2. Drawing will help a child use his hands with precision.
        3. Manual training will give children practice in the use of tools.

3. TOPIC OUTLINE

I. Disagreements in the educational field.
    A. Content.
    B. Aims.

II. Mistaken notions of the chief aim of education.
    A. Culture.
    B. Earning a living.

III. Education to improve the quality of the populace.

IV. Subjects which will lead to improvement.

   A. Language.

      1. Power to express thought.
      2. Early knowledge of things.

   B. Formal manners.

      1. Improvement of behavior.
      2. Development of consideration for others.

   C. Development of skills.

      1. Physical exercise.
      2. Drawing.
      3. Manual training.

The preceding outlines illustrate the two types most commonly used. They differ in that the *sentence outline* so phrases each item that it makes a complete sentence, whereas the *topic outline* gives each item little more than a label or title. The sentence outline is more useful for outlining material which you are reading, as may be seen from the way in which this one was derived. When you are preparing to write a paper, the topic outline may prove the more useful.

That shown here is not highly developed. It is the kind you might be able to make after you have begun to read your sources and when the pattern has begun to emerge, but before you are ready to write. You should make such a preliminary outline with wide spaces between the divisions, into which you can insert the details of evidence, fact, or illustration that will best serve your argument.

The advantage of making your outline early is that it will guide you in reading and note taking. You may find that in some division of your subject you need to read further. It also gives you a pattern by which to sort your notes. Keep enlarging and improving your outline with all necessary subdivisions until you have finished your reading. Then go over it carefully and correct any inconsistencies or faults of structure. Decide what details you will use and discard the others. The resultant corrected outline is ready for presentation to your instructor, if that is required, and in any case it is ready for use in the writing of your paper.

For both sentence and topic outlines the scheme of organization is the same:

I. ....
  A. ....
    1. ....
      a. ....
      b. ....
    2. ....
      a. ....
      b. ....
      c. ....
  B. ....
II. ....

If you need subdivisions beyond the third degree you may use *i, ii, iii,* and *x, y, z,* for subseries under these. It is seldom that an outline is that complicated.

4. SUGGESTIONS FOR OUTLINING

Observe the following precautions:

A. Make certain that all the members of one sub-division are of the same degree of importance.

Suppose that the topic outline had read:

IV. *C.* Development of skill.

    1. Physical exercise.

  D. Drawing.

    1. Manual training.

Such an arrangement would have been faulty for two reasons:

1. As "drawing" is one means of developing skill recommended by the author, it should not have been placed in an equal or co-ordinate position with "development of skill."

2. "Manual training" is not a form or sub-division of drawing, therefore it should not be placed in a position inferior or subordinate to "drawing."

Look at the topic outline again and see how these items are arranged.

B. Strive for parallel phrasing in co-ordinate parts of the outline.

Notice the following:

B. Formal manners.

    1. Improves behavior.

    2. Consideration for others.

Notice that "Improves behavior" consists of a verb and its object while "Consideration for others" is just a phrase. If we should place a verb in item 2, the two will be parallel:

    1. Improves behavior.

    2. Develops consideration for others.

C. Sub-division in an outline ordinarily demands that there be two or more parts under each heading. Notice the following:

III. Education to improve the quality of the populace.

  A. Subjects which will lead to improvement.

If the topic outline had been organized in this fashion, there would have been no second topic of equal rank with *A* to place under *III*. When you meet such a situation you must either combine the minor heading with the major heading under which you have placed it or elevate it to the rank of a second major heading.

CHAPTER XIII

MANUSCRIPT PREPARATION

*T*HE SUGGESTIONS which follow are designed to help you to make the best possible initial impression upon the reader. It is too bad when a well written paper is untidy, hard to read, or amateurish in form. Experience has shown that certain things are necessary to make a manuscript readable. Unless you are sure you can improve on them, follow the standard forms.

1. FORMAT

A. Manuscripts generally should be written on paper 8½ x 11 inches in size.

B. If the manuscript is hand written, use only black or blue-black ink. Write legibly.

Avoid breaks between the letters of a word, and do not run words together. Make your capital letters sufficiently distinct from lower-case letters. Make your marks of punctuation carefully, that the reader will be able to distinguish between a period and a comma, between a colon and a semicolon, and between a hyphen and a dash.

C. If the manuscript is typewritten, double space it.

Be sure to leave enough space after punctuation marks: One space after a comma or semicolon; two spaces after a colon, period, question mark or exclamation point; no space between the quotation marks and the material quoted; two spaces after the second pair of quotation marks; no space before or after a hyphen when not used for word division at the end of a line. If your typewriter is not supplied with a dash, use a double hyphen for a dash. Leave at least an inch margin at the left side. Do not crowd words at the right of the page or at the bottom. The title should be written at least two inches from the top of the first page, with the body of the composition beginning no less than three spaces below it. On subsequent pages there should be an inch margin at the top. The pages should be numbered at the top; Arabic numerals are preferred.

D. Paragraph indentation should be uniform.

Five spaces is the usual amount for typewritten manuscripts. Indentation in a handwritten manuscript varies with the size of the handwriting, but it should be clearly perceptible to the reader. A distance of one-half to one inch is enough for most handwriting.

2. PRESENTING SOURCE MATERIAL

In preparing your long paper you have gathered information of various kinds, some of which you want to use directly. The question is how best to present it. Let us suppose that your paper is concerned with the cost of naval construction and you want to prove that the government can build ships for less than private companies. You have secured some comparative figures of government and private bids for the same ships. If you say that the bids of the government on two battleships during the year 1942 were ten million dollars lower than the bids of two commercial companies, without any reference to the source of your information, that is not sufficient. Your reader infers that you have gathered this information directly from the incident, which is not true—or, if it is information which you obviously could not have obtained directly, your reader will be annoyed with you for not divulging the source of your facts and may be inclined to distrust them.

You may do one of three things:

1. **You may give the information and your source of it in an indirect quotation, in something like the following form:**

> According to testimony given at hearings of the Naval Committee in the Senate, it was shown that the bids of private shipbuilding companies were over ten million dollars higher than the estimates of the government navy yard. This fact was reported by the Associated Press in a story copyrighted June 16, 1942, and appeared in the Springfield (Mass.) <u>Republican</u> of that date on page 16.

2. **You may give only the indirect quotation in the text of your paper and then place the information about the source of the statement in a footnote:**

> According to testimony given at hearings of the Naval Committee in the Senate, it was shown that the bids of private shipbuilding companies were over ten million dollars higher than the estimates of the government yard.[3]

> [3] Springfield (Mass.) Republican, June 16, 1942, p. 16. Reported by the Associated Press.

3. **Finally, you may quote the information directly,** in this case either from the Associated Press account or from the official report of the Senate Committee hearing:

> "Mr. Mortimer J. Easly of the Navy Department at a hearing of the Senate Naval Committee, when asked about the comparative size of the bids of private companies and government navy yard estimates on the cost of building the two most recently projected battleships, informed the committee that the bids of the private companies were over ten million dollars higher than that of the government navy yard."[2]

> [2] Springfield (Mass.) Republican, June 16, 1942, p. 16. Reported by the Associated Press.

3. QUOTED MATERIAL

A. Poetry quoted in a text should appear line for line just as it was in the original. If the line of poetry is too long to be written on a single line of the page, the left-over portion should be indented. Maintain the stanza divisions of the original.

```
And she paused on her way to gather the fairest
      among them,
That the dying once more might rejoice in their
      fragrance and beauty.
Then, as she mounted the stairs to the corridors,
      cooled by the east wind,
Distant and soft on her ear fell the chimes from the
      belfry of Christ Church.
                        --Longfellow, Evangeline.
```

B. An extended prose quotation should be separated from the text proper by beginning it on a new line and indenting again the normal distance of paragraph indentation. In a published book, long prose quotations are usually centered and often set in smaller type. Something of the same effect may be secured in typescript by single spacing. A long prose quotation centered and set off in this fashion need not be enclosed in quotation marks, provided the language of the text shows that it is a quotation and proper credit is given in a footnote. Such quotations must follow the original word for word, and punctuation must be reproduced exactly. Omissions may be indicated by the use of suspension points.

```
      The Burlington and the Union Pacific and all the
Eastern industrial power which these two names
represented in Nebraska were still in control.
Mr. Olney, the Burlington's General Counsel, had
been made Attorney General by Mr. Cleveland.  He
wrote the frightened Mr. Perkins:

            The (Interstate Commerce) Commission . . .
      is, or can be made, of great use to the rail-
      roads.  It satisfies the popular clamor for
```

> a government supervision of railroads . . .
> Further, the older such a commission gets to
> be, the more inclined it will be found to
> take the business and railroad view of things
> . . . The part of wisdom is not to destroy the
> Commission, but to utilize it.[6]

4. FOOTNOTES

The purpose of footnotes is threefold:

1. To separate borrowed material from your own and to acknowledge the former. This is simple honesty and forestalls any suspicion of plagiarism.

2. To permit the reader to verify for himself or to read further in a source. Thus you also disclaim responsibility for errors in the material you are using.

3. To make a necessary explanation without interrupting the body of the paper. You may even wish to disagree with quoted material.

A. Footnotes are indicated by Arabic numerals placed a little above and to the right of the word commented on.

Usually the number is placed at the end of the sentence to which the footnote refers unless the sentence is so long that it eventually gets away from the precise item to be explained. When a footnote is used to give the source of quoted matter, the number should appear at the end of the quotation. If the footnote refers to the title of a work, it should be placed immediately after the title. It is desirable to number the footnotes consecutively throughout the paper.

EXAMPLES

1. De Neve had accepted the governorship of California rather under protest, and his resignation was now on file with the commanding general.[5]

2. Durant came out from New York "dressed in the style of a frontier dandy. He wore a slouch hat, velvet sack coat and vest, corduroy breeches and top boots, all his clothing being of a costly character."[3]

3. Mr. Krutch's book, Samuel Johnson,[2] is a bold attempt to follow in the track of one of the world's greatest biographies.

B. In the footnote itself the number appears first, so indented that it is on a line with the paragraph indentation.

In published books and articles the number preceding the footnote is superior (above the line), just as is the reference number in the text itself. If your manuscript is handwritten, you will find that it is best to employ the superior number; if your manuscript is typewritten, put the footnote number (but not the reference number in the text) on a line with the note itself. See page 432.

C. In a theme or class paper the footnote should appear at the bottom of the page which contains the passage to which it refers.

The note or notes should be separated from the text itself by a line at least two inches long, with at least one and preferably two spaces on either side of the line.

EXAMPLE

. . . He lived in the Wittelsbacher Palais[1] in semi-state, entertained lavishly at Leopoldskron,[2] built a few fantastic houses, still patronized the arts, went to Italy, travelled. He had become Maecenas . . .

---

[1] Long the residence of his grandson, Ludwig III, and later the seat of the Communist Government in April, 1919.

[2] Now Professor Reinhardt's palace near Salzburg.

D. Footnotes referring to source materials are of two styles, depending on whether or not the paper has a bibliography.

If it has none, the necessary bibliographical information will have to be given in the footnotes; but if it has a bibliography the footnotes will need only to identify the immediate references. Thus the chief province of the footnote is the *immediate reference* (giving volume, page, column, line, or otherwise locating a quotation or borrowing), whereas the province of the bibliography is the *general information* about any source (the author, exact title, edition, place of publication, publisher, and date). In the bibliographical footnote these are combined.

EXAMPLES

Complete Reference When There Is No Bibliography:

W. A. Craigie, *English Spelling: Its Rules and Reasons* (New York, 1927), p. 96.

O. Jespersen, *A Modern English Grammar* (Heidelberg: Carl Winter, 1931), II, 163.

H. L. Mencken, *The American Language* (4th ed., New York, 1936), p. 54, n. 6.

J. S. Kenyon, "Some Notes on American *R*," *American Speech,* I (1926), 329–39.

Marvin Barloon, "Steel: the Great Retreat," *Harper's Magazine,* August 1947, p. 145.

Shortened Reference When a Bibliography Is Appended:

Craigie, *English Spelling,* p. 96.

Jespersen, *Modern English Grammar,* II, 163.

Beals, "Swastika Over the Andes," p. 178.

These models will be found adequate for most occasions. If an ampler treatment of footnotes is desired, consult *A*

Manual of Style, University of Chicago Press, or the manuals published by various government departments.

E. After a footnote has referred to any source once, a number of abbreviations are permissible in subsequent references to the same source.

When two or more successive footnotes refer to the same place in the same work, it is not necessary to repeat the author and title in the second footnote; use the word *ibid.,* (Latin *ibidem*—the same) as a label. If the same work but not the same page is referred to, write: "*ibid.* p. 231."

If you are referring to a work the second time, but references to other works have come between the first and the second reference, you may give simply the name of the author followed by *op. cit. (opere citato*—"in the work cited") or *loc. cit. (loco citato*—"in the place cited") if the reference is to the same page. For example:

Robertson, *op. cit.,* p. 79.

If there have been a great many references between the first and second citations of a work, it is better to give again a shortened form of the title.

F. Other useful abbreviations which may be used in footnotes are:

cf., "compare."
ed., "editor" or "edition."
f., after a number, "and the following page."
ff., after a number, "and the following pages."
　(*f.* and *ff.* are frequently italicized.)
fig., "figure."
i.e., "that is."
l., "line."
ll., "lines."

n., "note."

pp., "pages."

passim after the title of a book or article, "scattered throughout."

q.v., "which see."

sic, "thus." Sometimes inserted in a quotation [*sic*] to indicate that an expression, an error, or a misspelling exactly reproduces the original.

tr., "translator."

viz., "namely."

Vol., "Volume."

The section devoted to abbreviations in a good abridged or unabridged dictionary will furnish other abbreviations. Notice that some are conventionally italicized, others not.

The modern ideal for footnotes is to make them as brief and concise as is consistent with their giving the necessary information. A sample page from a student's long paper, showing proper footnote form, is reproduced below (page 432).

5. BIBLIOGRAPHY

If the complete bibliography is to appear at the end of the paper, the form should follow the pattern of the complete references just given (page 427), naming the author, title, edition (if other than first), place of publication, date of publication, and the number of volumes included in the work. In a very complete bibliography the number of pages in the preface and in the work proper are also added. Some manuals recommend the practice of including the name of the publisher only for books which have appeared within the last twenty years.

The order of the items will, however, be different. In a term paper footnotes come in the order dictated by your use of sources. But a bibliography must be alphabetical.

The author's surname will thus precede his initials and will be separated from them by a comma. There will be no reference at the end to a particular page; if pages are mentioned at all, they will be the inclusive pages of some periodical article or of one member of a collection. If the author is not known or is unacknowledged, alphabetize by the title. Unless your bibliography is very long you need not separate books from periodical articles.

If the source material upon which the paper is based is highly variable in its reliability and accuracy, a short critical note after each item, giving the writer's estimate of the value of the work, may be desirable. One having such notes is called an *annotated bibliography*.

EXAMPLE

Green, Samuel J., *Westward to the Rockies* (Boston, 1903). An early work which contains much information that is still valuable, but some of its conclusions are no longer valid.

Johnson, G. Bruce, *Our Expanding Frontier* (New York, 1926). Written for the general reader rather than for the scholar.

Wrigley, Thomas, *Early Settlers in Iowa* (Chicago, 1915). The information here should always be compared with that in the *Dictionary of American Biography*.

Making correct footnotes and bibliography is an exacting task, a real test of your accuracy. Every period, comma, parenthesis must be in the right place according to the pattern you are following; and you must follow your pattern with absolute consistency. Variations in typography and punctuation have been worked out so that a reader's eye can run down a list and easily pick out the thing he wants, ignoring other features.

Notice that the titles of volumes are italicized. Periodicals are treated in the same way, each year's publication being considered a volume. The title of a complete unit that is a subdivision of any volume—for example, a magazine article or one of a collection of essays—is quoted, then the name of the volume follows. A sample bibliography from a student's paper is on page 433.

6. WRITING OF NUMBERS

We wonder when to spell and when to use figures, when to hyphenate, and what mathematical signs are permissible. The following practices of treating numbers have found most general agreement.

A. Dates, street numbers, page, chapter, and division numbers are never spelled.

On October 16, 1939, I came to New York.
My address is 92 Haley Court.

In formal social correspondence dates are regularly spelled out.

1. **To designate the day of the month:** June 1, April 2, September 3, July 4 are preferred to June 1st, April 2nd, September 3d, July 4th.

However, numbers above ten used as street names are frequently expressed in figures followed by *st, nd, d,* or *th.* When house numbers are used with such street names, leave ample space between the house number and the street name.

164   128th Street

B. For any one composition or article, set an arbitrary limit (ten, one hundred, or one thousand) below which you will spell out all numbers and above which you will use figures.

explains the principle of rocket propulsion.

Rockets operate on the principle stated in Sir Isaac Newton's Third Law of Motion: Every action must be accompanied by a reaction of equal force pointing in the opposite direction. This is precisely the same force which kicks a canoe back into the river when the occupant jumps ashore. The gases, in jumping away from the rocket, kick it back.[3]

Basically, then, since rocket propulsion does not depend on the existence of atmosphere, it is seen to be feasible. But there are several additional problems to be solved before space travel can be realized. These relate to temperature, navigation, the effects on the human body, and danger from meteorites.

The popular conception is that space is extremely cold, and that this would call for some method of heating a space ship so as to preserve the life of its occupants. Fortunately, this is not true. The fact is that "travel through interplanetary space has nothing to do with weather."[4] Space is neither cold nor hot, in our usual sense; it simply has no temperature at all, because there is no atmosphere to hold temperature. The upper part of the earth's atmosphere is very cold, but the rapid ascent of a space ship would create friction enough to neutralize the effect of falling temperature; and once the ship had left the atmosphere behind, it would have entered an almost perfect vacuum -- a poor conductor -- and would retain all its heat.[5]

How would the ship be turned or directed through space? The devices used on airplanes would be ruled out from the start, because they too depend on the resistance of atmosphere, which the space ship would soon have left behind. However, the answer to this problem is relatively simple.[6] Suppose there is a wheel about the size of a bicycle wheel

3. "Rocket to Moon," p. 80.
4. Ibid.
5. Philp, p. 117.
6. Ley, p. 237.

Quotation several lines long, indented, single-spaced, not in
quotation marks.

Footnote numbers following the quotation or reference, and superior.

Body of typewritten paper, double-spaced.

Short quotation worked into body of paper, put in quotation marks.

Sources referred to but not quoted.

Line separating text from footnotes; footnotes brief, there being a
bibliography; number 4 uses abbreviation, referring to exactly the same
place as preceding footnote.

BIBLIOGRAPHY

"Army to Test Nazi Rockets," Milwaukee Journal, Apr. 1, 1946, p. 5

Ley, Willy, Rockets; The Future of Travel Beyond the Stratosphere
(New York: Viking Press, 1944).

Philp, Charles G., Stratosphere and Rocket Flight (3rd ed., London:
Sir Isaac Pitman and Sons, Ltd., 1937).

"Rocket Soars to 43 1/2 Miles," Madison Capital Times, Mar. 21,
1946, p. 1.

"Rocket to Moon," Newsweek, May 22, 1944, XXIII, 80-1.

The bibliography is short, therefore it groups books and periodicals
in a single list.

The bibliography is alphabetical. Since some articles name no author,
they are alphabetized by title.

No page references are given for books; page references for periodical articles are inclusive, whereas in footnotes they refer to the
particular part quoted or used.

433

The one-hundred limit is perhaps the most frequent, but the frequency and size of the figures have a great deal to do with the choice. Follow your scheme consistently. It is permissible to write out in full any number that can be expressed in two words: *fifty thousand, one billion.*

1. **Use a hyphen in compound numbers from twenty-one to ninety-nine.**

fifty-six   two hundred (and) thirty

2. **Use a hyphen between the numerator and denominator of a fraction unless either part is written with a hyphen.**

six-sevenths   six sixty-sevenths

C. Avoid sentences which have in them some numbers spelled out and others written in figures.

UNDESIRABLE: A total of seventy-five items was chosen for consideration by the 260 judges.

UNAVOIDABLE: We found that the three pages contained 15,396 letters.

D. Never begin a sentence with a numeral.

So revise the sentence that it begins with a word or spell out the number if it is not too large.

FAULTY: 254 days were required for the journey.

REVISED: Two hundred and fifty-four days were required for the journey.

OR: The journey required 254 days.

E. A great many numbers cited within a short space should be expressed in figures.

Of the 121 disputed words, 48 were nouns, 36 were verbs, 29 were adjectives, and 8 were adverbs.

The prices of the three articles were $8.32, $10.41, and $11.64 respectively.

F. Do not spell *and* record in figures the same number except in legal and commercial papers.

Observe the following business forms:

RIGHT: I enclose a check for eight dollars ($8.00).

RIGHT: It is hereby agreed that the minimum rate shall not apply until five hundred (500) cubic feet have been purchased at the maximum rate.

G. Round numbers and those mentioned by way of illustration should be spelled out.

He ran about seventy-five yards.
The test is valid in ninety-nine cases out of a hundred.

7. ABBREVIATIONS

Formal writing permits very few abbreviations. Avoid them in your themes. Certain very common abbreviations are acceptable, but even these should be used with caution. For example, the abbreviations listed on pages 428 and 429 of this chapter are permissible in footnotes. Certain other abbreviations are permissible in one use but not in another.

RIGHT: I went to consult Dr. Klein.
WRONG: I went to see the Dr.

RIGHT: The train leaves at 9:15 p.m.
WRONG: I am leaving this p.m.

The abbreviations that are most generally permissible

are the courtesy titles *Mr., Mrs., Messrs., Rev., Hon.,* when used with proper names; abbreviations for academic degrees, Ph.D., M.A., D.C.L., LL.D.; also A.D., B.C., a.m., p.m.

Avoid the use of the ampersand (&) as an abbreviation for "and" in your themes.

8. PROOFREADING

No themes should be handed in without having been subjected to at least one rereading. It is best not to reread the theme immediately after writing it. Let it grow cold; errors in spelling and punctuation will then be more certain to catch your eye; awkward repetitions and ambiguous sentences will stand out. Moreover, if you type your themes, your instructor will not be inclined to accept the plea of a typographical error as an excuse for faulty spelling.

Although a list of proof marks is given on the back endpaper, a few of the most common correction signs are indicated below.

A. If you decide that a new paragraph should begin with a sentence which is now a part of some other paragraph, place the sign ¶ or *Par.* in the margin and also before the word with which the new paragraph is to begin. If a paragraph division is to be removed, write *No* ¶ or *No Par.* in the margin.

B. If you find it necessary to insert new material in the context, write it above the line where it belongs and indicate the point at which it is to be inserted by placing a caret (∧) below the line.

The train sped out of Los Angeles, and climbed swiftly
over the Rockies,
up the old Santa Fe Trail, and across the state of Kansas.
∧

PROOFREADING

This scheme for inserted material is for not more than a line. For a greater amount of material to be inserted, put it on a separate page and mark it with the number of the page followed by the letter *a*. Then indicate the place of insertion on the original page, and at the bottom of the original write, "p. —a follows."

C. Cancel words by drawing single lines through them and placing the sign ϑ (delete) in the margin. Do not use brackets or parentheses to indicate omissions.

D. If your paper, after a rereading, requires attention of a more violent nature than the foregoing instructions will take care of, you had better rewrite it.

Appendix

BUSINESS
LETTERS

BUSINESS LETTERS

Every business letter contains six parts:

1. The heading
2. The inside address
3. The salutation
4. The body of the letter
5. The complimentary close
6. The signature

1. THE HEADING

The heading contains two essentials, the writer's address and the date. The address is usually placed on two lines and the date below it.

Letter A has a block heading; Letter C has an indented heading. Notice the difference:

593 Oakland Avenue
Fort Wayne, Indiana
June 3, 19—

35 High Street,
 Cleveland, Ohio,
  March 1, 19—

A

Heading	593 Oakland Avenue Fort Wayne, Indiana June 3, 19—
Inside Address	Miller Publishing Company 956 Bowdoin Street Springfield, Illinois
Salutation	Gentlemen:

     Since I am leaving Fort Wayne permanently and moving to Missouri, I should like to request that my copy of the *Garden Magazine* be sent, henceforth, to 619 Water Street, Joplin, Missouri.

Body

     I should like, also, to take this opportunity of telling you how much I enjoyed Mr. Herbert L. Atkinson's article on growing dahlias, which appeared in the August number. I wonder if you would be so kind as to give me his address, since I would like to ask him about a few points which were not fully discussed in the article.

Complimentary Close Signature

       Very truly yours,

       Andrew C. Johnson

       Andrew C. Johnson

B

MILLER PUBLISHING
COMPANY
956 Bowdoin Street
SPRINGFIELD, ILLINOIS
June 9, 19—

*Inside
Address*

Mr. Andrew C. Johnson
619 Water Street
Joplin, Missouri

Salutation

Dear Mr. Johnson:

Thank you for notifying us so promptly of your change of address. The November issue of the *Garden Magazine* is off the press today, and it should reach you at your new address in a day or so.

We regret that you will not be able to communicate with Mr. Atkinson by mail for at least three months. He left last month for Guatemala, where he is to be engaged in gathering specimens of plant life from the jungle. The last mail, which was to reach his party at Belize, was sent from the office ten days ago.

Body

We do not know what his address will be after he returns to this country, but as he keeps in constant communication with us, any letter addressed to him in care of this office will be certain to reach him.

*Complimentary
Close
Signature*

Respectfully yours,

Charles F. Stockton

CFS/np

Charles F. Stockton

443

C

35 High Street,
Cleveland, Ohio,
February 1, 19—.

Heading

Salutation Dear Mr. Johnson,

Your letter of October 20, 19—, concerning my article in the *Garden Magazine,* has just been forwarded to me. The questions you raise about the texture of the soil are very interesting indeed, and *Body* I should like to talk with you at length about them. I am to lecture in Joplin before the Garden Club on the twenty-fifth of this month. Could we not arrange to meet for a visit after the lecture? I shall be at my present address for the next two weeks.

Complimentary Sincerely yours,
Close
Signature

Herbert L. Atkinson

Herbert L. Atkinson.

Inside Mr. Andrew C. Johnson,
Address 619 Water Street,
Joplin, Missouri.

THE INSIDE ADDRESS

Most commercial correspondence, at least that from a firm to an individual, is written on letterhead stationery, as illustrated in Letter B. Where the heading is not printed on the stationery, the block form of alignment is now generally preferred.

When printed letterhead stationery is used, the date may be placed in the center of the page, about one-half inch below the last printed line, as in Letter B, or it may be placed toward the right, where the full heading would normally come:

CHARLES SCRIBNER'S SONS

PUBLISHERS

597 FIFTH AVENUE   **NEW YORK, N. Y.**

May 31, 19—

Now observe the punctuation in the headings of Letters A and C. Letter A employs only two commas, the first between the city and the state, the second between the day of the month and the year. This is called *open* punctuation. Letter C has, as well, a comma at the end of the first two lines and a period at the end of the last. This is known as *close* punctuation. Today the open form is generally preferred.

Notice that neither the names of the states nor the months were abbreviated in any of the letters, and that *Street* and *Avenue* were always written out in full.

2. THE INSIDE ADDRESS

Either block alignment or indentation is permissible, but American business usage strongly favors the block alignment. Either open or close punctuation is permissible. The heading and the inside address should be aligned and punctuated alike. Do not employ block alignment for one and indentation for the other.

The usual position of the inside address is two or three spaces below the heading, but in personal correspondence and even in some business letters it may be placed below the signature, as in Letter C.

In writing the inside address, follow the form used by the organization to which you are writing. If *Corporation* or *Company* is abbreviated on its stationery, follow the same practice.

Some title should be used with the name of every person addressed. *Mr., Miss, Mrs.,* or *Messrs.* should be employed when titles such as *Professor, Dr.,* or *Reverend* are not applicable.

3. THE SALUTATION

The salutation is placed two or three spaces below the inside address (depending usually upon the length of the letter), flush with the left-hand margin of the body of the letter.

The salutation *Dear Mr. Blank* is the one now most commonly employed in business correspondence. *Sir* is archaic; *Dear Sir* lacks a personal touch, but may be used in writing to someone with whom you have had no previous correspondence. In writing to a firm, *Gentlemen* is the appropriate salutation, unless the organization happens to be composed entirely of women, in which case *Mesdames* should be used. *My dear Mr. Blank* is considered somewhat more formal than *Dear Mr. Blank*.

The most frequent punctuation after the salutation is the colon, although the comma may be used with open punctuation. The colon and dash together are somewhat old-fashioned.

4. *THE BODY OF THE LETTER*

The three specimen letters illustrate three different types of spacing and alignment. Double spacing is used most frequently for short letters. Longer letters are usually single-spaced, with double spaces between the paragraphs.

The block form, without any paragraph indentation, Letter B, is used less frequently than the indented form but appears to be gaining in favor. When it is used, the rest of the letter is entirely in block form. It is used only with single spacing, although there may be double spacing between paragraphs.

There is much variation in business practice as to the width of indentation. Some business firms begin the first paragraph immediately below the end of the salutation (Letter A) and indent the same number of spaces for all subsequent paragraphs. This is not practical when the salutation is more than one and one-half inches long. Others choose a standard of five or ten spaces and maintain it, irrespective of the length of the salutation.

One comment about the style of business letters must be made. The type of letter which began, "Yours of the 15th inst. rec'd, and contents noted. In reply would say—" and which closed with a "Hoping that we may have the pleasure of continuing to serve you, I beg to remain," is outmoded. Every attempt is made by the modern business correspondent to avoid such clichés as *your esteemed favor, at hand, and oblige*. Facts are stated simply, clearly, and in everyday English. The participial preparation for a leave-taking of the type, "Trusting that we may hear from you again," sometimes followed by "I am" or "I remain," has been a little slower in disappearing, but it too is on the wane. Today, when a correspondent has said what he has to say, he stops.

5. *THE COMPLIMENTARY CLOSE*

As the name indicates, this portion of the letter consists of one of several polite phrases which have been handed down by custom. The phrases which may be used are:

Very truly yours
Yours very truly
Sincerely yours
Yours sincerely
Faithfully yours
Yours faithfully
Cordially yours
Respectfully yours
Yours respectfully
Truly yours
Yours truly

Of these phrases, *Very truly yours* has perhaps the greatest currency in American business correspondence, with *Sincerely yours* a not too close second.

The complimentary close is placed two lines below the body of the letter and begins about in the center of the page. In typewritten letters, if the paragraph indentation is begun at the end of the salutation, an effort is sometimes made to align the complimentary close with the indentation for the paragraph. Sometimes also in letterhead stationery, the date is so placed that alignment with the complimentary close is possible.

The complimentary close is always begun with a capital letter and punctuated at the end with a comma. Only the first letter of the first word should be capitalized.

6. *THE SIGNATURE*

The signature follows the complimentary close. If the letter is to merit serious consideration at all, the signature must be written with pen and ink. Notice that Letter A has only the autograph signature, but that Letters B and C have, in addition, the typewritten signature below the autograph. A glance at the signatures of any half-dozen letters you have received recently will be enough to convince you of the necessity of a typewritten signature also. Signatures are written so frequently, they are often illegible.

Letters B and C illustrate two forms of alignment for complimentary close and signature. Letter B is block and open; Letter C is indented and close. The block form is more common than the indented, and the open form (no punctuation after the signature) is more common than the close.

7. THE ENVELOPE

The address on the envelope should follow the style of the inside address. The return address placed in the upper left corner is always in block form, if it is not printed.

INDEX

451

INDEX

Direct quotations, 11, 23; enclosed in quotation marks, 306–310; first word capitalized, 311

Disjunctive, 107, 220, 259; subject, agreement of verb with, 220

Don't, 331, 341

Double capacity, words in, 124

Double comparatives and superlatives, 332

Double negative, 332, 352; *can't hardly,* 337; *not,* 332, 352

Double reference, 96, 102, 103

Doubling a final consonant, 323

Down, 187

Due to, 341

Each, every, number of, 222

Each other, 341, 342

Economics, special references, 401

ed., used in footnotes, 428

Education, special references, 402

Effect, 130

Effect to cause, paragraph developed through, 67

Effective, 131

Effectiveness, paragraph, 57–61; sentence, 109–114; whole composition, 21–25

Effectual, 131

ei or *ie,* 323

Either, number of, 218, 219, 342

Either . . . or, number of verb with, 220

Elimination, method of paragraph development, 68

-else, use with compound indefinite pronouns, 342

Emigrate, 131

Emphasis, see Effectiveness; indicated by italics, 70, 311

Emphatic form of verb, 203, 204

Encyclopedias, listed, 397

End punctuation, 271–273

Ending of a paragraph, 57–59; of a sentence, 114; the theme, 25, 26

Engineering, special references, 402

Enthuse, 342

Envelope of business letter, 446

Errors of subordination, 110, 111

Errors of usage, glossary of, 330–364

Etc., 334

Etymology, 170, 171

Even, position of, 103

Every, everybody, everyone, number of, 222

Everyplace, 342

Exact word, 133–135

Except, 130

Exclamation point, use of, 272, 302, 308

Exclamatory sentence, punctuation of, 272, 273

Exercises, abstract and concrete words, 149, 150; agreement of pronouns with antecedents, 223; agreement of verb with subject, 223; comma fault, 91, 92, 281, 282; dangling modifiers, 109; diction, 156–158; fragmentary sentences, 85,

458

INDEX

INDEX

INDEX

INDEX

COMMON PROBLEMS

[A list for reference]